PERSPECTIVES ON GENDER
IN EARLY CHILDHOOD

"I don't see liking trucks as a boy thing.
I see it as a liking-trucks thing."

PERSPECTIVES
on
GENDER
in
EARLY
CHILDHOOD

Edited by Tamar Jacobson

Foreword by Bryan G. Nelson

Redleaf Press®
www.redleafpress.org
800-423-8309

Published by Redleaf Press
10 Yorkton Court
St. Paul, MN 55117
www.redleafpress.org

First edition 2011
Cover design by Jim Handrigan
Interior typeset in Adobe Caslon and Gill Sans and designed by Jim Handrigan
Printed in the United States of America
17 16 15 14 13 12 11 10   1 2 3 4 5 6 7 8

Library of Congress Cataloging-in-Publication Data
Perspectives on gender in early childhood / edited by Tamar Jacobson.
    p. cm.
  Includes bibliographical references and index.
  ISBN 978-1-60554-021-4 (alk. paper)
  1. Sex differences in education. 2. Gender identity. 3. Early childhood education—Social aspects. I. Jacobson, Tamar.
  LC212.9.P465 2011
  372.1822—dc22
                          2009041829

Printed on acid-free paper

CONTENTS

FOREWORD

Opening Our Minds and Hearts
to New Perspectives on Gender

— Bryan G. Nelson —

"Is it a girl or a boy?"

This simple question at the announcement of a baby's birth speaks volumes about the impact of gender in our daily lives. People want to know—they *must* know whether a new human is female or male. This need to know a newborn's gender occurs even before the child's birth: parents are asked whether they want a baby boy or girl; they need to choose clothing—pink or blue?

Identity is dramatically shaped by one's perceived gender. In many cultures and time periods, what one can and cannot do is determined by characteristics called "feminine" and "masculine." Frederick William, an eighteenth-century Prussian king and father of Frederick the Great, beat his son for wearing gloves in cold weather because it was "an effeminate behavior." When helmets first showed up on football fields, Pudge Heffelfinger, Yale's three-time All American from 1889 to 1891, said, "None of that sissy stuff for me." Helmets are now standard protective gear for football. Further, not until 1875 were women in the United States legally defined as "persons." Women did not receive the vote in the United States until 1920. In the book *Modern Woman: The Lost Sex* (1946), authors Marynia Famham and Ferdinand Lundberg argued that women who worked sacrificed their essential femininity. Before the

1900s, wristwatches were considered effeminate because men carried only pocket watches. When World War I fighter pilots adopted them for tactical reasons, they became acceptably masculine.

In our society, some styles, conditions, and behaviors for men and women haven't changed. The disparity between wages paid to women and those paid to men persists. In 2004, women's wages in the United States were 76.5 percent of men's wages. The care of young children and housecleaning continue to be done primarily by women. We also continue to see increasing numbers of men injured or dying as a result of their work in dangerous occupations and their participation in contact sports, such as boxing and football. Violence against men whose behavior is perceived as effeminate is also on the rise.

Norms for men's and women's appearance are narrowly defined by most cultures. In a recent court case in Texas, a four-year-old boy who wore his hair long was suspended from his school because his parents would not cut his hair—the length of his hair violated the dress code in his suburban Dallas school district. A girl would not be suspended for having short hair. Gender perceptions and expectations take root at an early age.

To appreciate the need for this book, one only has to visit an early education classroom and watch young children's play. You will see boys running around or predominantly playing in the block areas and girls with dolls in the dress-up or dramatic play areas. Is it considered acceptable for boys to dress-up as women? Sometimes, but not really. Do girls play with trucks or blocks? Not as often as the boys. Early education creates powerful environments that can positively or negatively influence a child's perception, understanding of, and attitude toward gender roles. We need this book to help develop a better understanding of young children and gender identity.

At the same time there are signs that gender expectations of men and women are changing in the United States today. For example, currently there are more women than men graduating from medical and law schools. We see more women joining the military and going into combat zones. There are more female professional athletes. For the first time in history, more women than men will soon be working outside the home and there are more single-parent fathers caring for their children than ever before. While this change (hopefully) will bring increased freedom to both men and women, it also may create an increased confusion regarding what one's roles should be.

Fortunately there is hope, knowledge, and information available in this book you've chosen to read. Tamar Jacobson, editor of *Perspectives on Gender in Early Childhood*, leads the way by sharing a powerful personal story about her emerging understanding of being a woman. The vulnerability modeled by Jacobson pushes us to consider our own path toward self-discovery. I think you'll find the journey rewarding in that it will bring you to new understanding of yourself, others around you, and the world that we live in. To authentically work with young children you must be open to all the possibilities that make up who you are. The new information you discover will be both exciting and challenging. Exciting because you may enjoy an activity that you previously thought of as unavailable due to perceived gender constraints. Challenging because you may need to let go of previously held expectations of children.

Finally, *Perspectives on Gender in Early Childhood* is needed to help expand our knowledge and understanding of gender and its impact on children. We all need guidance and support by reading about new theories, research, and practices that challenge our thinking while offering practical ideas for the classroom. This book will provide you more than self-reflection (which is certainly important); it will also provide practical approaches to making meaningful changes to your work.

INTRODUCTION

Understanding Our Gender Identity:

CONNECTING THE PERSONAL WITH THE PROFESSIONAL

— Tamar Jacobson —

Acquiring gender identity is complex. Many different sources are involved in helping us understand what it means to be male or female—a man or a woman. Young children are strongly influenced by significant adults in their lives: mothers, fathers, siblings, grandparents, extended family members, caregivers, teachers, guardians, and neighbors. They are also shaped by forces in society, and affected by media and cultural mores.

Most of my recent writing explores how feelings and life experiences affect teacher interactions with children in classrooms (Jacobson 2003; 2008). For this book about gender perspectives in early childhood, quite naturally, I have been thinking about the topic of gender quite a bit of late. Specifically, I have been thinking about what it means to a woman or a man and how our gender identity affects our interactions with each other and the children in our care.

My gender identity is a subject that causes me not a small amount of discomfort, for it is directly related to my own feelings of self-worth, self-perception, notions about my sexuality, and, even, fears of intimacy. Indeed, it exposes me to my deepest shadows and vulnerabilities. It is at the very core of my being, the foundation of who I am, and how I interact with the world—personally and professionally. My gender identity affects my entire worldview and is directly related to feelings of empowerment or powerlessness.

For example, most recently I have been participating in some important meetings at work. Early on in one of them, I realized that when surrounded by scholarly men who appear to be older than I am, I started to feel like an eight-year-old girl and became intimidated to the point of paralyzed silence. Indeed, I felt like an idiot and was terrified to voice any opinion. After the first meeting, I shared these realizations with female colleagues, who, although they expressed dissimilar feelings, were most understanding and accepting of mine. At following meetings in the days ahead, with awareness of my emotional issues attuned and available, I was able to overcome my discomfort and thus participate, making contributions that were professional and productive.

Where do I begin to think about how I developed my identity as a woman? I start with thinking about how significant adults in my life influenced my development in my earliest years and helped me shape my identity as a woman.

UNDERSTANDING THE MALE INFLUENCES
IN MY LIFE

My father was fifty-five when I was born. Growing up I experienced him as an old man, a grandfather-type figure. He was quiet and gentle and laughed nervously. He has been dead for over twenty-five years and yet on Father's Day I often think about him. My parents divorced when I was four and from then on until I left home at eighteen, I lived with my mother and stepfather, visiting my father on weekends and sometimes taking a short trip or vacation together. My stepfather communicated with me mainly through teasing and joking. His relationship with my mother was volatile and passionate. I did not think of him as a father figure, but rather was afraid to bother him with my presence. For example, he would constantly tease me about how much I ate or talked. I felt trivialized and small with him. Neither man was a role model or father figure for me.

And so, I chose my brother. Although he was only six years older than I was, my mother adored him, and I decided, very early on, that it was wise to adore whatever or whomever she adored. It just made life easier somehow, or so I thought. He became for me the epitome of manhood. His beliefs became mine. Indeed, his entire way of thinking about life was imported into my brain, poured into my veins. He was my greatest influence. I spent all my life longing for him to notice and acknowledge me. My brother was as unaware as I was that I gave him that role. What a disaster for our relationship. There I was with all sorts of wild and needy expectations, and there he was with his life, plodding along unaware. Not a good recipe for the survival of a healthy sibling relationship!

Father's Day is always complicated for me. I feel as if it is split into three men from my childhood, each influencing me in different ways. In fact, I do not remember experiencing the warm, supportive love of a father, and if I yearn for it, as of course I do from time to time, I do not really know what I am actually yearning for. Most likely, it is a movie- or television-type father figure or a character from a novel that I long for. As a result, relationships with men have been complicated for me throughout my life. At first I saw men as either Prince Charming or the devil. I learned very early on to be coquettish and cute, flirtatious and playful, and to sacrifice my needs for a man to like me. In addition I transferred the adoration of my brother to all other men. They must all be superior to me in every way, especially in intelligence, but also by being more rational and more vulnerable. A trilogy of men appeared in my childhood psyche: one, old and gentle with large wrinkled hands, somewhat unapproachable, who seemed startled, even physically jump-ing back if I tried to hug or kiss him; another, teasing and distant; and the third, intelligent and rational. I was unable to feel belonging or emotionally safe with any of them. Today I am orphaned of two of them—my father and stepfather have died. Many of my relationships with men in my life were illusions concocted in my brain to help me survive.

During the women's liberation movement, a world of complex-ity and emotional choices opened up to me. I wandered through the feminist door in wonder and relief as I began to shed the requirements I had set for myself and relearn the world of human relationships. Men became whole and complex, human and approachable, as I struggled with being authentic without fear. There were, of course, years of con-fusion as I transitioned out of the old and into the new ways of perceiv-ing my emotional psycho-socialization process. I explored my identity, sexuality, and spirituality—in short, the entire concept of my self. The search and struggle is not nearly over. There is still so much relearning to do because I came to this stage late in my life. It feels promising and hopeful to me, though, because I know that I still have much more to discover and uncover about my self.

TRANSFORMATION THROUGH READING

I became a feminist late in my life. Up until that time I had believed that a woman's place was to settle behind her man, taking care of children and hearth, and sacrificing career and education so that the man could better himself first. Indeed, I had practiced that fervently, doing everything in my power to get it right. For example, I remember when I was twenty-three, back in the early seventies, sitting in my brother's living room one evening after dinner. His friends, all seeming so much more scholarly and intelligent than I was, were discussing current issues of the time. When one of them spoke from a feminist perspective I became indignant and waxed prolific about the joys and delights, the duties and obligations of a dedicated wife being able, nay privileged even, to wash the floors, making them clean for her husband's well-being. I blush to remember it. I had always been an avid activist, believing in social justice and equal rights for all—*all* that is, except women, but way more personally—*except me.*

A few years later when I returned to Africa with my two-year-old son to visit my aging father, I spent the day with the mother of my best friend, Nan Partridge, a woman who had tremendously influenced the way I thought about social justice when I was an older teenager (Jacobson 2003). During our visit, Nan gave me a book to read called *Meet Me in the Middle* (Clinebell 1973). Back then I was struck by Clinebell's description of interdependence—a true *equality* of the sexes.

> Certainly it means that both sexes will have to give up some things. Men will have to give up dependence on women as an automatic servant class and will have to move over to make room for women in public life. Women will have to give up their helplessness and dependence for identity on men. . . . it means hanging loose about sex roles—what Maslow describes as a "desexualizing of the statuses of strength and weakness, and of leadership so that either man or woman can be, without anxiety and degradation, either weak or strong, as the situation demands. Either must be capable of both leadership and surrender." (Clinebell 1973, 31–32)

I felt the stirrings of feminism as I read the book at the time. It felt more than comfortable to read about women and men being interdependent. It was enlightening. I did not realize then that I would first have to emancipate my own mind toward the notion of me deserving equality in order to come even vaguely close to the idea of *interdependence*. The journey ahead would be long indeed.

It would be almost twenty years after reading Clinebell's book before I would embrace feminism and start the journey of self-emancipation and liberating my mind of our patriarchal system that had been hammered so deeply into my consciousness growing up. I discovered that the male-privileged and -dominant system was deeply ingrained in me, and, even now at the ripe old age of sixty I still have to work very hard at shedding those self-destructive beliefs. Lately, I notice all kinds of complicated and complex feelings. For example, how my self-worth was always tied up in looking pretty or being attractive or sexy—whatever all these things mean. In other words, a dominant male view was the one I sought out or felt was all-important and meaningful.

I tried to match my self-worth against all of those preconceived notions and found myself lacking. I was unable to take myself seriously. The belief that I must constantly sacrifice my *self* for one *him* or another, seemed honorable and was all consuming. Later on, in my own book, *Confronting Our Discomfort: Clearing the Way for Anti-Bias in Early Childhood*, I wrote about bell hooks describing the "strongest patriarchal voice" in her life as that of her own mother (Jacobson 2003). "When I began to resist male domination, to rebel against patriarchal thinking (and to oppose the strongest patriarchal voice in my life—my mother's voice), I was still a teenager" (hooks 2000, x). I identified very much with hooks's description, as it was true for me, too, except that I started to rebel when I was in my thirties—two decades *after* being a teenager! I have often thought that my mother tried to protect me so that I could succeed in our society, by teaching me that men were more important, vulnerable, and needy, and should be taken care of more seriously than women. Indeed, to this day I am uncomfortable when my life partner makes dinner after he and I return home from work. I can still hear my mother's voice in my mind expressing concern that men are tired after a hard day at work. Somehow, I learned to expect that it is a woman's duty to continue working in the home even if she returns from a long, hard day outside of it.

Two other books helped transform me into a feminist. The first, *Mother Daughter Revolution: From Betrayal to Power* (Debold, Wilson, and Malavé 1993), discusses in depth mothers who try to protect their teenage daughters by preparing them for a male-dominated society in a similar way as my mother did with me. I read the second book for a qualitative research course in graduate school. *Educated in Romance: Women, Achievement, and College Culture* (Holland and Eisenhart 1990) pretty much solidified my becoming a full-fledged feminist.

As I was reading *Educated in Romance* I realized the authors were describing my life, from the decisions I made to the way I viewed my place in the world. The authors describe how young women start out college with ambitions and dreams to become architects, political scientists, anthropologists, and so forth. Then, they quickly change course toward nurturing professions like teaching or nursing to make it easy to follow their romantic partners wherever they might go, sacrificing their own careers for those of the men they have fallen in love with. Some of the things the women say in their interviews might have come directly from my own lips. The book spoke to me deeply because at the time I was experiencing much guilt for having left country and husband, and dragged my teenage son with me across the world so that, finally, I could give myself the education I had always dreamed of. I remember gasping as I read, tears streaming down my cheeks, feeling validated and supported, with fear and guilt pushed aside for a few moments.

Of course, I understand that it was not the books per se that changed me. Rather, the words reached me at a point in my life's journey that was the culmination of events, my therapy, and psychological development. It became a revelation, a huge "aha" period in my life, and I have never been the same since. Indeed, books have often been the catalyst in changing my life in most significant ways.

FEMINISM FOR ME

For me, being a feminist means being free from the patriarchal system, choosing *against* dominance, elitism, and exclusion, but opting *for* empathy and compassion for *all* human beings. It also means realizing that women are often their own worst enemies. Because socialization in childhood is so powerful, women have bought into the patriarchal system to survive and succeed. Rebelling against the system often calls for drastic external acting-out for men and women alike to counteract that societal teaching in our early years. After all, it is less than a hundred years since women achieved the right to vote. There is still a lot of relearning for all of us to do.

Dominance and privilege cause everyone pain, including boys and men. What a burden it must be for men to feel like they must repress emotions or hide their vulnerabilities and human frailty. How challenging to feel that they must always be the breadwinners and carry the burden of their family alone. Interdependence makes so much more sense for both men and women. Interdependence encourages a relationship between the sexes where each depends on the other and each is open and helpful to the other, emotionally and physically—supporting, encouraging, and sometimes taking over when the other is feeling weak or unable. My mother used to say that men have to go to war, therefore women must be strong in the home. Today, women are also able to go to war, and men find themselves taking care of home and children.

We can never know what it is like to walk in the shoes of another person—or a whole people—but we can listen to all our stories in the hope of better understanding one another. And, thus, become interdependent as Clinebell (1973) suggested over thirty years ago. Or as bell hooks says in *Feminism Is for Everybody: Passionate Politics* (2000, x): "Imagine living in a world where there is no domination, where females and males are not alike or even always equal, but where a vision of mutuality is the ethos shaping our interaction. . . . Feminist revolution alone will not create such a world. . . . But it will make it possible for us to be fully self-actualized females and males able to create beloved community, to live together, realizing our dreams of freedom and justice, living the truth that we are all 'created equal.'"

No matter how we think about the genders or the "isms," if we are intentional in our self-exploration, we are bound to discover that our beliefs, prejudices, and attitudes affect how we interact with the boys and girls in our classrooms.

GENDER IDENTITY AFFECTS OUR INTERACTIONS WITH CHILDREN AND FAMILIES

I have been writing about how early childhood experiences, emotional memories, and biases affect my interactions with people I teach, whether they are young children or college students (Jacobson 2003, 2008). In my books I talk about the connections I make between personal and professional behaviors. One of the examples I describe relates to my early childhood experiences and memories of ballet dancing. When I was eighteen months old, growing up in Africa, my mother and grandmother took me to learn ballet dancing (Jacobson 2008). From then on until I was ten years old, I attended classes and even appeared in public performances in our town. My mother would tell me about how I would become famous and how she would sit in the special audience box and watch me dance. Thus, it became a childhood dream to one day perform on world stages.

When I was ten, ballet dancing was suddenly taken away from me. I remember being told that I was becoming anemic and did not have time to play with friends like other children did. Forty years later memories of my childhood dancing years revisited me during one of my classes when an undergraduate student described how, after having an accident, she gave up a career in dance to become a teacher. I wrote about it in my journal:

> As I write this I have just realized why I was so emphatic with one of my students recently. She had described in class that until she had been involved in a car accident she had studied ballet and jazz dance. Now she was going into the teaching profession. I asked her if she was well enough to dance and she nodded her head vigorously, but said that she did not have the confidence any longer. I became quite excited and exclaimed vehemently that she must return to dancing and follow her heart. I went as far as to say that I hoped I could talk her out of teaching during the semester and get her back into dancing. I wonder . . . was I really talking about myself? (Jacobson 2008, 116–17)

Writing in my journal after the class I realized how passionate I had become as I advised my student to return to dancing instead of becoming a teacher. Reading back what I had written, I realized a connection between my own childhood relationship with ballet and what I was telling my student. As one of my dissertation advisors used to say to me, *"Take my advice, I don't use it!"* My words of advice came from my own life experience and probably did not have much to do with my student's life choices or what was good for her at the time. Sometimes we are as unaware as I was before I wrote in my journal about the dancing student in my class. It is crucial for us to uncover these feelings and biases so that we can become more intentional in our behaviors and more authentic in our guidance with young children.

I have no doubt that the ways in which teachers interact with girls and boys are connected to their own experiences of gender identity. For example, when I was starting out as a first-year teacher over thirty years ago, long before I began a psychological exploration of my self, I found that I was unsympathetic to little girls in my preschool class. In fact, I found that they got on my nerves! They always seemed preoccupied with silliness and prettiness, and I was often impatient with their stories and needs. On the other hand, I found myself more inclined to like the boys in my class. They seemed more interesting, and I certainly took them more seriously.

I started psychotherapy when I was a young adult, and as I began exploring early emotional memories and experiences and unpacking the mystery of my childhood, I realized how complex the influences of the significant women in my life (mother, sisters, stepmother, and grandmother) were on my development. Indeed, I began to make connections between how I perceived my own femininity and the girls in my classroom. As I look back, I now understand that at some level I have always been unsure of what it means to be a woman. I have been affected by my earliest relationships with the significant adults—both men and women—in my life, and, thus, my interactions with young children are often based on those influences.

Gender identity is also tied up with a person's sexuality and comfort with intimacy in general. However, this is not the place or time for me to examine or share what effect my gender identity has had in my personal life and intimate relationships. But it is certainly appropriate to discuss how my professional behaviors are influenced. I must admit it is quite a challenge to unlearn some of the gender biases I acquired as a young child. For example, while I definitely welcome, accept, and rejoice in the fact that women can join any profession they choose, I often find myself in awe of women who become architects, astrologers, mathematicians, doctors, lawyers, politicians, engineers, pilots, bus drivers, and construction workers, as well as those who serve in the military.

If I had completely embraced gender equality in my heart and soul, I would not be in awe of those women. Rather, their occupations would seem natural to me. I would take them for granted, just as I do when men enter those professions. By the same token, I find myself appreciating men who become nurses or child care teachers, whereas it is unremarkable for me when women enter those professions. Therefore, I wonder whether I convey that ambiguity to young children in subtle, unconscious ways. For example, am I really comfortable with girls playing in the hollow block corner, wearing hard hats and shouting out raucously? Or do I feel the need to shush them or even to redirect their play to something quieter, more demure, and, dare I say it, more feminine? Do I feel comfortable when little boys cry or need support, or do I subtly encourage them to hold back their emotional expression?

I am always proud of myself when I take out my toolbox and fix a faucet or do something as simple as hammer a nail into the wall! I never take it for granted. How can I? I bought my first toolbox when I was forty-five years old. I had just gotten divorced and had moved into an apartment on my own. During that year, I built myself a desk and learned to fix all manner of things in my home. I realized just how much helplessness I had learned as a girl. I felt empowered and more confident each time I was able to take responsibility for the tasks I used to think belonged only to men. I wonder, when I was a young teacher of preschool girls back in the seventies and early eighties, if I encouraged them to fix things or become curious about math and science. I doubt it, because at that time I did not feel capable of such manly tasks myself. I am sure that in subtle and even intentional ways, I directed girls to domestic and nurturing types of play. I shudder to think of it now!

Now, I find that I become agitated when I hear adults commenting about little girls' appearance with statements like "How pretty you look," or "What a pretty dress . . . ribbon . . . shoes . . . " I would prefer to encourage and support girls about how intelligent, curious, or strong they are, or about their ability to solve problems. This has become a new bias. Yet I am sure that girls also like to know how they look to others, since society still puts a strong emphasis on appearances, clothes, and body shapes.

I still have much work to do to find a balance between my biases, learned and unlearned, old and new. But one thing is for sure: education and self-reflection have given me numerous, different options about how I think about and understand gender identity. In my book *"Don't Get So Upset!" Help Young Children Manage Their Feelings by Understanding Your Own* (2008), I describe specific actions to take when we decide to research our own self, especially when making connections between our earliest emotional memories and our inter-actions with the young children we care for and educate. Here are some questions to help you learn about how you acquired your gender identity:

- How did I learn about becoming a woman or a man?
- What are my earliest memories?
- What was fun or painful for me as I learned about these aspects of my identity?
- How do I agree or disagree with my parents' ideas about gender?
- If I disagree, how did I develop my own ideas?
- What and who were significant influences on me?
- As a parent, what would I want to teach my children about gender identity?
- What stereotypes would I want to avoid?
- Which aspects of stereotypes would I want to embrace?

When teachers enter the classroom, we bring our self with us. We do not get to leave our self outside the door. Our personal feelings, early childhood memories, prejudices, values, beliefs, and attitudes accompany us as we struggle to guide young children to become future citizens of a world that is developing more rapidly than we can imagine. All around the country, I have heard from teachers about how they try to leave their personal self outside the door of their classrooms. In other words, they believe that to be professional, they must separate out or compartmentalize their personal lives.

Can we be authentic and intentional in our relationships and behaviors if we leave such an important part of our self at the door in order to separate the personal from the professional? Instead, I think we need to embrace our personal life, our inner self. We must constantly work to make valuable connections between our earliest memories, experiences, biases, and values learned, and how we interact with children. Then we might be able to offer children numerous, different options about how they think about and understand gender identity and the choice to change their worldview.

GENDER PERSPECTIVES IN EARLY CHILDHOOD

The authors included in this volume have come from different parts of the United States (Arizona, Texas, and Hawaii) and the world (Finland). All talk about gender from different perspectives. All have done some type of research to explore and understand more clearly how children learn about their gender identity from the teachers who teach them. There is no one prescription for how the authors do this. Rather, an assortment of ideas, reflections, and suggestions have come out of caring for and educating young children in an ever-changing and evolving world.

We start out with an in-depth examination of the history of gender education in our field. The chapters that follow discuss ways teachers talk or behave with children that either reinforce gender stereotypes or try to change traditional modes of communication about gender; explore how girls and their teachers relate to learning mathematics; examine the portrayal of gender through children's books and how picture books and literacy activities influence the development of gender identity; and talk about gender roles and healthy sexual development. In addition, the authors give concrete suggestions to help us become more aware of how and why we shape children's understanding of their gender identity.

From Plato to Vivian Gussin Paley, Blythe Hinitz and Dorothy Hewes describe the history of gender in early childhood beginning with Spartan and Roman education and continuing to the current debate about the different physical needs of boys and girls ("Practical Applications from the History of Gender and Early Childhood Education"). This chapter provides a foundation for the complexity of gender perspectives in early childhood. Hinitz and Hewes show us that through the ages societal influences were powerful in shaping our expectations about gender roles and gender identity. As I read the in-depth account of gender history in this chapter, I am in awe of our profession and the important task we have in caring for and educating young children. I am even more convinced that teachers' self-reflection about their relationships and interactions with children together with acquiring knowledge about girls' and boys' developmental needs are key to unlearning biases or stereotypes from a very early age.

Eila Estola discusses gender with early childhood teachers from two different child care centers ("Discussing Gender"). Estola hails from Finland, and in the introduction to her chapter, she describes the early childhood policies of her country. It is thought provoking to compare the differences between early childhood education systems and policies in the United States with those of another country and especially interesting to note the similarities between us when it comes to gender stereotyping. Estola explores different aspects of gender bias through descriptions of discussions with teachers of young children. She asks readers to reflect on many different questions that arise. For example, how do we support the individual development of both masculine and feminine qualities in children when most of the care and education of young children is predominantly the responsibility of women? Estola identifies gender-based rules among the children and teachers, and discusses teachers as role models who should, therefore, examine their own behaviors.

While Estola's chapter is based on observing the discussions with teachers from different child care centers, Jeanne Marie Iorio and Hema Visweswaraiah contribute a chapter that analyzes how conversations between children and teachers construct understanding about gender ("Do Daddies Wear Lipstick? and Other Child-Teacher Conversations Exploring Constructions of Gender"). The authors suggest that disrupting the social construct of gender is crucial for helping children develop different ways of looking at traditional gender roles. To help us understand what they mean, Iorio and Visweswaraiah describe detailed conversations where the teacher deliberately provokes discussion that might change children's ideas by offering other realities that children have not yet seen. The authors identify a number of items for teachers' self-reflection, including documenting and examining one's own practice and encouraging conversations about gender-related topics to occur in a trusting environment.

"Most of us, gender-bending and gender-conforming alike, experience the confines of gender identity as both positive and negative," concludes Gail Masuchika Boldt ("One Hundred Hotdogs or Performing Gender in the Elementary Classroom"). She arrives at this supposition after asking numerous questions upon observing what children were saying and doing about gender in her classroom. The larger question Boldt's conclusion asks is "Why . . . in spite of my critical attention to stereotypes in literature and daily life, did the children continue to express preferences, attitudes, and behaviors that seemed so clearly delineated by gender?" (p. 90). This chapter first offers a narrative about a kindergarten class at group time where the author shows us that gender is ever-present in the classroom. Dr. Boldt discusses the notion that children and adults perform gender norms in behavior, desires, and gestures and that the reasons we are compelled to perform gender norms constantly are complex and enforced from birth. An interesting discussion follows showing how our gender performance is constantly nurtured through rewards and punishments. It is up to the teacher to create a safe environment for children to converse and explore their gender identity through authentic interactions with teachers who admit to their own struggles with performing gender—through experiences both positive and negative.

Josh Thompson and Stephen Garretson observe that our directors and principals, mentors, and coteachers—mostly women—helped us find our places in the profession ("Encouraging Men in Their Conversations with Children"). "Our parents, particularly our moms, and our wives supported the development of our voices and our lives among children. Our fathers contributed to our construction of our gendered identity—what it means to be male, even in a world of female early childhood educators" (p. 102). Thompson and Garretson invite us to encourage men in their conversations with children. They discuss the different ways men converse with young children, share their experiences as male teachers in our predominantly female profession, and talk about how they acquired their gender identity. As I read this chapter, I am reminded of my own many biases about male teachers in early childhood classrooms, including how I used to have to confront my discomfort when I witnessed rough-and-tumble play. I am most grateful for Thompson's and Garretson's suggestion that their female counterparts might have to think outside the box and find out more about the language of men in the lives of children.

Two of the chapters in this book take a look at how children's books and literary experiences determine gender roles or help boys and girls specifically learn literacy and socio-emotional skills. Clarissa M. Uttley and Cynthia A. Roberts detail how gender identity is portrayed in children's books by analyzing the roles of the heroes in the stories as well as the types of roles taken by the characters ("Gender Portrayal in Early Childhood Children's Books"). For example, they show how the male characters in children's books are more adventurous and independent than the female characters, who are nurturing and dependent. This is particularly interesting to me because a few years ago I wrote about the same type of stereotypical gender roles in Shel Silverstein's *The Giving Tree* in my own book *Confronting Our Discomfort: Clearing the Way for Anti-Bias in Early Childhood* (2003). Because books can affect gender role socialization, Uttley and Roberts suggest a list of books that can support children in developing healthy gender identities.

In contrast, Debby Zambo uses picture books as a way of helping boys and girls develop not only literacy intelligence but socio-emotional skills as well ("Using Picture Books and Literary Experiences to Help Boys and Girls Develop Literacy and Socio-Emotional Skills"). Using the illustrations to describe different feelings, Zambo gives the reader strategies to help young children self-regulate their emotions, while at the same time nurturing their love of reading. The ideas and strategies that Zambo offers are based on knowledge about how children develop emotional intelligence and how emotional memory and brain development affect children's identity. In addition, the author shares a wealth of information about how girls and boys process and express emotions differently.

The next two chapters explore why boys seem to do better in math and science than girls. Sylvia Bulgar opens her chapter ("The Role of Early Childhood in Gender Differences in Mathematics") with a historical perspective on gender inequity in mathematics, including roles and position statements from national organizations like the National Association for the Education of Young Children (NAEYC) and the National Council of Teachers of Mathematics (NCTM), and the effects of No Child Left Behind legislation and testing procedures. This information serves as a strong basis for her report of the research she conducted in primary grade classrooms in New Jersey. Her conclusions are powerful and important, and they reinforce for all of us the need for concrete "experiences that will help all children develop abstract notions of the mathematics in which they are engaged" (p. 173). In other words, it is in early childhood classrooms that we can build a strong foundation for girls, as well as for boys, to succeed in mathematics when they enter higher grades, where the gap between girls and boys widens.

Debra Dyer, on the other hand, gives us a specific tool to help us teach concrete mathematical concepts to young children in early childhood classrooms—block building ("Block Building in the Primary Classroom as a Gender Equalizer in Math and Science"). Dyer offers practical strategies and ideas about how to use the blocks, including suggestions for making the block center "female friendly." She writes, "Using block building as both a preinstructional strategy and as a way to consolidate new knowledge can be highly motivating and interesting to all students" (p. 184). Both Dyer and Bulgar talk about the importance of creating equal opportunities in math and science for boys and girls.

"Sexuality is, at its essence, about relationships. Children who have a healthy sense of themselves . . . have a good start at developing relationships with others," (p. 202) write Donna Couchenour and Kent Chrisman ("Healthy Sexuality Development and Gender Roles in Early Childhood"). They believe that gender identity and healthy sexuality development are inextricably linked. They go on to explain that while the prominent observable differences between the sexes at infancy are biological, environmental and socially constructed influences begin once the baby has been identified as a boy or a girl. In a discussion about how children construct meaning about gender identity, the authors suggest that teachers can inspire gender-balanced experiences with the types of projects they assign as well as by avoiding sexist comments and providing critical responses to the influences of media and commercialism.

Janis Strasser and Lisa Mufson Koeppel share detailed and specific ways that teachers can organize their activity centers to promote gender equity ("Creating Preschool Classroom Environments That Promote Gender Equity"). After discussing the different ways boys and girls play in the preschool years, the authors describe what to do and what to place in each center, whether it is in the art area or dramatic or outdoor play. They include types of pictures to hang on the walls and resources, such as books or prop boxes, needed for each center. In each section Strasser and Koeppel suggest specific questions for teachers to ask themselves as they organize their preschool environment. Some of the questions deal with ways in which we talk to children; for example, "Are high-level answers to questions probed for in girls as well as boys? (that is, Why do you think that happened? How else could we solve that problem?)", or "Are children commended on their courage and bravery not just for their physical achievements but for their emotional accomplishments as well?" (p. 214). One of the questions Strasser and Koeppel suggest teachers ask themselves—"Are girls given as much wait time as boys?"—relates directly to the next chapter.

In intriguing descriptions of anecdotes and analysis, Sonja de Groot Kim shares observations made over an extended period of time in a suburban child development center ("Lessons Learned Early: Girls Wait"). Describing in detail toddlers and their teachers, de Groot Kim shows how over and over girls are subtly taught to wait for the boys. Her observations and analysis emerge as she focuses specifically on the teachers' interactions with the children because, as she says, "their interactions seemed to set the tone for what transpired in the classroom" (p. 239). We are asked to look at the evidence the author provides through her thorough descriptions of what happened, her own comments, and questions that she asked herself throughout her research. De Groot Kim asks us to determine from the evidence she shares whether the teachers might be sending messages to the children that could be construed as gendered messages. This chapter is powerful because it shows that even when teachers are competent, caring, and conscientious, they still might unconsciously expose very young, impressionable children to gender-related messages. Dr. de Groot Kim's hope is that we will become more aware of our own differentiated responses to the young children in our care.

In the final chapter, Shaun Johnson wonders, "how can the counsel of educators be taken seriously that children can grow up to be whomever they want to be if the educators' own profession is marred by an ongoing adherence to traditional and conservative gender values?" (p. 249) ("Men in Education: Reframing the Gender Issue"). Johnson asks a number of provocative questions throughout his chapter as he explores the broader issue of gender disparity in teaching, including discussions about status and prestige, salary and benefits, and physical contact with children. Johnson calls on us to rethink the gender issue in education, saying, "It is now for us to decide: Is there something inherent about teaching that makes it more attractive to women or are we as its professionals defining teaching so narrowly that only a slim sliver of the male population joins it?" (p. 252). As I read this chapter, I find myself questioning much of what I thought I knew about gender stereotypes, feminist theory, and, especially, reasons for the scarcity of men in early childhood settings. In fact, I find myself thinking about ways I might change my teacher education courses and "refocus on the cultural conditions that leave [men] out of the classroom in the first place," as he suggests, instead of focusing "simply on so-called boy- or girl-friendly teaching strategies" (p. 263).

CONCLUSION

Gender identity is at the core of our being, the source of expectations for ourselves and those that society has of us. Societal forces and cultural norms, as well as the way our family members guided and taught us our beliefs, values, biases, and attitudes, have all gone toward shaping our gender identity. We learned to fit in and acknowledge the expectations of our gender roles in order to survive and succeed in society. Some of our most beloved role models taught us these expectations.

Each time I read the chapters in this book, I reconfirm the importance of the work that teachers and caregivers of young children do for such long hours every day of the week, year in and year out. The pay more often than not does not support a family, and many of you are doing all you can to keep body and soul together as you devote your energy, knowledge, and emotions to the young children in your care. And now, here we come, my colleagues and I, to tell you that some of what we all have learned since our own early childhood is no longer useful—indeed, is even harmful! We ask you to rethink, relearn, reflect, and change the way you feel and believe for the good of us all. The very fact that you are reading this book makes me hopeful that you will try to make these changes for the good of those young children you care for and educate so diligently. I am most grateful for your tireless efforts and dedication. Thank you!

Being a teacher is an awesome profession and an awesome responsibility because we are the people who can give our students different options about how they think about and understand gender identity, and we can influence the all-important choice to change their worldview. In the words of William Ayers (1998, xvii):

> The fundamental message of the teacher is this: You can change your life. Whoever you are, wherever you've been, whatever you've done, the teacher invites you to a second chance, another round, perhaps a different conclusion. . . . To teach consciously for social justice, to teach for social change, adds a complicating element to that fundamental message, making it more layered, more dense, more excruciatingly difficult to enact, and at the same time sturdier, more engaging, more powerful and joyful much of the time. . . . And so the fundamental message of the teacher for social justice is: You can change the world.

I am grateful for my colleagues' contributions to our different perspectives on gender and early childhood. It is my hope that this collection of chapters will shed some light and insight, as well as stimulate discussion and reflection about how young children learn about their gender identity. No matter what the subject—mathematics instruction, literacy, dramatic play, or social studies—teachers' interactions set the tone for what happens in classrooms, and they decide which messages are transmitted to children unconsciously or intentionally. We have the power to reinforce gender stereotypes or we can choose to abandon those stereotypes and develop more humane, just, and fulfilling ways of relating to one another. Whether our scholarship is qualitative and descriptive or quantitative and accounted, the way in which we reflect and synthesize our findings will be determined by our biases, early emotional memories, or life experiences, as well as by knowledge gained. Self-reflection, therefore, is key to unlearning systems and traditions that are no longer useful for us and that cause discrimination, social inequality, and injustice.

REFERENCES

Ayers, W. 1998. Foreword. In *Teaching for social justice: A democracy and education reader,* eds. W. Ayers, J. A. Hunt, and T. Quinn. New York: Teachers College Press.

Clinebell, C. H. 1973. *Meet me in the middle: On becoming human together.* New York: Harper and Row.

Debold, E., M. Wilson, and I. Malavé. 1993. *Mother daughter revolution: From betrayal to power.* Reading, MA: Addison-Wesley Publishing Company.

Holland, D. C., and M. A. Eisenhart. 1990. *Educated in romance: Women, achievement, and college culture.* Chicago: University of Chicago Press.

hooks, b. 2000. *Feminism is for everybody: Passionate politics.* Cambridge, MA: South End Press.

Jacobson, T. 2003. *Confronting our discomfort: Clearing the way for anti-bias in early childhood.* Portsmouth, NH: Heinemann.

———. 2008. *"Don't get so upset!" Help young children manage their feelings by understanding your own.* St. Paul, MN: Redleaf Press.

ONE

Practical Applications from the History of Gender and Early Childhood Education

— Blythe F. Hinitz and Dorothy W. Hewes —

The history of gender studies in early childhood education foreshadows many of the chapters in this book. From ancient days to the present time there has been gender-differentiated dress, child rearing, play, and education.

Gender differences in Spartan, Athenian, and Roman education have been discussed in the literature. Plato, for example, recommended spontaneous play, under careful supervision, with boys and girls together up to the age of six years. Separate education was to begin at that time. The artwork of the Middle Ages depicted children as "small figures in adult dress," leading to the controversial writing of Ariès, disputed by Shahar and deMause (see Lascarides and Hinitz 2000). Jewish children of the Middle Ages and Early Modern Period attended gender-segregated schools. Boys were educated to become part of the prayer community, while girls' learning and skill development prepared them to assume traditional women's roles. Later, during the 1600s and 1700s, boys and girls in Europe and the New World were dressed in identical white gowns, which were long in their earliest years and shorter as they reached the age when they were learning to walk. In the eighteenth century, or later in some places, boys were not given "breeches" (trousers) to wear until they were five to seven years old. In paintings of the period, boys sometimes had dogs and girls had dolls. In his letters, Locke was quite specific about the differentiated discipline and education of boys and girls.

During the Victorian Age in the United States, doctors who emphasized that both boys and girls needed vigorous exercise that led to deep breathing recommended clothing reform. The Rational Dress Society was established in 1881. They recommended shorter dresses that would not hinder infant development (Smith-Rosenberg 1986). An article in the *Cincinnati Enquirer* of November 27, 1880, describes the Music Hall performance of a group of children from the Kindergarten Association. They marched, sang songs, played traditional kindergarten activity games, and used rhythm instruments to accompany an adult orchestra. The article states that as they marched in "the sight was both a novel and a pretty one. The little girls, whose ages ranged from three to six years, were attired, some in pure white, others in indigo blue, and others in plaid. Another sweet little costume was set forth by the addition of a tiny lace collar. The boys one and all, excepting the little toddlers who hadn't graduated from frocks into pants, all wore large white collars in true naval style."

GENDER DIVISIONS IN SCHOOLS

Descriptions of the colonial period in the United States note that both boys and girls attended "Dame schools" and church-sponsored elementary schools. Although primary schools were open to children of both genders in all of the colonies, the curriculum taught to boys and girls differed, because their education was considered preparation for their adult roles and duties. The literature about Froebel's schools differs in its descriptions of whether boys and girls attended his elementary-level school together. However, there is no dispute that, from its inception, the kindergarten enrolled students of both genders. Nor is there differentiated discussion of the children's play with the Gifts, or their engagement with the Occupations.

The movement toward group programs for younger children included the nursery school begun by the McMillan sisters in England and the Casa dei Bambini founded by Montessori in Italy. In both instances, the children had undifferentiated involvement with the materials and participation in the activities. When these three programs (kindergarten, nursery school, and the Montessori Method) were brought to the United States, boys and girls continued to participate equally in all aspects of the curriculum (Hewes 1998). Histories of the development of kindergartens, nursery schools, and child care centers in the United States from the 1800s into the 1960s focus primarily on philosophy, curriculum, facilities, and materials—or teacher education—with little attention paid to gender issues.

The decade of the 1960s saw criticism of the equality and relevance of school experiences. "In defining sources and manifestations of inequality, we have come to recognize sex as one basis for 'sorting' children and for providing differential opportunities. As we become aware of changes in the roles of women and men, we see that such sorting on the basis of sex limits the optimal growth of *all* children. . . . As the roles and lives of women have changed, so have those of men. With women's increased entry into the labor force, many men have assumed new responsibilities in maintaining home and family" (McCune and Matthews 1976, 179–80).

DEALING WITH SEX ROLE STEREOTYPES

Research completed by Maccoby and Jacklin in 1974 concluded that a number of traditional beliefs about nonreproductive sex differences were myths. Among these were the views that girls are more "social" and "suggestible" and have lower self-esteem than boys; additionally, that girls lack motivation to achieve, differ from boys in learning processes, and are less analytical than boys. However, Maccoby and Jacklin (as cited in McCune and Matthews 1976, 180) did find evidence that

- males are more aggressive than females
- girls have greater verbal ability than boys
- boys excel in visual–spatial and mathematical ability

The February 1976 issue of *Childhood Education,* titled Overcoming Sex-Role Stereotypes, endeavored to assist schools in changing the organization of their physical environment and curriculum and their administrative and personnel practices. It looked at how schools transmit sex roles, presented space ideas for what teachers can do, and suggested resources to support nonstereotypical education (Cohen 1976).

In October 1976, a group of leaders came together at the Conference on Non-Sexist Early Childhood Education. For the first time, work that had been going on all over the country was shared on a national scale. Barbara Bowman, Monroe Cohen, Lilian Katz, Selma Greenberg, Letty Cottin Pogrebin, and many others shared their research that supported ideas about sex differences in the use of space; the political, cultural, and psychological aspects of the topic; play; and parenting. The edited volume of the conference proceedings provided a blueprint for the action that followed (Sprung 1978).

During the 1970s, early childhood educators began to look at sex-role stereotyping, and a few research projects were initiated. Among the first was a study done by the Women's Action Alliance, begun in 1973, as a result of women's concern that their children were being forced into rigidly stereotyped roles, even in preschool. The goals of the Non-Sexist Child Development Project were

- to present men and women in a nurturing role so that children understand parenting as a shared responsibility.
- to show women and men performing a wide variety of jobs so that children understand that people are free to choose their work from an enormous variety of options unhampered by sex typing.
- to encourage girls as well as boys to engage in active play and to encourage boys as well as girls to enjoy quiet play.
- to help boys and girls respect each other so that they can be friends throughout childhood and into adulthood. (The authors continue, "We do not mean that children of opposite sexes will always play together. Girls will want to be with girls and boys with boys much of the time. However, we feel that our social mores encourage this separation of the sexes rather than minimize it. We also feel that the way girls are presented in children's materials as passive, fearful creatures who strive constantly for adults' approval helps to create the derisive attitudes boys have towards girls.")
- to encourage the full physical development of all children.
- to encourage boys and girls to develop and be able to express a full range of emotions. It is mostly boys who are shortchanged in this area.

                                                        (Sprung 1975, 1–2)

The child development literature is replete with statements such as the following: "By the age of two, girls are becoming slightly smaller and lighter than boys, a difference that continues until puberty. Tests of motor and perceptual development show no significant differences between boys and girls until after they reach the elementary school age of six" (Santrock 1988, 260). However, historically and currently, these statements tend to be ignored by those with gender-specific political or educational agendas. Recent brain research has been cited by several practitioners to bolster their interpretations of "the mismatch between boys and conventional education" (Gurian and Stevens 2006, 87). Many genetic and socialized differences between the male and female brain have been identified in the literature, including the following:

- verbal/spatial differences (boys generally have more cortical areas dedicated to spatial-mechanical functioning)
- different chromosome markers
- different types of ganglion cells space (causing boys to rely more on pictures and moving objects when they write)
- differences in development of the prefrontal cortex and the frontal lobe (causing girls to be less impulsive than boys)
- boys' brains go into neural rest states many more times each day than girls' brains do (boys' brains go into a less active mode that "negates learning and performance")
- boys' brains tend to lateralize and compartmentalize brain activity, causing less cross-talk between hemispheres (causing many boys to have a single-task focus, to concentrate best when they follow a step-by-step sequence, and to take more time than girls to transition between tasks)
- the male physiological system has less oxytocin (causing boys to tend toward greater impulsivity, more competitiveness and aggression, and to have "less desire than girls to comply to please others, including teachers") (see King and Gurian 2006, 59; Gurian 2006; Gurian and Stevens 2004; Gurian and Henley 2001; Gurian and Stevens, 2005)

The debate and discussion is not limited to the professional literature, having found its way into popular print and online media. For example, the Sesame Workshop Web site includes a discussion of gender stereotyping, divided by chronological age group. In the discussion of the development of two- to five-year-olds, Flatter states that children have absorbed gender stereotyping by the time they are two years old because the clothing and toys a baby is given are chosen by

adults "with an eye toward gender." Among the cultural factors Flatter (n.d., 1) describes in this article is the tendency of boys to choose a
toy gun over other playthings by the time they are two or three years
old. Tyson (n.d., 1–2) describes the ages six to eleven years as a time
when gender identity is consolidated. She maintains that children, consciously or unconsciously, may "pattern themselves more closely after
one sex or the other." Tyson concludes that "when people allow their
thinking about gender definitions to expand, women and men can then
choose the best qualities of both sexes."

GENDER-APPROPRIATE PLAY OPPORTUNITIES

Play is an area where the differentiation between boys and girls can be
blatantly apparent. A number of authors, including Baker and Ehrhart
(1973) and Erikson (1950) have described dissimilarities between males
and females. It has been said that males engage in rougher types of play
and are more intrusive, and females are more passive and engage in
calmer, more passive play.

In *You Can't Say You Can't Play,* Vivian Gussin Paley (1992)
recounts her discussion with kindergarten through grade five students
after she initiated the above rule in her kindergarten classroom. Some
children felt that everyone should be able to play together, while some
thought it was fair that boys or girls could play in single-sex groups.
However, as Penny Holland (2003) discovered, the zero-tolerance
policy about war, weapon, and superhero play can cause difficulties in
the early childhood classroom, particularly for boys (see also Carlsson-
Paige and Levin 1990).

During the late 1970s and the 1980s adult male violence figured into
the nature-versus-nurture debate. It caused child care and kindergarten
teachers to ban superhero and conflict play from their classrooms because
of the unsubstantiated belief about a connection between these types of
play and aggressive behavior. Holland's (2003) review of the literature
found little research to corroborate a causal link between toy gun play,
for example, and aggression. In fact, her own research into the relaxation
of the zero-tolerance policy found that children are empowered both to
deepen their own thoughtful play and encouraged to say "no" when they
do not like what is happening. The exposure of teachers' distorted perceptions of the number of play incidents, and the identity of those involved in
war, weapon, and superhero play in their own classrooms, led to extensive

reflection and discussion among the practitioners involved. In the majority of the child care centers studied, when the zero-tolerance policy was relaxed, there was more free play among boys, leading to enhanced social skills, inclusion, more imaginative play, and friendships.

Some of the author Hinitz's graduate students have made the following points in debating the issue of young children's superhero play:

Pro
- Children may use superhero play to express themselves.
- Children can develop language skills by creating sequential stories.
- Children can develop cognitive skills through cooperation.
- Children can develop gross motor skills when they run, jump, tumble, and climb to act out a story.
- Children can develop affective skills when they gain power over their fears.

Con
- Superhero play excludes children.
- Danger and safety issues exist, possibly due to lack of adult supervision.
- Teacher intervention is often necessary.
- It may lead to children becoming scared, out of control, or even hurt.
- Children may engage in the same violent play day after day without bringing in new or creative ideas of their own.
- Children's self-esteem and trust are affected.

EFFECTS OF SCHOOL POLICIES AND PROGRAMS ON CHILDREN

Holland (2003, 99) reminds us that "zero-tolerance relies on the use of adult power in the real world to enforce a moral and behavioral imperative against powerless children operating in a fantasy world." She echoes Montessori who, in a 1932 address to a convention at the International Office of Education in Geneva, Switzerland (later published as *Education and Peace*), said that "in the child, we can find the natural human characteristics before they are spoiled by the harmful influences of society" (Wolf 1989).

Montessori maintained that adults attempt to mold children to societal patterns by forcing them to develop different characteristics and behaviors, which causes conflicts between parents or teachers and children. In this struggle (for example, the execution of a zero-tolerance policy), the adult usually triumphs over the child, "and when that child becomes an adult, he bears, graven forever, the marks of that infamous peace that follows war, which is, in reality, a painful adaptation" (Wolf 1989).

Montessori believed that if education recognizes the intrinsic value of the child's personality and provides an environment suited to spiritual growth, a new child emerges "whose astonishing characteristics can eventually contribute to the betterment of the world" (Wolf 1989). She asserted that an education that is merely a blind struggle between the strong and the weak produces inefficient adults, and therefore, school conditions that foster strife and conquest between persons of unequal status should be replaced with more nourishing and supportive ones. She further stated that "the child who has never learned to act alone, to direct his own actions, to govern her own will, grows into an adult who is easily lead and must always lean upon others" (Wolf 1989). Montessori, in this address delivered between two world wars, elaborated on her philosophy, contending that "the cause of war does not lie in armaments, but in the adults who make use of them. . . . Docile citizens engage in warfare, not because of hatred, but because they have been ordered to do so" (Wolf 1989). Approximately seventy-five years later, Gartrell concurred, stating, "Some children, especially high-energy boys, face increasingly inappropriate programs, which offer lots of seat-work and little movement. It is as if some teachers are rehearsing their young students for the sit-down academic world to come. Children who are *kinetic* or total-body learners suffer. They need active classrooms that affirm and accept them" (Gartrell 2006b, 1; see also King and Gartrell 2003, 106–24). Gartrell believes that "programs are developmentally appropriate only if they support *all* [emphasis added] children, not some or even most" (2006b, 2). He echoes Kessler and Swadener (1992, xxi) who state that the debate

> between those advocating what the NAEYC calls "appropriate" versus "inappropriate" practices . . . can be viewed as a debate between two or more different interest groups lobbying for a particular set of values, taking different political positions, and representing different philosophical schools of thought. What appears to be a debate between those who are well informed by current

research in child development, and those who are not is, in reality, a debate between individuals who hold different values about the purposes of schooling, what counts as legitimate knowledge, and presumably the nature of the good life and the just society.

Some concern has been expressed about the "takeover" of boys' issues by conservative groups. This position is exemplified by the work of Weaver-Hightower. Writing in the journal *Men and Masculinities* (2008, 289–90), he cautions us against falling prey to the conservative "strategy of providing simple solutions," such as "buying the right toys, reading the right books, and spending a few extra hours fishing at the creek." He additionally cites the strategies of using the language of character traits, such as respect, responsibility, and resourcefulness, and providing "boy friendly" literature as a means of "reinforcing traditional masculinity, rather than allowing masculinity to adapt to the social changes going on." Weaver-Hightower suggests that the "suturing of the boys' debate to conservative, authoritarian populist discourses distracts teachers, parents, and researchers from the more progressive goals of working with boys . . . for progressive ends."

A different position is taken by Judith Smilg Kleinfeld, a member of the Independent Women's Forum (a conservative research and educational institution) and founder of the Boys Project, a not-for-profit group formed to address the female-male gender gap in educational achievement. The project counts the controversial Diane Ravitch, Christina Hoff Sommers, Michael Thompson, William S. Pollack, Michael Gurian, and Leonard Sax among its board members. If these names seem familiar, it is because the majority of them have authored books and articles about boys' issues in popular as well as professional periodicals (see for example Kleinfeld 1998; Sommers 2001; Pollack 1998).

TEACHER PERCEPTIONS
OF GENDER DIFFERENCES

Research on preschool teachers' perception of gender differences, conducted by Hyun and Tyler (1999, 28), found that "in some ways, preschool teachers may reinforce young children of both sexes for 'feminine' rather than 'masculine' behavior. In classrooms, obedience is usually valued and teachers generally discourage assertiveness." The authors go on to critique "institutionalized 'feminine bias'" as causing "a certain degree of discomfort for boys in school." They argue that this type of bias may be even more harmful for girls, causing "possible long-term negative consequences for their sense of independence and self-esteem." The authors remind teachers that "because a feminine bias exists and influences pedagogical practices, teachers need to be extremely careful to maintain gender-congruent experiences and a gender-fair learning environment."

A more recent qualitative Australian study looked at how gender was created and sustained in an urban kindergarten from a feminist post-structuralist point of view. Mindy Blaise (2005, 105) discusses examples of how the young children in this setting constructed themselves "as gendered beings, socially, culturally, and politically." Blaise states that "these alternative ways of understanding children and how they 'do' gender might also challenge teachers to question child-centered cur-riculum." She asserts that the pervasiveness of the heterosexual matrix and gender discourses in classrooms must be recognized. She believes that it will be necessary to move beyond the biological and socialization frameworks by including such alternative perspectives as feminist post-structuralism to find the complexities of gender and recognize the mul-tiple ways in which children "do" gender. She concludes that it will then become possible to enact pedagogies leading to "gender equity strategies that will successfully change the current gendered social order in our classrooms and society" (105–6).

CULTURAL FACTORS IN GENDER CHARACTERISTICS

A program that appears to have had positive and negative consequences for boys as well as girls is Project Head Start. The work of Cynthia and Martin Deutsch has been cited for its suggestion that low-income chil-dren who attended Head Start did better in school than those who did not, and that, by adulthood, the advantages of Head Start favor males more than females (Deutsch et al. 1981). Santrock believes that because "the preschool program stressed verbal skills, inquisitiveness, and self-confidence . . . the boys were rewarded for showing these characteristics, but in many instances, girls were punished for showing similar behav-iors. Some teachers, for instance, even complained that the girls were too assertive and asked too many questions" (Santrock 1988, 239; see also Lazar et al. 1982).

One group of boys in particular has had, and continues to have, a difficult struggle in early childhood classrooms. Black boys have been disproportionately singled out for their manifestations of gender-based development, and family- and culture-based experiences. Haynes, for example, includes preschool as one of the three phases of development during which critical events influence the lives of Black males. He states that "during the pre-school years, Black males need caring and attentive adults in stable environments to whom they can look for guidance." He further states that families can be strengthened from within and without, including family support groups, big brother programs, and other experiences with "responsible, reliable and well-adjusted adult [Black] males" among the possibilities (Haynes 1993, 129, 134; see also Morgan 1995, 205–13).

The lack of these support systems leads to data such as that presented by Gilliam (2005, based on the National Pre-kindergarten Study) that four-year-old Black boys are expelled from public prekindergarten programs twice as often as Latino and Caucasian children, and they are over five times as likely to be expelled as Asian American children. In a later study, observers for Barbarin and Crawford (2006) found that in some prekindergarten and kindergarten programs, single children were isolated by their teachers to control their "difficult and disruptive" behaviors. The observers reported that "the children who were separated and excluded were almost always boys of color." The authors conclude that "failure to acknowledge the role of race in our society has perils. Programs flirt with failure if they ignore how some classroom practices may seem to stigmatize and denigrate children because of their race. Early in life too many children of color, particularly boys, come to learn that they are not valued by society. Their present and future well-being depends on the commitment of early childhood professionals at all levels." In their article, Barbarin and Crawford ask whether the observers' reports of successful teachers highlighted the work of those who had graduated "from teacher preparation programs that prepare them to work with children from a wide range of cultural backgrounds" (80, 86).

PREPARING TEACHERS TO DEAL WITH GENDER INEQUITY

Current national professional standards for initial teacher preparation programs expect all accredited higher education institutions to integrate multicultural and gender-related coursework into their programs. The criteria for teacher certification in most states include required study of these fields. However, that was not always the case. The New Jersey Project, Integrating the Scholarship on Gender, created in 1986, was among the first programs in the nation to encourage and engage teachers and scholars as institutional change agents to foster curriculum transformation. A possible response to Barbarin and Crawford is found in Hinitz (1996), which discusses the further infusion of diversity content (including nonsexist content) into the early childhood education course titled Guiding the Learning Experiences of Young Children, following attendance at the summer seminar of the New Jersey Project. In describing what students gain from the infusion of this content, the author states that students "have access to the printed materials, media, and hands-on experiences that will assist them in incorporating such ideas and content into their personal lives as well as into their teaching" (Hinitz 1996, 268). In the late 1990s, some sourcebooks for teachers of young children promoted learning activities to foster equity. It was an attempt to counter the belief that "females and males have distinctive characteristics, and that one gender has the right to more power and resources than the other" (Schniedewind and Davidson 1998, 8). The books included information about and suggestions for changing the physical environment, textbooks and media, and the curriculum (Schlank and Metzger 1997).

UNDERGRADUATE RESEARCHERS CONTRIBUTE TO THE FIELD

Undergraduate student researchers are the wave of the future. Their research both confirms the findings of previous studies and branches out in new directions. Several members of the Discipline Specific Research Seminars in Early Childhood Education have chosen projects in the sphere of gender education. One study—Using Technology in Early Childhood Professional Education: Combating the Effects of Media Violence and Supporting Boys' Learning—was presented as part of the workshop at the National Association for the Education of Young Children (NAEYC) Professional Development Institute held in June 2008 in New Orleans (Hinitz et al. 2008).

The study utilized observation instruments and a questionnaire to look at a number of factors that can have a negative effect on boys' school experiences, including

- less active play with few large-muscle activities
- little or no rough physical play
- a requirement to sit still for long periods of time, to listen, and to retain information given orally
- a requirement to work at a desk or table rather than on the floor or at a place of one's own choosing
- an emphasis on quiet activities like puzzles
- having few books or magazines on topics that interest boys
- having few male materials or props for dramatic play
- making woodworking rarely available and having fewer messy activities such as using fingerpaint, playdough, papier-mâché, or clay
- the absence of hands-on math and science activities

Students in kindergarten to grade three classrooms were observed to answer the following questions:

- Is the classroom setup beneficial to boys?
- Are psychomotor activities such as block and dramatic play permitted?
- Is there room for active play?
- What types of activities are boys involved in?
- How are the boys interacting with their peers?
- Are there specific instances of gender stereotyping?

The student researcher found that in many instances, activity choices were restricted and boys were not given the full opportunity to explore and engage in physical activity. Their need for more space in the classroom was rarely addressed. The space in play areas in the kindergarten and first grade classrooms was insufficient for the types of play boys wanted to engage in. The second and third grade classrooms had a specific requirement for everyone to stay seated throughout the day.

Classroom teachers were surveyed about differences they saw between boys and girls in the classroom. They were asked about actions that were permitted or prohibited for boys and/or girls. Although teachers believed it was difficult to say that one gender was functioning at a higher level cognitively, socially, or emotionally than the other, they did see distinct differences between them. Corroborating other research in the literature, they stated that girls were more advanced in literacy and boys were more spatially oriented. The overall consensus was that girls are more mature socially, are very talkative, and that they form cliques. Teachers said that girls preferred to have leaders in their groups. Boys were viewed as very active and aggressive, and they often acted inappropriately. However, the teachers felt that boys worked better as a team and that they are more sensitive than girls, but they do not often let others see that. The teachers agreed that all children develop differently; therefore one can never make generalizations about the genders. They also said that each year's class varies from the previous one. By self-report, teachers said they tried to treat all children equally by applying rules and regulations in a similar manner to everyone. Children of both genders were expected to follow directions and behave in the same way. Teachers stated that they would adapt rules and expectations according to situations that arise, but they would never base the adaptation on gender.

WHAT IS BEST FOR BOYS AND GIRLS?

Room arrangement, daily schedule, classroom management and discipline techniques, teaching methods, observations, evaluations, and assessments all have an impact on what happens to boys and girls in classrooms. However, factors such as differentiated childrearing, dress, play patterns, and socialization may have a greater impact on boys than girls. We therefore need to draw from the historical record the pedagogy that works, and from current and future research supports for both the boys and the girls in our early childhood education programs.

REFERENCES

Baker, A., and W. S. Ehrhart. 1973. Hormonal aberrations and their implications for the understanding of normal sex differentiation. Paper presented at Society for Research in Child Development, Philadelphia.

Barbarin, O., and G. Crawford. 2006. Acknowledging and reducing stigmatization of African American boys. *Young Children* 61 (6): 79–86.

Blaise, M. 2005. A feminist poststructuralist study of children "doing" gender in an urban kindergarten classroom. *Early Childhood Research Quarterly* 20 (1): 85–108.

Carlsson-Paige, N., and D. E. Levin. 1990. *Who's calling the shots? How to respond effectively to children's fascination with war play and war toys.* Philadelphia: New Society.

Cohen, M. D., ed. 1976. *Growing free: Ways to help children overcome sex-role stereotypes.* Washington DC: Association for Childhood Education International.

Deutsch, C., M. Deutsch, T. Jordan, and R. Grallo. 1981. Long-term effects of project Head Start. Paper presented at the annual meeting of the American Psychological Association, Los Angeles.

Erikson, E. H. 1950. *Childhood and society.* New York: Norton.

Flatter, C. n.d. Gender: Two to five. Sesame Workshop. http://www.sesameworkshop.org/parents/advice (retrieved June 7, 2006).

Gartrell, D. 2006a. Boys and men teachers. *Young Children* 61 (3): 92–93.

———. 2006b. Boys and men teachers. *Beyond the Journal.* May. http://journal.naeyc.org/btj/200605/GuidanceBTJ.pdf.

Gilliam, W. S. 2005. *Prekindergarteners left behind: Expulsion rates in state pre-kindergarten programs.* New York: Foundation for Child Development.

Gurian, M. 2006. Learning and gender. *American School Board Journal* 193 (10): 19–22.

Gurian, M., P. Henley, and T. Trueman. 2001. *Boys and girls learn differently: A guide for teachers and parents.* San Francisco: Jossey-Bass.

Gurian, M., and K. Stevens. 2004. With boys and girls in mind. *Educational Leadership* 62 (3): 21–26.

———. 2005. *The minds of boys: Saving our sons from falling behind in school and life.* San Francisco: Jossey-Bass.

———. 2006. How are the boys doing? How boys learn. *Educational Horizons* 84 (2): 87–93.

Haynes, N. M. 1993. *Critical issues in educating African-American children.* Langley Park, MD: IAAS Publishers.

Hewes, D. W. 1998. *It's the camaraderie: A history of parent cooperative pre-schools.* Davis, CA: Center for Cooperatives.

Hinitz, B. F. 1996. Guiding the learning experiences of young children: A course in early childhood education. In *Creating an inclusive college curriculum: A teaching sourcebook from the New Jersey project,* ed. E. G. Friedman, W. K. Kolmar, C. B. Flint, and P. Rothenberg, 263–69. New York: Teachers College Press.

Hinitz, B., B. Sprung, M. Froschl, and J. Chesney. 2008. Using technology in early childhood professional education: Combating the effects of media violence and supporting boys' learning. Presented at the National Association for the Education of Young Children Professional Development Institute, New Orleans.

Holland, P. 2003. *We don't play with guns here: War, weapon, and superhero play in the early years.* Philadelphia: Open University Press.

Hyun, E., and M. Tyler. 1999. Examination of preschool teachers' biased perception on gender differences. Paper presented at the annual meeting of
   the American Educational Research Association, Montreal, QC.

Kessler, S., and B. B. Swadener, ed. 1992. *Reconceptualizing the early childhood
   curriculum: Beginning the dialogue.* New York: Teachers College Press.

King, K., and M. Gurian. 2006. Teaching to the minds of boys. *Educational
   Leasdership* 64 (1): 56–61.

King, M., and D. Gartrell. 2003. Building an encouraging classroom with boys
   in mind. *Young Children* 58 (4): 33–36.

Kleinfeld, J. S. 1998. *The myth that schools shortchange girls: Social science in the
   service of deception.* Washington, DC: The Women's Freedom Network.

Lascarides, V. C., and B. F. Hinitz. 2000. *History of early childhood education.*
   New York: Falmer Press.

Lazar, I., R. Darlington, H. Murray, J. Royce, A. Snipper, and C. T. Ramey.
   1982. Lasting effects of early education: A report from the consortium
   for longitudinal studies. *Monographs of the Society for Research in Child
   Development* 47 (2): 202–04.

Maccoby, E., and C. Jacklin. 1974. *The psychology of sex differences.* Stanford,
   CA: Stanford University Press.

McCune, S. D., and M. Matthews. 1976. Building positive futures: Toward a
   nonsexist education for all children. *Childhood Education* 52 (4): 178–86.

Montessori, M. 1932. Education and Peace. Chicago: Regnery.

Morgan, H. 1995. *Historical perspectives on the education of black children.*
   Westport, CT: Praeger Publishers.

Paley, V. G. 1992. *You can't say you can't play.* Cambridge, MA: Harvard University Press.

Pollack, W. 1998. *Real boys: Rescuing our sons from the myths of boyhood.* New
   York: Random House.

Pollack, W., and T. Shuster. 2001. *Real boys' voices.* With contributions by J.
   Trelease. New York: Penguin Books.

Santrock, J. W. 1988. *Children.* Dubuque, IA: W. C. Brown.

Schlank, C. H., and B. Metzger. 1997. *Together and equal: Fostering cooperative
   play and promoting gender equity in early childhood programs.* Boston: Allyn
   and Bacon.

Schniedewind, N., and E. Davidson. 1998. *Open minds to equality: A sourcebook
   of learning activities to affirm diversity and promote equity.* 2nd ed. Boston:
   Allyn and Bacon.

Smith-Rosenberg, C. 1986. *Disorderly conduct: Visions of gender in Victorian
   America.* New York: Oxford University Press.

Sommers, C. H. 2001. *The war against boys: How misguided feminism is harming our young men*. New York: Touchstone Books.

Sprung, B. 1975. *Non-sexist education for young children: A practical guide*. New York: Citation Press.

———, ed. 1978. *Perspectives on non-sexist early childhood education*. New York: Teachers College Press.

Tyson, P. n.d. Gender: Six to eleven. Sesame Workshop. http://www .sesameworkshop.org/parents/advice (retrieved June 7, 2006).

Weaver-Hightower, M. B. 2008. Inventing the "all-American boy": A case study of the capture of boys' issues by conservative groups. *Men and masculinities* 10 (3): 267–95.

Wolf, A. D. 1989. *Peaceful children, peaceful world: The challenge of Maria Montessori*. Altoona, PA: Parent Child Press.

TWO

Discussing Gender

— Eila Estola —

This chapter is based on an inquiry conducted within discussion groups of early childhood teachers in two child care centers funded by the Academy of Finland no. 208745. These child care centers were in regular middle-sized (around sixty to seventy-five children in three or four groups), municipal-owned settings. In both centers children's ages ranged between one and six years.

The poststructural research has shown the significance of gender in the lives of young children. From the very first moments of their lives babies are treated as either girls or boys. Gender construction begins at a very early age as girls and boys are divided by guiding them to separate, diverse practices in their everyday lives (MacNaughton 2001). Thus the concept of gender refers especially to cultural and social phenomena and focuses on the behavior and the ideas of what it means to be a man or a woman. Children are guided to adopt different values, since the ideal of a good girl and of a good boy differ from one another. A "good" girl is caring, empathetic, and responsible, while a "good" boy is guided to use reason, to not display his emotions, and to be sporty and independent (Noddings 1986).

In this chapter I describe some issues early childhood teachers considered significant as they spoke of gender issues in child care centers. My practical aim is to encourage practitioners to reflect on their own practices by illustrating how discussions can support such critical reflection.

THE FINNISH CONTEXT
OF EARLY CHILDHOOD EDUCATION

Finland is known as one of the twenty richest countries in the world, and as a country of relatively small differences between the rich and poor. This sparsely populated country has only 5.2 million inhabitants, is located in Northern Europe, and shares its borders with Sweden, Norway, and Russia. Finland is a member of the European Union. The nation is bilingual, with a Finnish-speaking majority and a Swedish-speaking minority. In addition, there are other small minorities, for instance, those who speak Sámi, as well as the Romany citizens. The 100,000 or so population of immigrants in Finland represent 150 nationalities. Compared to many other European countries, Finland can be considered a rather homogeneous country when examining its population.

Finland and other Nordic countries have had a special ideology of social justice to support the welfare of all their citizens. Since this ideology has an impact on gender equality and on equality in general, I will briefly describe it here. Society tends to care for everyone, especially those who are helpless: children, elderly, sick, handicapped, and other vulnerable people. In addition, many social and health services as well as education and schooling are free and available to everyone. These services are organized by the state, municipalities, or other public institutions. To finance all these services the inhabitants pay relatively high taxes (Moore, Antikainen, and Kosonen 2005).

From the gender equality perspective, Finnish family policy has made it possible for women to work outside the home by creating a safe environment for children to grow in and by guaranteeing parents the material and psychological resources to bear and raise children. The Ministry of Social and Health Affairs with its research agent have a central responsibility for the education and care of children under the age of six. Child care fees are in relation to family income but are priced very reasonably from no fee to about 150 euros (about 208 U.S. dollars) per month. Free preschool education for six-year-olds has been a reality since 2000 (Organization for Economic Co-Operation and Development 2000, 58; see also Estola et al. 2007).

Early childhood education is based on the so-called "educare" concept in which care, education, and instruction are combined. A core curriculum for early childhood education, care, and preschool guide local authorities in preparing local center-based and child-based curricula. Early childhood teachers are trained in universities, have bachelor's degrees, and many finish their master's degrees as well. Full-time child care centers (more than four hours a day) maintain a minimum ratio of one trained adult per four children under the age of three, and of one early childhood teacher or nurse for every seven children over the age of three. In part-day services, the ratio is thirteen children over three years per one early childhood teacher or nurse.

Historically speaking, the Finnish child care system has roots in educational and social policies that follow the Fröbelian philosophy of offering high-quality education for small children through play and other activities, and by caring for children in need of support. The roots go relatively far in the past since the first Fröbelian "kindergarten" in Finland was established in 1886. Finnish child care has connections with labor policy as well, by offering good child care so that parents are able to work outside their homes. The child care system in Finland is predominantly public. Mainly municipalities provide for these services; additionally, the Lutheran church provides private child care programs and play groups (Kess 2002; Välimäki 1998). Some families prefer home-based child care for their children over the public services. Some municipalities help these families in funding their choices and by finding suitable people to work in their homes.

Preschool constitutes an important link between child care and school education and is mainly organized in child care centers. Pedagogical methods rise from early childhood education. At the end of 2003, 96 percent of six-year-olds were in preschool education. Academic skills are not considered more important than play. Nevertheless the total literacy level for the Finnish population is nearly 100 percent.

Early childhood education and care services are meant to serve the needs of families and to support families in their education. Equity and equality are greatly appreciated at the highest government levels. The national guidelines remind us that constant change in society must be taken into account. The national core curriculum gives frames to local and unit-specific curricula as well as an education plan for every individual child. Close cooperation between parents and educators is considered a prerequisite for good education. Child care centers should support families in their education and take into account the opinions and views of the parents. Surprisingly, nothing precise about gender equality is said explicitly. Instead, regulations use the word "child" and mention equality as a principal for organizing education (National Curriculum Guidelines on Early Childhood Education and Care in Finland 2003).

In many ways, Finland has a very high-quality educational system. Finland has also succeeded in the Program for International Students Assessment (PISA). What is somewhat surprising is that the political and general discussion of gender equality questions has not focused much on education in early childhood education or even primary schools. Research has been done (for example, Lappalainen 2004; Värtö 2000) and some projects conducted (for instance, Leinonen 2005), but the common concerns of gender equality and equity seem to focus more on working life as well as vocational and higher education.

CHALLENGING GENDER ISSUES IN EARLY YEARS

It is characteristic of the public discourse that official guidelines speak of "the child" and of respect for each child's individuality as a unique personality. Critical education and many poststructural theories have, however, shown that the life of each child is connected to many historical, societal, and cultural factors that situate the child. Gender, ethnicity, language, and social class are some of those factors that must be taken into account when talking about the concept of the child. All educators know that the basic values, habits, and attitudes are learned during childhood. For that reason, gender-sensitive education and equality of education should be taken seriously during the early years of childhood.

Research shows that several gendered practices still exist in child care centers. Change is difficult since most of these practices are unconscious: educators have been socialized into them during their own childhood. Often official, societal discourses naturalize gender differences by arguing that these differences have biological grounds and therefore the differences are permanent. Even in such cases where gender-sensitive education is emphasized and gender is understood especially as a social construction, educators often act in a gender-blind manner (Gordon, Holland, Lahelma, and Campling 2000; Lappalainen 2004). Educators often argue that they treat children as individuals—not as girls and boys—and that they are, in fact, gender blind: educators are not aware what guides girls to tasks where they can learn care, responsibility, and other orientations, but support boys in being active, sporty, and competitive. Although two- and three-year-old children are quite conscious of their gender, most children play with gender roles, crossing the borders and enjoying it. However, strict and stereotyped gender roles can prohibit individuals from fulfilling their own ideas and activities (Vuorikoski, Törmä, and Viskari 2003). Thus educators have a lot of power to make a difference by being gender sensitive.

In gender-sensitive pedagogy, the basic idea is to expand gender roles in such a way that children are treated as individuals, not according to the stereotyped gender role. In their interview study, Sandberg and Pramling-Samuelsson (2005) point out how playing with dolls is now not as popular as it was previously. Similar worries have made some other researchers ask how we should promote caring instead of violence (Sunnari, Kangasvuo, and Heikkinen 2002). These worries inspired me as well as three master's dissertations that were conducted on gender issues in Finnish child care centers (Palatsi 2005; Parkkonen 2006; Rantanen 2006).

THE RESEARCH PROCESS

The research material was collected in 2005 from discussions in which early childhood teachers talked about girls, boys, and children in general in early childhood. Gender was the main focus of the discussions. Methodological commitments were in the narrative approach, in which the stories were understood as coconstructions between the participants and the researchers. The stories are not static, but interactive, and the purpose of the storytelling as well as the audience may color what is told (Clandinin and Rosiek 2007).

Two groups of early childhood teachers in two child care centers were recruited to meet three times in the winter of 2004. The first group consisted of four female teachers and one male teacher; the other group was one female and one male teacher. Their ages ranged from about thirty to fifty years, all having several years' work experience. In each group meeting I was present with my three students. At least one of the students had been working or had some practical training in the child care centers and thus was familiar with the participants.

Based on our methodological commitments we understand that by telling, listening, and sharing stories the storytellers can find new perspectives in the ways they understand gender and education. In addition to our research interest, we believed that the participants could also get something back by having the opportunity to discuss and reflect on their thoughts relating to gender.

The meetings were organized as thematic group discussions. We did not have any concrete questions; instead we spoke in advance of our interests and concerns. We discussed how previous research has shown that children play fewer caring games, such as playing house, and that the popular culture is rapidly entering into children's daily lives. Since caring is historically and culturally connected to women's activities and their moral orientation, and the media is sexualizing women more and more, the question arises on how to promote gender equality in early childhood education. We also gave some papers to the participants to read, of which the most important was a report on Hjalli pedagogy (Ólafsdóttir n.d.). From an ethical standpoint we adopted views from critical pedagogy in that we wanted to offer the option for insights rather than only collecting material and then leaving the participants on their own.

Our relationship with the participants became informal. We perceived our roles as participatory, although from time to time we offered some research results for discussion. In that sense, the discussions also had an in-service function. The meetings were held in the child care centers during the day (in a room without the children) and each meeting lasted for about an hour and a half. The meetings were tape-recorded and later transcribed. The atmosphere of the sessions varied and a rich variety of stories were told. Sometimes the shared stories evoked diverse critical self-reflections:

> I think of my own unreflected assumptions and thoughts. For example, during the fall period when there's a new group, and we start doing pencil exercises. I notice that a certain boy has absurdly exact and clear handwriting and feel a glimpse of satisfaction because of it. But with a girl, I consider it quite natural that she's dexterous and crafty with her fingers. This is the case with me. I could even make a list of those children.

Here, a teacher reflects on her own stereotypes. It is well known that teachers often have stereotyped expectations of girls being handy with pens and that they do well in arts and crafts generally. (At the end of this chapter I will explore further the matter of the discussion group as a learning environment.)

The narratives from the teachers tell us that gender is at the same time cultural and personal. Teachers can choose the cultural narratives and they do so at least partly based on their own biographical story. This was obvious in cases where teachers justified and explained some of their views by referring to their own experiences.

For instance, one male teacher mentioned that he has instructed children in how to dance, since he himself had learned folk dances as a youngster. A female teacher explained that since she plays soccer, it is easy for her to play the game with children. Another female teacher told us that during her childhood her parents never questioned her choice to study math or physics. Even though these personal stories are encouraging examples of "exceptional" choices, they also voice the stereotyped cultural story of what is usual or ordinary.

Teachers work in child care centers amongst many, often-contradictory expectations that include gender issues. Families have diverse understandings, each child care center has its own culture, the media and different levels in society have their own discourses—and in the midst of all this each educator has his or her own views. No matter how good their intentions are in promoting equality and using gender-sensitive methods, educators find it can be hard work to put them into practice.

TEACHERS FACE GENDER ISSUES
WITH PARENTS

Official guidelines advise professional caretakers to support families in raising their children (National Curriculum Guidelines on Early Childhood Education and Care in Finland 2003). In practice this means that early childhood teachers and other professional practitioners should listen carefully and take into account what parents or guardians want. Even though daily educational practices of child care centers usually do not arouse many questions or problems, parents may have strong opinions on topics closely connected to values and basic views on life. Sometimes early childhood teachers feel that what parents want is not always best for their child. Gender issues can be one of those conflicting topics. Two examples I provide here shed light on parents' concerns when their sons, in the parents' eyes, are not boyish enough. The third example is from a female early childhood teacher who tells of a father and his sporty daughter who plays ice hockey.

The father was especially worried about his son, even though the boy was nearly perfect. I even asked, "How do you make kids like that, so smart, calm, and considerate?" But because the boy didn't like team sports, the father was extremely worried. I felt that if the child was so good in so many ways, what on earth did it matter if he didn't like to play ice-hockey? It is typical for parents to create these pressures.

After finishing the account, the storyteller's male colleague commented that "the father should give thought to accepting the child as he is." This episode is a multivoiced and vivid story of a parent's expectations of his children as well as his expectations of himself. The father seems to have stereotyped role expectations of how a "good" boy should act: sporty! The teacher telling the story describes the boy very positively, almost as an ideal child. Her male colleague seems to accept this characterization and suggests that the father should accept the child as he is.

It is often said that crossing the boundaries of stereotyped role models is easier and considered more acceptable for girls than for boys. There were no stories in our material where parents worried over girls who didn't behave as "traditional girls" should. On the contrary, a boy who is interested in academic skills or is empathetic is often the target of bullying or becomes marginalized. The next episode describes the worries parents had when their son wanted to wear girls' dresses.

A female teacher and her male colleague had the following discussion:

FEMALE TEACHER: The boy is now in a group of three- to six-year-old children. He likes to pretend being a girl, likes wearing skirts, takes the role of a girl. His parents—mother—interferes if we let him play so.

MALE TEACHER: We haven't really paid much mind to it.

FEMALE TEACHER: Yeah, we haven't really told him that "No, you can't play like that" . . . in some ways we've tried to guide him, but on the other hand we've let him play, perhaps against his parents' will. It hasn't been that big of a deal for us.

This discussion shows that some parents worry if a five-year-old (the age of the boy in question) crosses over gender roles. Parents give instructions to the educators of the child care center. This becomes a moral dilemma for teachers who do not consider this "border crossing" a problem because the official guidelines bind teachers to respect the parents' opinions and to support parents in their children's education.

Later on, the teachers reflected on how the peer group reacted. The teachers told us that boys are more strict, they laugh and make mean comments, whereas girls are more empathetic or indirect. During dramatic play, the girls just give the boy a traditional gender-based role.

MALE TEACHER: It could be that the role casting is actually sourced from the girls so that he has the role of the prince . . .

FEMALE TEACHER: Yeah, they gave him another role than that of the princess, which he might have wanted to have . . . I can imagine that he would still like to be a princess . . .

From an educational point of view we can ask whether the main problem was resolved or not. The girls treated the boy in a stereotyped way. And the teachers had the dilemma of what to do, since the boy's parents did not care for their son acting like a girl. The example confirms that behaving against hetero-normative expectations, against the heterosexual matrix, as Butler (1990) says, will be questioned in the community. In this case it was the other children who "guided" the boy toward the traditional gender role. Obviously the children had already learned much of the binary gender system. My empathies lie on the boy's side: How does he feel? From the educational point of view these kinds of situations are good opportunities to guide children toward more flexible views on gender issues. Nevertheless, it is not easy to negotiate these borders, since crossing gender roles often produces homophobia (Bedford 2009).

In the next extract, a male early childhood teacher tells a story of a father who brought a hockey stick for his daughter to use at the skating session at her child care center. The episode seems to confirm that it is more accepted for girls to be boyish than for a boy to be girlish. At the end, the teacher notices how important it is that each child be supported as an individual person. In this case the father taught the teacher to be sensitive to the needs of each individual child.

The father took hockey sticks and skates with him and took it for granted that she's [his daughter] going to play. It was rather interesting to realize that the fact that she took a hockey stick did astound me: I wouldn't have guessed it. It was so clear for her, that of course she uses a hockey stick, that of course the roles can be reversed. It ought to be like this, that you support a child as he is and avoid leading him to a certain direction, to certain expectations.

The three examples above show that the gender issue is present when teachers cooperate with parents in various ways. Some parents have traditional gender role expectations, while some are ready to break the borders. Sometimes parents' views make early childhood teachers defend gender-sensitive education. Sometimes parents challenge early childhood teachers' own expectations and practices, making them aware that they do not always manage to be as gender sensitive as they might have thought. I consider it important that parents express their own views, since these kinds of confrontations can promote gender-sensitive education.

GENDER ISSUES AND ROLE PLAYS

Children learn and practice the world of adults through role-playing. Playing in general is known as a basic way to learn how to interact with other people, as well as how to think, negotiate, and solve problems (Hyvönen 2008). From a gender dimension it is important that all play domains are not culturally divided into separate "boys" or "girls" games, since this narrows children's possibilities to develop their full potential. However, even young children know that the world is quite dichotomous, that even toys are "for boys" or "for girls."

Teachers discussed games in general, especially domestic role plays, which we had mentioned as one of our interests. We were interested in them since different ways of playing house, like cooking, playing with dolls, shopping, and cleaning, are all ways in which children can learn many caring activities and moral attitudes. Domestic role-playing has also been considered as "something suitable for girls," although some recent studies have shown that boys can enjoy role-playing as a cook just as well as girls (Sandberg and Pramling-Samuelsson 2005). Some Finnish projects in child care centers (Haataja 1992) have pointed out that one gender can be more able in some areas and thus dominate that area. In these cases the other gender often drops out of that activity. As an example, there were ways to play house that were often dominated by girls, while construction games, ice hockey, and soccer were more often dominated by boys.

In our study, early childhood teachers in the second child care center reflected on the consequences of disassembling the domestic play corner to give more space for "sporty" boys. When we, as researchers, asked about these caring activities amongst the children, the teachers considered and discussed their own practices from recent years in organizing places for domestic role-play. One female early childhood teacher recalled that in the past the staff had constructed diverse play activities to inspire the children. She worried that they had thrown away something valuable when they began to accept and promote all kinds of "hustle and bustle." (This turn of events was brought on by a debate in Finland in which child care centers were said to better suit the nature and character of "good" girls rather than that of "active and sporty" boys. The debate started after some writings pointing out that educators in child care centers should pay more attention to boys [for example, Sinkkonen 1990]. This kind of passionate discussion among practitioners and professional journals encouraged the staff to develop activities especially for boys.)

The different ways early childhood teachers promote, inspire, and motivate children into diverse activities has, of course, a strong impact on what happens in child care centers. From this perspective, joint discussions can be eye-opening moments. One early childhood teacher explained how domestic role-play usually begins:

> The initiative often comes from the adult, like "How about we nurse a baby?" and three- and four-year-old girls join in, but very seldom are the boys asked to participate . . . maybe sometimes they join in later but . . . yeah . . . I haven't asked them in the beginning.

During the discussion the teacher seemed to realize that she does not encourage boys to play house; the teacher recognized her own gender-based behavior.

The next fragment of the discussion gives examples of the available and desirable roles in playing house:

> FEMALE TEACHER: Well, for instance if a three-year-old boy plays house, he's easily the dad, which is what we all agreed on and accepted, but you hardly ever see a five- or six-year-old boy playing house.

FEMALE COLLEAGUE: Uh-huh, hardly ever.

FEMALE TEACHER: Yeah, but in general no one really plays house anymore, not as much as they used to, not even the girls.

RESEARCHER: So what do the girls play instead?

FEMALE TEACHER: Mice, animals that run and bustle about the floor, mama cats and baby cats . . . As if they're playing house inside the animal kingdom. And boys end up playing wild animals, like lions and lynxes, not cats or dogs.

At these child care centers, playing house is popular only among younger children. In the episode above, the teachers mention how three-year-old boys like to play fathers, but as they grow older the role of father is not as appealing any more. According to the teachers, the popularity of playing house has decreased enormously. Also, in the study by Sandberg and Pramling-Samuelsson (2005), preschool teachers reported that playing with dolls isn't as common anymore, even if the teachers organize places designated for playing with dolls. Instead, animals have taken over the corners that are meant for playing house. Even then, gender-based dichotomies are obvious: girls are pets, but boys want to be wild animals.

Toys have a very important part in how children play. In theory, practitioners usually have the competence to choose pedagogically the best toys for children, and to consider tools and means that are developmentally appropriate. In practice, however, it seems that the toy industry with its heavy commercial activities has an impact on the daily practices in child care centers. In the next excerpt, a female early childhood teacher who has a comparatively long career speaks of organizing games and taking care of toys:

This product-based culture has clearly influenced things, something that we grown-ups at the child care center have grown tired of. There's so much stuff that no one really takes care of. . . . Playing house used to be arranged neatly; things were put in their places; children would clean up after themselves. But now we have all this commotion with trainees and such, it takes an awful lot of work to keep things in order and in play condition. . . . It's not out of the ordinary that things needed to play house with, dishes and such, are all over the place. . . . They're just thrown around, not really taken care of. Everything is disposable: this is something that really stands out in the children's day-to-day lives.

In the middle of a throw-away, consumerist culture children do not learn to take care of their toys. This might have happened among the workers in the child care centers as well. It is not surprising that this early childhood teacher was nostalgic for "the good old days." She refers to the times when child care centers had more workers and staff had time to organize special play-corners. Does this have anything to do with the gender issue? I think it does. It seems that especially care-taking dramatic play, such as playing house, shopkeeper, or hair dresser, in which a variety of good organizational skills are necessary, has decreased. This means that activities in which children could easily learn empathy and other habits of helping and taking care of others have decreased. In this sense, the resources in the learning environments have diminished children's play.

Adults are important role models for children. The examples they set most probably influence children's play as well. Men are often said to exemplify the male model in child care centers. At its worst, this argument can simply mean expectations of a stereotyped role for a male early childhood teacher—he should be in charge of duties that culturally have belonged to men, such as keeping discipline (Sikes 1997). From a gender equality perspective it is important that both female and male early childhood teachers have flexible tasks. Therefore, we must ask, What kind of male and female role models do we want?

In this section I have some examples of how the teachers describe their own efforts in being nonstereotyped role models. A male teacher talks about showing love and caring in physical contact, such as with touches and hugs:

> I've tried to—not meaning it's something that I have to specifically *try* to do because it would be difficult for me—but just in case someone has the idea that somehow it's more difficult for us men to give hugs and embrace. . . . It goes both ways: sometimes children come to us (adults) to be hugged, snuggled and held; and sometimes it's us adults that are the hug-deprived ones . . . that we gently tousle their hair or something like that, to show affection.

The fragment reveals that hugging and touching by a male teacher can astonish some. In any case, some days children really need this kind of physical contact, according to the teacher. This behavior of breaking the ice is very important since caring activities are not essentially gender-based virtues, but nevertheless have been gendered. Men in child care centers can face contradictory expectations and prejudices. On one hand they are expected to be "male role models," and on the other hand they are often expected to participate in all the activities, also those traditionally typical for women (Sandberg and Pramling-Samuelsson 2005, 304).

At the other child care center, a male teacher told us how he had tried to explain to the boys how it is important to listen to the girls' wishes. An example of such a situation occurred during the music sessions where children could ask for certain songs to be sung: boys would boo if girls requested "girly songs."

The next example from a female early childhood teacher is an unusual story about her role as a teacher:

> I was playing hockey, but I don't usually do that since I don't really care for it, and well, some hardcore sport boy from our child care was like, "You play hockey too?" and I told him, "Of course I do." So I've played with them now on a couple of afternoons and really done my best to play well. Me and a couple of boys from our group, we've played against these sport fanatic boys as a team, and now they're annoyed that they haven't been able to beat us. At least the questions of whether or not I play have stopped, but there's still someone who thinks that "women can't play, it can't be possible."

The story is very interesting. This female teacher does not like ice hockey, although she knows how to play it. Apparently at the child care center she is a good player. This female teacher gives an example of a sporty female person, and she does it on purpose with educational motives to show that a woman can play ice hockey as well as boys. She breaks the cultural stereotype, just as the man did in the previous example by hugging.

From the equality perspective it is necessary that practitioners in child care centers break stereotypes with their own examples. This is the way false opinions of essential differences between boys and girls can be disproved (see also Noddings 1995; Naskali 2001; Ruddick 1995). The options for both girls and boys are widened, and children can choose for themselves, basing their choices on their interests and skills rather than gender.

POPULAR CULTURE AS A GENDER MODEL

During our discussions the participants spontaneously spoke about how popular culture and media in general shape children's everyday lives. Modern media play a surprisingly strong part in many young children's lives. Children are conscious of teenage fashion, music, and hairstyles. In this respect, gender issues seem, at least occasionally, different from the traditional norm. Early childhood teachers feel that popular culture has an impact, especially on boys:

> MALE TEACHER: It feels like there are these fads, like baggy pants and such . . . and a lot of effort is put into having "the" hairstyle.

> FEMALE TEACHER: Yes, the hair . . . they start grooming it at home, checking themselves in the mirror, water-waving their hair and looking soooo stylish. There might be five, six boys at once just arranging their hair.

> MALE TEACHER: It's kind of nice that boys pay attention to things like that, to a certain extent. Yes, and very, very boyish though.

Here, male and female early childhood teachers discuss boys' fashion and how the ideal of a man has changed. Boys consider it acceptable to concern themselves with clothing and hairstyles. Also, the male teacher thought it was nice that boys took care of their appearance, but to certain limits: a boy must look like a boy.

The conversation points out that pop culture is familiar to the children. The teachers told as well how boys adopt heavy metal bands as their music idols, which is a way to present masculinity in child care centers. Thus pop culture has arrived at child care centers. Children are critical and conscious of their bodies. At the same time children have become a consumer-marketing group (Tolonen 1999, 73–74; Wilska 2001, 68–69). Some Finnish researchers (Laine 2000) have noticed that marketers carefully follow what children want and what they'd like to be to direct advertising toward children. This happens even though children should be under special care and protection, not objects of commercialism.

Nonetheless, the ideals of masculinity have changed during the last decades. A male early childhood teacher told us his story:

Gender-based ideas have changed. It was the winter of '92, and I was a trainee for the first time with this group of three- to five-year-olds. A lot of the children asked me, "Why do you have earrings if you're a man?" or "How can you have a ponytail even if you're a man?" I just told them, "Well, sure men can have earrings and ponytails." In this group it's no longer an issue [that] I have earrings, but why do I only have *one* earring.

These short fragments give concrete examples of changing images of a good-looking man. Media and popular culture seem to have a significant role in this change. Children adopt fashion, hairstyles, music, and other popular culture images easily. In our material the participants talked especially of boys as popular culture consumers. Why so? It is impossible to know, but we can make some assumptions regarding the matter. Maybe there is nothing new on the subject of girls being fashion conscious—for instance, we know how schoolage girls can have eating dysfunctions. From this perspective, boys are newcomers in the field of popular culture. The story of the male early childhood teacher's earrings seems to support this change. Fifteen years ago a man with one earring was a stranger, if considered a man at all. But now he is a stranger for a different reason: he is supposed to have two earrings!

JOINT DISCUSSIONS AS LEARNING ABOUT GENDER

It is well known in the field of narrative research and socioconstructivism that stories and language not only represent a phenomenon, but construct it as well. Through stories and language, early childhood teachers present gender as a certain kind of phenomenon. Some of my earlier examples note when during the discussion teachers seemed to realize something relevant to them in their own behavior. Here I'll give further examples of teachers' self-criticism as they view their practices with children. The discussions depict the practices that thus become visible and can be a kind of prerequisite for change.

A previous example concerned an early childhood teacher who realized she had never thought that some of her assumptions had been gender stereotyped: "If I think of my own unreflected assumptions and thoughts . . ." She continues by telling of these stereotypes: when a boy has clear and neat handwriting, she feels satisfaction, but the same scenario with a girl is considered natural, because girls are naturally dexterous. The teacher concludes that she could even make a list of children toward whom she has acted like this, and finishes off by saying, "So this is clearly the case with me."

The next eye-opening moment reveals other stereotyped and well-known educational practices: girls are educated to be more responsible for themselves and their equipment and cautious of other things. A part of these stereotypes is also the thought that girls can do these ordinary daily chores independently. Boys, however, have to be cared for by adults; they are assisted and are allowed lapses from preciseness; they do not have to be as meticulous as girls do. The next fragment from a female teacher offers an amusing as well as a worrysome example of how boys learn to be helpless and careless:

> Responsibility, when you think about it, for instance, when I think about homework: you never hear a girl saying 'My book is at home, my mother forgot it there.' But you do tend to hear that from boys.

The final example is a female teacher noticing how self-evident it is that girls can manage all these daily routines, while boys get special, positive attention:

> It's sad, though, that when the boys learn to do something, like fastening a zipper or something that does affect the course of the day and any other day at the child care, then it's noticed and praised; but of all these abilities—the ones that girls can already handle and do automatically—they can go unnoticed.

CONCLUSION

From a gender perspective, child care centers create their own special environments because they are mostly occupied by women. According to some studies, only about 2 percent of the nursing and teaching staff in Finnish child care centers is male. This emphasizes how children come to understand childrearing and caretaking to be the responsibility of women. Therefore it is important to carry out the gender and equality-based view in educational practices and to support the individual development of both masculine and feminine qualities in children no matter which gender the adult happens to be. When supporting individuality, the educator must be aware of his or her own—even hidden—behavior toward a child's actions. Thus one can prevent one's own gender-based, stereotyped-based behavior.

The way that teachers talked about gender issues in the research groups proves that teachers are ready to reflect on their own educational practices from a gender perspective. For the sake of promoting equality in child care centers, educators should examine their own behavior. One option is to ask some critical questions about one's own behavior. A teacher can, for instance, start by asking the following questions and them talking about them with colleagues.

- Do I treat girls and boys differently?
- Do I reprimand boys more?
- Do I help boys more?
- Do I let girls get away with being rowdy and loud?
- Am I equally encouraging to girls and boys?

In our research we were concerned about whether activities in which children can learn ethics of caring are decreasing. Indeed, it seems that this is happening and is why educators should encourage both girls and boys toward caring activities not only by organizing caring play such as playing house, hospital, or hairdresser, but also by paying attention to caring in general. Teaching children to care should be done in a gender-sensitive way since both girls and boys need encouragement in this respect. Discussing gender issues in groups can support educators in this important and difficult task.

REFERENCES

Bedford, T. 2009. Promoting educational equity through teacher empowerment: Web-assisted transformative action research as a counter-heteronormative praxis. Acta Universitatis Ouluensis E103. Academic diss., University of Oulu, Oulu, Finland.

Butler, J. 1990. Gender trouble: Feminism and the subversion of identity. London: Routledge.

Clandinin, D. J., and J. Rosiek. 2007. Mapping a landscape of narrative inquiry. Borderland spaces and tensions. In Handbook of narrative inquiry: Mapping a methodology, ed. D. J. Clandinin, 35–75. Thousand Oaks, CA: Sage Publications.

Estola, E., A. Lauriala, S. P. Nissilä, and L. Syrjälä. 2007. The antecedents of success: The Finnish miracle of PISA. In *International research on the impact of accountability systems: Teacher education yearbook XV*, eds. L. Deretchin and C. Craig, 189–206. Lanham, MD: Rowman and Littlefield.

Gordon, T., J. Holland, E. Lahelma, and J. Campling. 2000. *Making spaces: Citizenship and difference in schools.* Houndmills, UK: Macmillan Press Ltd.

Haataja, M-L. 1992. *Tasa-arvokasvatusprojekti neljässä kajaanilaisessa päiväkodissa 1987–1990.* Loppuraportti. Oulun yliopisto: Kajaanin täydennyskoulutuskeskus.

Hyvönen, P. 2008. Teachers' perceptions of boys' and girls' shared activities in the school context: Towards a theory of collaborative play. *Teachers and Teaching: Theory and Practice* 14, (5–6): 391–409.

Kess, H. 2002. The child's right to early childhood services in Finland. In *International developments in early childhood services*, eds. L. K. S. Chan and E. J. Mellor, 71–79. New York: Peter Lang.

Laine, K. 2000. *Koulukuvia, Koulu nuorten kokemistilana.* Jyväskylä: Kampus Kirja.

Lappalainen, S. 2004. They say it's a cultural matter: Gender and ethnicity at preschool. *European Educational Research Journal* 3, (3): 642–56.

Leinonen, E, ed. 2005. *Opetuksen ja ohjauksen tasa-arvoiset käytännöt. Sukupuolen huomioiva opas kasvatuksen arkeen.* Women IT-projekti. Oulun yliopisto.

MacNaughton, G. 2001. *Rethinking gender in early childhood education.* Thousand Oaks, CA: Sage Publications.

Moore, E., A. Antikainen, and T. Kosonen. 2005. Research review of restructuring in health and education in Finland. In *A literature review of welfare state restructuring in education and health care in European contexts: Implications for the teaching and nursing professionals and their professional knowledge*, eds. I. Goodson and C. Norrie, 25–47. Luxembourg: EU Sixth Framework Programme.

National Curriculum Guidelines on Early Childhood Education and Care in Finland. 2003/2004. Helsinki: Stakes. http://www.stakes.fi/varttua/english/e_vasu.pdf.

Naskali, P. 2001. Sukupuolitettu subjekti pedagogisella näyttämöllä. Näkökulmia feministiseen pedagogiikkaan. *Aikuiskasvatus* 4: 284–93.

Noddings, N. 1986. Fidelity in teaching, teacher education, and research for teaching. *Harvard Educational Review* 56 (winter): 496–510.

———. 1995. *Philosophy of education.* Dimensions of Philosophy Series. Boulder, CO: Westview Press.

Ólafsdóttir, M. P. The Hjalli pedagogy. The Hjalli Pedagogy Information Website, http://www.hjalli.is/information/.

Organization for Economic Co-Operation and Development. 2000. *Early childhood education and care policy in Finland: Background report prepared for the OECD Thematic Review of Early Childhood Education and Care Policy.* Paris: Organization for Economic Co-Operation and Development. http://www.oecd.org/document/49/0,2340,en_2649_34511_1941745_1_1_1_1,00.html.

Palatsi, P. 2005. Sosiaalinen sukupuoli lastentarhanopettajan hoivadiskurssissa. Master thesis, University of Oulu.

Parkkonen, M. 2006. *Maskuliinisuus päiväkodissa.* Master thesis, University of Oulu.

Rantanen, K. 2006. *Sukupuolistereotypiat lastentarhanopettajien puheissa.* Master thesis, University of Oulu.

Ruddick, S. 1995. *Maternal thinking: Toward a politics of peace.* Boston: Beacon Press.

Sandberg, A., and I. Pramling-Samuelsson. 2005. An interview study of gender differences in preschool teachers' attitudes toward children's play. *Early Childhood Education Journal* 32, (5): 297–305.

Sikes, P. 1997. *Parents who teach: Stories from home and from school.* London: Cassell.

Sinkkonen, J. 1990. *Pienistä pojista kunnon miehiä.* Helsinki: WSOY.

Sunnari, V., J. Kangasvuo, and M. Heikkinen, eds. 2002. *Gendered and sexualized violence in educational environments.* Femina Borealis 6. Oulu: University of Oulu.

Tolonen, T. 1999. Hiljainen poika ja äänekäs tyttö? Ääni, sukupuoli ja sosiaalisuus koulussa. In *Suomalainen koulu ja kulttuuri,* ed. T. Tolonen, 135–58. Tampere: Vastapaino.

Välimäki, A-L. 1998. Päivittäin. Lasten (päivä)hoitojärjestelyjen muotoutuminen varhaiskasvun ympäristönä suomalaisessa yhteiskunnassa 1800- ja 1900-luvulla. Acta Universitatis Ouluensis E31. Oulu: University of Oulu.

Värtö, P. 2000. Mies vastaa tekosistaan. . . . siinä missä nainenkin2. Maskuliinisuuksien rakentaminen päiväkodissa. Kuopion yliopiston julkaisuja E 79. Kuopio.

Vuorikoski, M., S. Törmä, and S. Viskari. 2003. *Opettajan vaiettu valta.* Tampere, Finland: Vastapaino.

Wilska, T-A. 2001. Tuotteistettu nuoruus kulutusyhteiskunnassa. In *Nuori Ruumis,* eds. A. Puuronen, and R. Välimaa, 60–70. Helsinki: Gaudeamus.

THREE

Do Daddies Wear Lipstick? and Other Child-Teacher Conversations Exploring Constructions of Gender

— Jeanne Marie Iorio and Hema Visweswaraiah —

I [Jeanne Marie Iorio] worked as a classroom teacher for over ten years in a variety of settings before becoming a professor. During my teaching, a theory was shared over and over again by the children, regardless of the site: "Boys have short hair. Girls have long hair." I would often try to disrupt this theory, pointing out girls with short hair and boys with long hair in the everyday classroom, pictures, and books. Yet, even after my attempts at challenging their theory, the children would stick to their mantra, "Boys have short hair. Girls have long hair." Children's constructions of gender and the responses of teachers to these constructions present a perspective that can be challenging. As children come to understand and describe gender, the presence of context, culture, and experience contributes to how they perceive gender (Wohlwend 2007; Lind 2005; Ochsner 2000; Dyson 1993; Heath 1983; Yelland 1998). Since teachers are part of children's everyday life, teacher response can add to the child's comprehension of gender. Through conversations between children and Hema Visweswaraiah (a preschool teacher), teacher and researcher reflections, and discussion, I hope to explore teacher influence on children's constructions of gender. I also will offer teachers a means to examine their own practice to influence creating opportunities for conversations about gender to occur.

DATA, METHODOLOGY,
AND THEORETICAL ORIENTATIONS

Data from the original study (Iorio 2007) was collected using observation, interviews, and a researcher's journal over twenty days, two hours per day, attempting to develop a deeper understanding of the people, process, and community involved with these child-adult conversations. The site of research was a preschool classroom utilizing emergent curriculum in a university early childhood center located in a culturally and economically diverse city. Therefore, the population of the center, including staff, children, and families, reflected the diversity of the city and the university. The children were primarily from middle-class families who use conversation between children and adults as part of their everyday activities. Inclusive practices, such as supporting children with special needs throughout the classroom communities, were part of everyday learning. The researcher, Jeanne, has a longtime commitment to the center as a previous preschool teacher for four years, coteaching with Hema, the adult participant and teacher in the original study.

Inspired by Vygotsky's (1962) theory on social constructivism, the following tenets framed the study: participants do construct knowledge; development cannot be separate from its social context; learning can lead development; and language plays a central role in development (Bodrova and Leong 1996). The researcher chooses to question accepted early childhood practices, attempting to see alternate possibilities and interrogate positions of power between children and adults (Foucault 1979; Lather 1991; Ellsworth 1997). Further, rethinking early childhood practices to include voice, identity, and social justice (Kessler and Swadener 1992; Grieshaber and Cannella 2001) frames the study.

CONVERSATIONS

The following conversations depict the teacher's influence on how children construct gender. Each section includes the narrative of the conversation, reflections by the teacher, and analysis of both the conversation and reflection. Practice is examined through the documentation and discussions of the conversations from the perspectives of the teacher and researcher as well as thoughts on how reflection can inspire everyday classroom teaching and learning.

Narrative: Do Daddies Wear Lipstick?

Outside, three-year-old Julie is sitting on the chain ladder, her arms are behind her, and her legs are bent with her feet resting on the chain links. Hema, the teacher, is kneeling at the bottom of the ladder, looking up at Julie. Julie is continually moving on the ladder, changing her body, sometimes standing on the chain link and then sitting. Julie and Hema are deep in conversation, first about party dresses and then about parties. According to Julie, for a party, she wears lipstick. Using knowledge of Julie's personal life, Hema asks about makeup in relation to her parents. Julie's father often appears on television in various news shows. Julie's personal experiences fuel her perspectives on gender and give context to her understandings.

HEMA: Does mommy wear lipstick?

JULIE: Yes.

HEMA: Does daddy?

JULIE: No (with a laugh).

HEMA: Why not?

JULIE: Daddies do not wear makeup. Last time my dad was on TV they put on makeup.

HEMA: When your daddy was on TV he wore makeup?

JULIE: Only because he was on TV.

HEMA: What kind of makeup did they put on? Did they put on lipstick?

JULIE: No.

HEMA: What was he wearing?

JULIE: Ummm. I don't know.

HEMA: That's funny! Daddy was wearing makeup. How come daddy does not wear lipstick?

JULIE: He would look silly.

HEMA: Don't clowns wear makeup?

JULIE: Yeah clowns wear makeup.

HEMA: So boys could wear makeup?

JULIE: They can't wear lipstick.

HEMA: Oh, they can't wear lipstick.

JULIE: Clowns can wear lipstick.

HEMA: Oh. Clowns can wear lipstick.

JULIE: Only clowns.

HEMA: But boys can wear other kinds of makeup.

JULIE: Only if they are on TV.

(Iorio 2007)

Julie continues to talk about how she saw her dad on television and then how her older sister Dianne joined her father on television. Hema asks if her older sister wore makeup on television. True to Julie's understanding of gender and makeup, she explains Dianne only wore lipstick.

Teacher's Reflection: Hema Shares Her Perspective on the Conversation

During this conversation with Julie I initially reacted as if the idea of a male wearing makeup was unusual, that is, "funny." However, immediately after that response, I attempted to challenge her concept of who could wear makeup. But the only example that came to mind was one that involved clowns, perhaps inadvertently equating boys' wearing of makeup to something not serious, such as clowns. I knew that I wanted to challenge her theory that "Daddies do not wear makeup," but as I look back on this conversation I realize that I was unable to formulate an example that she could relate to as ordinary in terms of boys wearing makeup.

I further realized that I missed opportunities to ask Julie to give a definition of makeup and to talk about the use of makeup. I feel that the basis of meaningful conversation originates from understanding another's perspective and, particularly with young children, it is of value to know, in their terms, how they perceive their world and why they perceive it in that way. I believe asking young children to share their views provides grounds for how to relate to them during conversation while also giving them a meaningful voice in the conversation. From that point I can begin to consider how I can relate to this perspective and either validate, enhance, or challenge it as an adult in this conversation.

It also occurred to me to consider how Julie might engage in a similar conversation now. Is the concept of gender relating to makeup the same for her three years later? What would have changed more, her concept of what makeup is for or her concept of boys wearing makeup? I often wonder if segregating the world into boys and girls is a way for young children to more easily make meaning out of their world. Does that segregation deepen or subside as they get older, and what is responsible for that trend?

The Researcher Reflects

The subject of makeup flows naturally from Julie's conversation on party dresses, reflecting the socially constructed idyllic version of femininity (Ashcraft and Sevier 2006; Ochsner 2000; Yelland 1998). As Hema uses knowledge of Julie's personal experiences to further the conversation, Julie shares what she believes about females and males. Hema attempts to challenge Julie's gender stereotypes but chooses at one point to talk about her father wearing makeup as funny. Her decision indicates a more traditional conception of male and female, possibly exerting her power in a dominant manner rather than in a negotiated mode. This is further emphasized as Hema compares wearing makeup to a clown, offering an option of a male wearing makeup as a pretend state of being, a male in a costume.

Yet, Hema does make the choice to use the clown example as an attempt to challenge traditional ideas of males and makeup when she follows the example with the question, "So boys could wear makeup?" Julie then uses the question as a means to further emphasize her own vision of gender in the world. Hema tries again to dispute Julie's theory by stating, "But boys can wear other kinds of makeup." Julie responds to the challenge by returning again to her personal theory on gender— males can wear makeup in extraordinary situations but not in the everyday. Hema's endeavor in setting up a space to challenge Julie does not impact Julie's comprehension of gender. Does the opening for further interpretations of gender become limited by encouragement of expression, a common practice in early childhood education?

Julie expresses how she interprets gender at this point in her life while Hema listens, responds to Julie's expressions, and utilizes Julie's words and theories. Further, there is an implicit acceptance that females do wear makeup in all contexts and that it may not be acceptable for females to not wear makeup, again emphasizing the model of the female as constructed by society. The decision to focus on the goal of encouraging expression through conversation does not challenge gender stereotypes and reinforces accepted societal limitations of males and females:

"Seemingly neutral child-centered techniques can maintain and even strengthen existing gender inequalities" (Wohlwend 2007, 73).

Hema's perspective on the conversation between Julie and herself offers a lens into the impact of reflection on teaching as well as the possible limitations of appropriate early childhood practices. As Hema engaged in conversation with Julie, expression became the central focus of the interaction. In this focus, socially constructed traditional ideals of gender were accentuated and accepted as normal—girls wear makeup as part of everyday life and boys only wear makeup in pretend situations. Hema shares her struggle to find an ordinary example of when males might wear makeup, indicating the constraints surrounding the current conventional conceptions of gender and implicit acceptance of society's view of when it is acceptable for a male to wear makeup.

The presence of identity formation is also part of Hema's reflection. Noting both Julie's current definition of makeup and her potential future comprehension, Hema sees the possibility of Julie's identity to be fluid and multiple, continually developing with different experiences and positioning herself within the world (Wohlwend 2007; Robinson 2005; Yelland 1998). Julie shares her vision of gender through the discussion of makeup, and Hema challenges her and then continues to listen to Julie's viewpoint. Hema's actions acknowledge the process of identity formation, often shifting and developing, and attempt to offer Julie alternative ways to see gender (Davies 1998; MacNaughton 1998; Lind 2005).

Narrative: Girls Go to the Hairdresser, Boys Go to the Barber

Hema and William, a four-year-old, are in a discussion about his new haircut. Hema is situated on the floor while William is standing and building using large natural wood blocks. Hema notices William's new haircut and initiates a conversation with him, asking him who took him to get his haircut. According to William, his father takes him to get a haircut, while his sister, Ruby, goes with his mother. William easily expresses how he sees the world from his family experiences, noting that a barber is for a male and the hairdresser is for a female. Hema respects his thoughts, yet attempts to deepen his thought process. Although William does not distinguish the separation because of gender, Hema hears beyond his words and questions this practice with William.

HEMA: So Daddy can't take Ruby to get a haircut?

WILLIAM: Well, sometimes daddies can take girls to get their haircuts.

HEMA: Oh, they can?

WILLIAM: Yeah. Do you want to know why I'm just making this up myself? Because my father is just very awesome at taking me for a haircut.

HEMA: So it's usually your father that takes you for haircuts. Does mommy usually take Ruby?

WILLIAM: Yeah.

HEMA: So it's just the way it works in your house?

WILLIAM: Yeah.

HEMA: But if my father wanted to take me for a haircut, would that be okay?

WILLIAM: Yeah.

HEMA: And if you wanted to take Ruby to get her haircut that would be okay?

WILLIAM: Well, girls usually don't get haircuts.

HEMA: What do they get?

WILLIAM: They go to the hairdresser for a haircut.

HEMA: That's a haircut, right?

WILLIAM: It's not the same as a barber.

HEMA: What's not the same as a barber? A hairdresser and a barber aren't the same?

WILLIAM: No, because the hairdresser sometimes does nails.

HEMA: A hairdresser sometimes does what?

WILLIAM: They paint women's nails.

HEMA: Oh, so the hairdresser paints nails. Men can't get their nails painted.

WILLIAM: Not really. They can get their nails filed.

HEMA: But not painted.

WILLIAM: No.

HEMA: Why?

WILLIAM: Because they don't go to the hairdresser.

HEMA: But what if they wanted to?

WILLIAM: That's the way it works.

(Iorio 2007)

At this point in the conversation, William's understandings are very strong. Even with Hema's questioning, he sticks to his beliefs, not backing down. Jeanne decides to enter into the conversation from behind the camera, uncomfortable with William's fierce notions of female and male. Hema responds to Jeanne's statement and continues the conversation. Again, she attempts to challenge William's views of gender.

JEANNE: My husband goes to the hairdresser. He doesn't go to the barber.

WILLIAM: That's cool.

HEMA: Is that cool? So what if a man wanted to get his nails painted? What would he do?

WILLIAM: That's just a story.

HEMA: What's just a story?

WILLIAM: What you just told me.

HEMA: That a man gets his nails painted?

WILLIAM: Yeah.

HEMA: No, it's not.

WILLIAM: The nails don't really get painted at the hairdresser. Only the hair gets cut.

HEMA: For who?

WILLIAM: For the persons who go there.

HEMA: But you said that the nails get painted when you go to the hairdresser.

WILLIAM: That's just for women.

HEMA: But why? That's what I am asking you. Why can't a man get his nails painted? What if one day you wanted to get your nails painted?

WILLIAM: I just don't like it.

(Iorio 2007)

William ends the conversation at this moment as a friend comes over and taps his shoulder. They move to another space in the room to play.

Teacher's Reflection: Hema Shares Her Perspective on the Conversation

After countless conversations with William, regardless of topic, it is evident that he is very resolute in his theories. Some of his strongest theories appear to be a result of his experiences at home with his mother, father, and little sister. This conversation about haircuts and hairdressers follows suit. Considering the passion with which William shares his theories, I am always very curious as to how they have developed to the point at which he is currently expressing them. When talking with William about haircuts, I asked him a number of follow-up questions and "What if . . . ?" questions. My reason for asking the follow-up questions was to clarify my understanding of his theory and to use his words for him to hear. I also asked the "What if . . . ?" questions in an attempt to challenge his theory. My intention was not necessarily to prove him wrong, as I could not state a right or wrong on this discussion topic, but more to offer him perspectives that he may not have considered and to see how he would respond to them. Is he curious or dismissive? Is he accepting or unyielding?

Without trying to diminish William's valid home experiences, I try to challenge his theories merely to offer him the thought that there are possibilities other than his experiences. Jeanne's part in the conversation is another offer that brings in home life, once again trying to push William to see a reality that is not his own. In this conversation and many like it with William and his peers, my intention is to validate their thoughts and ideas but also to challenge their theories with the hope that the concept of seeing another's perspective might reverberate with them in the future.

While I respect the tenets surrounding the child-centered philosophy, one of my goals as a teacher is to encourage children to envision a world that is different from their own. Does the idea of "child centered" mean accepting that those ideas that do not belong to a certain child are untrue and impossible? Is that not when we become single-minded and reinforce stereotypes? If we are trying to break stereotypes and encourage open-mindedness, should we not at the very least introduce the ideas that are not readily present while also accepting the child's current theories? The world is not centered on one person's beliefs; it is a wide assortment of thoughts, beliefs, and values. While a child-centered philosophy encourages confidence and ownership in young children, my goal in these conversations is to encourage the child to envision an alternative in a more realistic fashion, as he or she may one day be presented with it.

The Researcher Reflects

William feels comfortable articulating his beliefs. He continually supports his theories, going as far as to tell Hema that men having their nails painted is a fantasy. Throughout the dialogue, Hema tries to debunk William's understandings, pushing him to see beyond traditional perceptions of gender. Evidence of their shared power is illustrated within the interaction. Yet, when Hema begins to challenge William, an interesting element emerges, indicating a possible dichotomy of correct and incorrect theory.

This element is further indicated as I, Jeanne, enter the conversation, offering William another perspective through my experience with my husband. The sharing of the story was an attempt to give William an additional point of reference describing gender. At the same time, the inclusion of my story shows that William's experience is not always the case. As the adult, I positioned myself as correct in this moment. Although this could be considered an exchange of power between child and adult as well as a disruption of traditional conceptions of gender, it also could violate the early childhood practice of connecting home, school, and culture.

The tension between the early childhood practice of honoring families and cultures and challenging traditional gender stereotypes creates an interesting perspective of discussion. Embedded deep in the viewpoints of children as innocent and compliant, child-centered practice often becomes the vehicle for teachers' choices in curriculum and creating the classroom space. Hema's decision to offer William alternative viewpoints on gender disrupts accepted child-centered practices and traditional gender constructions in an attempt to broaden William's perspectives (Ashcraft and Sevier 2006; Lind 2005; Taylor and Richardson 2005; Davies 1998; MacNaughton 1998). Hema sees herself beyond the child-centered identity of "neutral guide" (Wohlwend 2007, 79) and more as a catalyst in a child's identity formation as well as the means to interrupt traditional gender constructions.

At the end of the conversation, William walks away from Hema, stating that he does not like Hema's interruptions in his theory, the possibilities of alternative ideas of gender beyond his experience. Hema does not chase him to continue the conversation. Rather, the suggestions of what could be otherwise are offered to William. He now has the option to consider an unknown and expand his vision of the world. This interaction further illustrates Hema's awareness of how she can influence identity formation and children's conceptions of gender outside of traditional constructs.

Narrative: Is God a Girl or a Boy?

Lucas, William, and Emma (all four-year-olds) and Hema are snuggled in a nook on the far side of the classroom. The nook is approximately three feet wide and less than two feet deep and is covered in pillows. The three children are sitting together, bodies comfortably situated, while Hema sits on the floor in front of them. They have been here for a while, conversing about various subjects from pirates to sharks to the origin of lightning. The focus on lightning brings up the chance that a lightning bolt could hit a person. William equates death with going to God. As one child names God a he, another challenges with the suggestion that God is a she. All the children express how they view God.

WILLIAM: You would go to God.

HEMA: You would go where?

WILLIAM: To God.

HEMA: To God. Where is he?

LUCAS: Or she.

HEMA: Or she.

LUCAS: He or she.

HEMA: He or she. Hmm. God could be a girl?

LUCAS: Or it could be a boy.

WILLIAM: Guess what?

HEMA: What?

WILLIAM: My family believes that there's only one God.

LUCAS: But it's not.

HEMA: But is that God a boy or a girl?

EMMA: There's no one God. My mom is God.

HEMA: Your mom is God? Oh.

LUCAS: There's all kinds of Gods.

WILLIAM: Well, my family believes there is only one God.

HEMA: That's what I asked you. Is it a girl God or a boy God?
Could other people believe different things, William? Like
Lucas believes that magic is not real and that there are differ-
ent Gods all over the world.

(Iorio 2007)

There are no responses for a moment and then Emma points to
the map hanging behind her. The subject switches again. Hema's questions have been shared and there does not seem to be a necessity for an
answer. These questions could be a possibility for future conversation or
just food for thought.

Teacher's Reflection: Hema Shares Her Perspective on the Conversation

This topic of God turned out to be a very short tangent within a free
flowing conversation that did not necessarily reach a conventional conclusion, as the topic quickly changed. However, when I looked back on
this conversation I came away with a great deal of insight as to how and
why I respond to children in some of the ways that I do.

"Could other people believe different things, William?" Similar to
the haircut topic, I am attempting to offer William the idea that there
could be theories and realities other than his own. In the haircut conversation, William was being challenged by me and Jeanne, two adults.
However, in this conversation two of William's peers are offering alternative perspectives. At no point in the conversation do I disagree with
any of the children and their theories about God's existence in the world
or God's gender, nor am I asking them to accept each other's ideas. I am
asking them to accept the possibility that there could be other answers
and that there are people like their peers who may believe a truth that is
different from their own.

As a preschool teacher I know that the three-, four-, and five-year-
olds I work with have had merely a glimpse of life and even at the age
of twenty-nine I have not experienced all there is to experience in the
world. By having conversations that challenge and disrupt theories, I am

not attempting to prove children wrong but to share with them the fact that there are people who believe and see things differently. I want to challenge the children in a safe environment so they can react, consider what they would say, and decide how they will perceive the experience. Can they handle the discomfort with ease? Will they grow to be accepting even if they do not agree? I wonder if these childhood conversations will reverberate with them at some point, or perhaps a succession of these conversations over time will build a broad framework for accepting what the world has to offer.

The Researcher Reflects

In this conversation, the theories of each child exist as part of the culture of the community. Through the interaction, the children are positioned as knowledge makers, sharing their visions of God and gender. Hema is present in the conversation and uses the discourse of the children to create an opportunity for expression of their constructs of spirituality and gender. What is notable in this conversation may not be the actual content but the atmosphere that is created where the children feel comfortable sharing their viewpoints—even relating to content that is not the usual early childhood fare (Blaise and Yarrow 2005).

Through the conversation, perspectives are shared. There is little agreement about the subject matter, yet the chance for each different perception to be conveyed is enacted. This illustrates the possibility of challenge beyond traditional ideas—much like Lucas's suggestion that God could be a woman or Emma's idea that God could exist in the everyday as her mother. These students are talking outside of traditional conceptions, questioning the possible positioning and power often accompanied by conventional ideas, creating a space for change (Lind 2005). Hema supports the conversations, responding to the children's thoughts and accepting, as noted in her reflection, that her own experiences may be limited. "We are not searching for an 'ideal' space, but one that is capable of generating its own change" (Ceppi and Zini 1998, 115). This conversation could generate change, create more conversations about experiences, develop an awareness of the limitations of a child's own stance, and offer an alternative view of gender roles and the world.

FURTHER REFLECTIONS

After considering each of the conversations between the young children and Hema, several ideas emerge as ways to think about practice in early childhood settings, particularly in terms of the teacher's role. As gender is described as a social construct, the disruption of this construct is critical to teaching and learning. The teacher is positioned to be the catalyst in these disruptions, offering children alternative ways to portray gender beyond accepted and limited societal viewpoints.

Hema's reflections on the conversations offer us an active example of how teacher reflection is essential to rethinking traditional conceptions of gender. As Hema struggles for new ways to describe masculinity in the conversation with Julie, we connect with our own limitations as teachers either in our education or experiences. Finding the discourse or the experiences that might offer another perspective into considering both femininity and masculinity calls for teachers to engage in teaching beyond standards and accepted early childhood practices (Cannella 2005; Rhedding-Jones 2002; Robinson 2005). It calls for teachers to expand into research and writing focused on other points of view that consider power and positioning.

Creating spaces for disruption and alternative conversation as Hema does when she challenges Julie and William about their theories or encourages the discussion of the gender of God frames teaching and learning beyond the traditional conception of the teacher holding all the power and knowledge. In these experiences, children are trusted as sources of knowledge as well as having the ability to consider another stance beyond their own. As teachers, we must consider how we position ourselves within our practice (Wohlwend 2007; Rhedding-Jones 2002; Robinson 2005; Yelland 1998). Do teachers really trust children to have opinions worthy of the world? Can children's knowledge be more important than the teachers'? Should teachers give children the power to engage in an emergent discussion without a specific goal or standard?

Hema shares her perspective on this process:

> My hope in these conversations and in nearly all the conversations that I have with young children is not to try to change their ideas, but merely to offer them other realities that they have not yet seen but may encounter at some point. I hope to do this while still encouraging and validating their notions and beliefs. As a practitioner, I find it my duty to create the space for these conversations

to occur spontaneously. However, the conversation cannot and should not end there. As teachers who spend a great deal of time with young children, it becomes critical that we revisit these conversations to understand our motivations and the impact that we have. There are many layers to these conversations, even the shortest ones such as the one regarding God, and they are not all evident after the first, second, or even third time a conversation is examined. The learning and understanding appear to deepen each time a conversation is revisited, and thus it is our job as teachers to continually analyze ourselves and our roles if we intend to truly glean the most from these conversations over time.

TAKING ACTION

Using the conversations and reflections as a means to think about gender in the classroom, several possibilities emerge as ways to take action. Although listed in a sequential order, there is not a specific sequence or time period for these actions to occur. Some may happen at separate times, at the same time, or even have a cyclical nature. Be open to the possibilities of what could happen as you engage in these actions.

1. Document your practice.
    For any actions to occur, practice must be documented. We began our reflections by looking at our documented practice. Our documentation was conducted using videotaping and audiotaping as well as journaling, but documentation can be as simple as writing down observations on paper. Finding what works for you is essential. Explore the uses of technology as a tool to record the everyday world of the classroom.

2. Examine your practice.
    Once documentation is complete, spend time looking at your practice. Reread your notes, watch the videos several times, listen to the audiotapes over and over. Write about what you notice, what questions are emerging, your reactions to the documentations, and possible ways to respond. This is an open-ended experience that should bring you discomfort, reflection, and evolution. Consider yourself teacher as researcher, engaging in analysis of the teaching and learning in your classroom.

3. Expand your visions of the world.
    Analysis of the documentation can reveal gaps in practice.
    These gaps should not be viewed as weaknesses. Consider these
    gaps as inspiration for your own engagement in the process of
    lifelong learning. Discovering new information, reading another
    viewpoint, visiting a different classroom or school are all ways to
    frame expanded visions of the world and offer children alternative
    perspectives on constructs like gender. When we begin to engage
    beyond the expected rhetoric of teaching and learning, we can
    find fresh approaches to talk and act in the classroom. This allows
    us to address all of our learners.

4. Create spaces and opportunities for conversations to occur.
    Constructing classrooms that encourage conversations to occur
    may mean letting go of our power as teachers and trusting the
    children to think while valuing their experiences and knowledge.
    Consider your own classroom and ask yourself, "Do I trust the
    children I work with each day? How do I know I trust these
    children?" As trust emerges, conversations between children
    and their peers as well as between children and adults will
    encourage alternative views of the world, disruptions of traditional
    constructs, and acceptance of the unknown.

At the beginning of this chapter, I discussed a theory that young
children often share: "Girls have long hair; boys have short hair." Considering Hema's experiences and reflections, as well as my reflections, I
realize the significance of disrupting this theory. Documenting the sharing of children's theories as well as my attempts at disruption could offer
me a lens to consider my practice. I may learn my own limitations as a
teacher—I may not be providing enough alternative perspectives for other
constructions of gender to exist beyond the traditional societal definitions.
Looking at these gaps calls for me to expand my own understanding of
gender. I want to explore a variety of viewpoints and perhaps study the
diverse processes children may engage in when creating theories. Using
the documentations, examination of practice, and discovered information,
I may be able to encourage alternative theories to be discussed, explored,
and developed, giving children the chance to develop identities beyond
the expected. My own reflections of teaching and learning are critical to
rethinking practice, trusting children, and ensuring that conversations
about constructions of gender are part of the everyday classroom.

REFERENCES

Ashcraft, C., and B. Sevier. 2006. Gender will find a way: Exploring how male elementary teachers make sense of their experiences and responsibilities. *Contemporary Issues in Early Childhood* 7(2): 130–45.

Blaise, M., and A. Yarrow. 2005. How "bad" can it be? Troubling gender, sexuality, and early childhood teaching. In *Critical issues in early childhood education*, ed. N. Yelland, 49–57. New York: Open University Press.

Bodrova, E., and D. Leong. 1996. *Tools of the mind: The Vygotskian approach to early childhood education*. Englewood Cliffs, NJ: Merrill.

Cannella, G. S. 2005. Reconceptualizing the field of early care and education: If "western" child development is a problem, then what do we do? In *Critical issues in early childhood education*, ed. N. Yelland, 17–39. New York: Open University Press.

Ceppi, G., and M. Zini, eds. 1998. *Children, spaces, relations: Metaproject for an environment for young children*. Modena, CA: Reggio Children and Domus Academy Research Center.

Davies, B. 1998. The politics of category membership in early childhood settings. In *Gender in early childhood*, ed. N. Yelland, 131–148. New York: Routledge.

Dyson, A. 1993. *Social worlds of children learning to write in an urban primary school*. New York: Teachers College Press.

Ellsworth, E. 1997. *Teaching positions: Difference, pedagogy, and the power of address*. New York: Teachers College Press.

Foucault, M. 1979. *Discipline and punish: The birth of the prison*. New York: Vintage Books.

Grieshaber, S., and G. Cannella, eds. 2001. *Embracing identities in early childhood education: Diversity and possibilities*. New York: Teachers College Press.

Heath, S. B. 1983. *Ways with words: Language, life, and work in communities and classrooms*. New York: Cambridge University Press.

Iorio, J. M. 2007. Rethinking child-adult conversations as aesthetic experiences. EdD diss., Columbia University.

Kessler, S., and B. B. Swadener, ed. 1992. *Reconceptualizing the early childhood curriculum: Beginning the dialogue*. New York: Teachers College Press.

Lather, P. 1991. *Getting smart: Feminist research and pedagogy with/in the postmodern*. New York: Routledge.

Lind, U. 2005. Identity and power, "meaning," gender and age: Children's creative work as a signifying practice. *Contemporary Issues in Early Childhood* 6 (3): 256–68.

MacNaughton, G. 1998. Improving our gender equity "tools": A case for discourse analysis. In *Gender in early childhood,* ed. N. Yelland, 149–74. New York: Routledge.

Ochsner, M. 2000. Gendered make-up. *Contemporary Issues in Early Childhood* 6 (2): 209–13.

Rhedding-Jones, J. 2002. An undoing of documents and other texts: Towards a critical multiculturalism in early childhood education. *Contemporary Issues in Early Childhood* 3 (1): 90–116.

Robinson, K. 2005. Doing anti-homophobia and anti-heterosexism in early childhood education: Moving beyond immobilizing impacts of "risks," "fears," and "silences." Can we afford not to? *Contemporary Issues in Early Childhood* 6: 175–88.

Taylor, A., and C. Richardson. 2005. Queering the home corner. *Contemporary Issues in Early Childhood* 6 (2): 163–73.

Vygotsky, L. S. 1962. *Thought and language,* trans E. Hanfmann and G. Vaker. Cambridge, MA: MIT Press.

Wohlwend, K. 2007. Friendship meeting or blocking circle? Identities in the laminated spaces of playground conflict. *Contemporary Issues in Early Childhood* 8 (1): 73–88.

Yelland, N., ed. 1998. *Gender in early childhood.* New York: Routledge.

———. 2005. *Critical issues in early childhood education.* New York: Open University Press.

FOUR

One Hundred Hotdogs, or Performing Gender in the Elementary Classroom

— Gail Masuchika Boldt —

I was observing in a kindergarten class. The children were sitting on a rug in a group, and the teacher was asking them a question and recording their responses on large chart paper. Her question was, "If you could choose to eat one hundred of something, what would it be?"

The responses started off well enough. The children had just spent part of the morning sorting cereal, pretzels, chocolates, and other small foods into piles of one hundred. The answers initially referenced this work:

"I could eat one hundred raisins," said one child. The teacher wrote, "Jill—one hundred raisins."

"No! I don't like raisins. I would like to eat one hundred Goldfish crackers," came a response. The teacher wrote, "Chantel—one hundred Goldfish."

"Yeah," tossed in another. "Or I would like one hundred Nerd candies." Onto the chart, "Ben—one hundred Nerds."

A boy sitting in the back row called out, "Well, I would eat one hundred hot dogs!" I looked at him. He was grinning and looking from his teacher to the other children and back to his teacher again.

"What?" called out a few classmates. "One hundred hot dogs? You can't eat one hundred hot dogs!"

The teacher weighed in, "Do you really think you could eat one hundred hot dogs?"

"Yes," the boy responded. "I know I can."

The teacher then added the words to the chart, "Tommy—one hundred hot dogs," and Tommy smiled triumphantly.

Now the floodgate was open. Boys' hands shot up across the group.

Jose, "One hundred hot dogs."

Ben, "I want to change my answer—one hundred hot dogs!"

Tony, "One hundred hot dogs."

Wesley, "One hundred hot dogs."

The laughter of many of the boys and a few of the girls grew with each hot dog response. Several children were becoming visibly excited in their movements and posture. The teacher was accepting the responses without comment, but some of the children, mostly girls, appeared to be increasingly uneasy or frustrated with the rising energy level, and a few of the girls attempted to bring things back in line.

"I would eat one hundred Froot Loops. They're little and a person could *really* eat them," Julie said, shooting a glare at a cluster of boys. Several girls nodded or spoke their agreement.

One of the girls, however, attempted to join in the fun. She called out, "I could eat one hundred hot dogs too." She looked around to the boys, presumably seeking smiling approval, only to find herself being thoroughly ignored. The teacher, however, smiled at her and recorded, "Chelsea—one hundred hot dogs." The teacher then quickly took a few more responses from the children and brought the activity to a close by announcing, "It was very interesting to hear what you might like to eat one hundred of. While I don't have one hundred hot dogs to offer any of you, you know that we have many of the other foods you mentioned, and after recess we will come back in to make a snack. You can choose or ignore foods from each of our bowls of ingredients, as long as in the end your snack has one hundred pieces in it. " With that, she sent the children off to line up for recess. In my field notes, I closed the observation with the following comment: "There is nothing that can't be turned into a performance of gender!!!"

My goal in this chapter is to raise questions about teachers' interventions into children's exchanges around gender in elementary classrooms. I use the previous vignette to argue that gender is ever-present in the classroom, that even in exchanges and activities that seem to have nothing to do with gender, children in our classrooms are constantly making assertions about the meaning of gender and the authenticity of their own and others' gender performances.

I will speak to the question, "If a teacher does interpret this exchange as being at least in part about gender, what, if any, response is called for?" To address this, I return to my own years of elementary classroom teaching and child rearing. My observations as a teacher and a parent lead me to believe that children are often able to talk about difficult gender issues in the abstract, in response to a book or an item on the news, in ways that are fair and nonstereotyped. However, when concerns arise over gender-related conflicts in the classroom itself, children (like adults) rarely see their own investments in gender in such neutral terms. Understanding children's behavior, beliefs, interests, and words in relation to gender through the lens of "identity performance" (Butler 1990; 1993) can help classroom teachers understand the significance of gender performance to children. Understanding identity performance is an important prerequisite to initiating discussions about gender in the classroom. I question the idea that the children's beliefs about gender and enactments of gender are less mature and more problematic than those of adults, and further argue that gender is an important category of being for both children and their adult teachers. I will raise questions about when to intervene, what form intervention might take, and what we can hope for from our intervention.

PERFORMING GENDER

Perhaps the most important perspective in gender studies in the past decades has been the move to understand gender—femininity or masculinity—as a performance, rather than an attribute. The work of Judith Butler (1990; 1993), a leading feminist theorist, informs us that while what we experience as natural in what it means to be a boy or a girl (or a man or a woman), we are in fact performing an idea of gender that has been made to seem natural to us since the day we were born. Children and adults signal their understanding of the rules of gender by performing gender norms in behavior, desires, gestures, talents, interests, and physical stylization such as gait, vocal styles, and postures.

We play games, speak, move, and express emotions in ways that feel like and appear to be our own, and that also identify us as having an ethnic, class, gender, and sexual identity. Butler argues, however, that these behaviors are not natural, but only appear natural because we repeat them so incessantly. This repetition creates the appearance of stable and taken-for-granted ways of being in relation to standard identity markers.

If gender is a performance of norms rather than an expression of who we naturally are, what is it that compels us to perform gender so incessantly? The answer to this is complex. The performances are, for one thing, socially compulsory—acting like a boy/acting like a girl—are not chosen, but are rather enforced from birth. From the time we are born, gender is used to explain to us who we are and why we are as we are. As young children, we learn to use meanings of gender—what we learn it means to be a boy and what we learn it means to be a girl—to understand ourselves and what is expected of us, and to gain social approval and pleasure. When, for example, my son and my niece were both babies, I noticed that while their behavior was very often the same—rolling over, spitting up, laughing, cooing—the things that others noticed and praised, and how they were described, were gender specific. My son's actions—pulling himself to standing, for example—were often interpreted as proof that he was a "strong boy" or a "typical active boy," while my niece, performing the same action, was more often praised for having a good disposition or for looking cute.

I am not alone in these observations. A whole body of work points to substantive and predictable differences in the way infants' and toddlers' behaviors are interpreted and explained through reference to gender (Mondschein, Adolph, and Tamis-LeMonda 2000; Connor-Greene 1988; Burnham and Harris 1992; Connolly 1995). From the time he was born, my son's gender-meaningless behavior was understood as a marker of "proper" gender; he was told that being a boy meant being strong and active and he was praised for it. Social approval was framed around reading his development as gendered, and this approval was a source of pleasure and meaning for him (and perhaps for his parents, as well). My niece, likewise, learned to experience being a girl as a primary source of meaning, pleasure, and approval. Gender functions in our society to tell us what sorts of behaviors, beliefs, and interests are "normal" within our identity groups; and in sharing those things with others, we get the rewarding satisfaction of that community's approval.

At the same time, however, we can never forget that along with the pleasure of identity there is always a threat. Butler (1990) reminds us of what we all know: that those who do not perform in gender-specific ways within an acceptable range are punished. The force of social sanction enacted through peers, family, friends, strangers, and professionals (teachers, counselors, lawyers, doctors) threatens to fall squarely on the heads of those who do not conform to the norms. Butler suggests that identifying and punishing "gender offenders" bestows the social privilege that comes with being perceived as normal to those who toe the line, and it also communicates what happens to those who step over the line. The driving threat behind demanding narrow gender performance comes from the punishing nature of homophobia. Boys who behave in ways that are not deemed masculine enough find themselves punished by the worried intervention of adults and by the social ostracization of other children who find them weird or accuse them of being "fags." For girls, the worry and accusation tend to be somewhat different: they learn to fear—or others fear for them—that in not being feminine enough they will be unattractive to boys and to the other girls who judge them by their perceived desirability to boys. It is important to note that all of us, regardless of how we experience and perform gender, have the potential to gain pleasure and even approval for who we are. I would not contribute to the difficulties of being a gender bender by suggesting that it is a life of unrelieved misery. But it is clear that some identities carry more of a burdensome threat of social reprisal than others.[1]

We perform identity, then, with both fear and pleasure. Insofar as any of us believe that gendered identity—doing it "right" as a male or a female—comes naturally to others, our own doubts and uncertainties can cause us tremendous anxiety. We can end up wondering what is wrong with us; we can end up fearing that others will notice our lapses and accuse us of not being proper females or males; we can fear the withdrawal of social approval, love, and protection. I have noted many times the look of confusion and worry on the face of this or that boy in my elementary class when he talks about liking something, only to have other boys say, "Oooooh. That's for girls!" The boy in most cases quickly backpedals from the position, stating something like, "I didn't mean that thing. I meant something else." Even when the child defends his or her position, it is fairly unlikely he or she will mention it again. Both boys and girls end up having things they like at home, privately, but rarely discuss publicly, or perhaps only with one or two trusted friends, or they abandon those likes altogether, claiming that they never really did like them or only liked them when they were "babies."[2]

When, however, our performances of gender are taken up approvingly by those around us we can experience relief and pleasures of all kinds. For example, a girl proclaims, "I love *My Little Pony*!" and the girls around her respond with enthusiasm, "I do too!" We can explore our interests in a community; the interests can create and solidify social bonds that give us feelings of warmth, belonging, and satisfaction. It is with these ideas in mind that I return to the kindergarten scene.

HOT DOGS AND MASCULINITY

In my field notes, I characterized the opening vignette as a "performance of gender." Tommy's proclamation of the obviously unlikely statement, "I could eat one hundred hot dogs," can be read as making an assertion of his masculine gender in at least two ways. Both hot dogs, themselves, and the ability to eat many hot dogs are easily understood as masculine claims. It's not that girls don't eat hot dogs; it is rather that as a cultural reference, eating hot dogs conjures a train of association both to phallic imagery and to activities that have been accepted as masculine—sports events and camping come immediately to mind. Even given that hot dogs are more often a children's food, eaten by both girls and boys, than an adult food, part of the absurdity of Tommy's statement is the size of hot dogs in comparison with the other foods named—Cheerios, raisins, and so forth. Tommy asserts a hearty, even macho appetite that leads to a Herculean feat of eating that is far from a feminine ideal. It is, after all, adolescent girls and not adolescent boys who are supposed to learn to curb their appetites, to only pick at their food on their first dates.

What is more important, perhaps, is that I read Tommy's statement—"Well, I would eat one hundred hot dogs!"—as a claim about what it means to be a boy in kindergarten. The claim I hear is this: "I am exactly what little boys are supposed to be—the little 'bad good boy.'" Ferguson (2001) argues that for boys in elementary school, there is pressure to be good, but not too good; to be naughty, but not too naughty. She argues that we do not want schoolboys to be out of control, but those boys who are too submissive and well behaved are also not quite the ideal. They are somehow seen as too feminine or too prissy or weak. After all, in the discourses of American boyhood, the boys we like best are just a little unruly, a little tousle-headed, slightly naughty and rambunctious in a charming, good-at-heart way. They are little rogues.

This is exactly what I am suggesting that Tommy signals to his classmates and teacher. He is not out of control. He answers the teacher's question, and the answer he gives, while clearly silly and impossible, is not rude or disgusting. It is not truly naughty. He signals to his teacher that he has heard the question and is complying, but only to a certain degree. He is not, after all, one of the goody-goody boys who comply completely with the demands of the female teacher (and here Ben signals that he understands this implied accusation by quickly changing his response). Neither, however, is he a boy who would go too far.

That this becomes a communal session of affirming "boyness" is clear in the responses of many of the other boys, as well as some of the girls. Many of the boys turn their attention away from the teacher and begin looking and grinning at Tommy and each other. One child after another requests and demands that his own answer is registered as, or even changed to, "hot dogs." It is not the answer on its own that threatens to disrupt the class order; the child did not, after all, say "one hundred boogers!" It is the momentum that is building in the response of the other children. The boys are creating a community around the assertion of themselves as people who could and would eat one hundred hot dogs, who could and would threaten to disrupt the class order by offering a slightly naughty response. As each boy adds his name to that "club," he receives the smiles and nods of approval of many of his male peers. The girl who attempts to join the club threatens to break the unity of this gendered pleasure, and she is rebuffed by being glared at or completely ignored. Meanwhile the gendered nature of the exchange is consolidated even further by the prim attempts of some of the girls to rally around the schoolgirl role of "little teacher," answering in a way that carries a clear reprimand to the boys and that attempts to restore order. The teacher, probably wisely, carries on, placidly writing down "one hundred hot dogs" and bringing things back into order through the recess break and the instructions for the next activity.

My decision to spend this much time discussing one event was driven by the determination to assert that gender is, in fact, far more present in our classrooms than we usually notice. The teacher in this particular scenario did not consider that she was participating in a gendered event until we talked afterwards. Even then, recognizing it as gendered, she didn't see it as especially significant. The question I want to explore next is: Was this a significant gendered event? If not, what would be a significant event? How should we talk to our students about gender and what do we hope to achieve?

My argument is that because we are performing gender all the time, everything that happens in our classrooms can be understood to have a gendered connotation, even if that connotation is not foregrounded, even if it is not the most important thing that is going on. In the hot dog conversation, gender was at the foreground of what was happening. A group of boys stole a few moments of pleasure and a sense of belonging, an exercise that in many ways is, in fact, a good thing. With this good-natured kindergarten teacher with many years of experience, the expression of high spirits was greeted with tolerance, even with a bit of enjoyment. There is one difficulty, however: to make it work, the boys seemed to feel that it had to be an experience that was exclusive to themselves. The girl who wanted to join in had to be excluded. This brings us to the great dilemma of gender identity.

GENDER AS EXCLUSION

In many cultures, including dominant western cultures, the meaning of gender has been established through exclusion. How do we know what it means to be "girl" or to be "boy"? If we attempt to define these things, there seems to be no escape from defining them through reference to what they are not. To be "girl" is to be "not boy." Even more doggedly and exclusively, to be "boy" is to be "not girl." Men and boys, whether primarily gender bending or gender conforming, have suffered from this exclusion. For gender-bending males, there are, as I've discussed, the social sanctions of being too "girly." For gender-conforming boys and men, "proper" masculinity carries the cost of anxious self-monitoring and self-exclusion from many potentially enjoyable ways of relating and being (Serriere 2008; Connell 2000; Kindlon and Thompson 2000; Pollack 1999). The suffering of women and girls has been in many ways more thorough because it has been more systematized in unequal status under the law. That is, in the equation of "boy/not girl" versus "girl/not boy," the girl/not boy side has been devalued, and denied equal protection, access, and privilege.

As a feminist in the 1980s and 1990s, I believed with many others in a two-pronged approach to dealing with the inequalities brought about by gendered exclusions. One prong was to work for change at the level of law and public policy. The second prong was to argue that difference was the result of socialization and that children could be raised to be gender neutral. As a parent and an elementary school teacher, I made this goal a particular concern (Boldt 2002).

It is, of course, important to understand that desires, interests, and styles are not inherently masculine or feminine. Both as a parent and as a teacher, I was insistent with children and adults that "anybody can like anything" and that "there are no such things as boys' things and no such things as girls' things." My intention was to de-stigmatize interests and behaviors that get stigmatized as gender bending. I wanted to open up the possibility that any of us might be able to enjoy and desire things we previously did not allow ourselves to consider.

My perspective was not without problems. No matter how often I proclaimed that dolls are not girl things and *Yu-Gi-Oh!* is not a boy thing, there are, in fact, few interests, behaviors, and desires that don't carry some gender connotation, that aren't likely to be more often done or desired by women or by men, by girls or by boys.[3] As a teacher, I considered it a triumph if I was able to get girls interested in computers, math, or science. I rarely considered that I did so by devaluing the pursuits that the girls often preferred in the place of these activities. I did not often question the value of computer use or interest in math or science. Nor did I have nearly as much concern about or success in getting boys interested in the sorts of things that girls called their own in school. For the girls to pursue the interests and skills that were dominated by the boys seemed to promise a step toward privilege, or at least the approval of the teacher. There has long been a more-or-less accepted role of "tomboy" for girls. There is no broadly accepted parallel identity for boys, however; for boys to associate themselves with things that are usually the province of girls is often experienced by both children and adults as threatening, and as a step away from power and possibility.

What was missing from my perspective was an understanding of the meaning and pleasure that both children and adults gain from their gender performances. While I continue to believe that gender differences are social constructs, I also now understand that gender is marked precisely by the creation of patterned differences. I no longer think it is valuable to try to convince children to deny the powers of "girlness" or "boyness" in their own lives and in the lives of others. I also believe, however, it is the teachers' responsibility to challenge the narratives that confirm that gender means exclusion and to provide alternatives both in action and in story in our classrooms.

TALKING (AND DOING) GENDER IN THE CLASSROOM

I cannot propose a solution that will allow us to talk about gender in our classrooms in a way that solves the problems of sexism. Rather, I believe that what we can do as teachers is to create environments in which we learn to negotiate gender. With this in mind, I offer two suggestions for thinking about gender in the classroom.

The first is to look at ourselves as teachers with as much honesty as we can muster. A common perception and bias in research and writing suggests that children are less perceptive and "mature" in their understandings of gender than adults. If we take a hard look at our own teaching practices, I believe we will find we are as likely to perpetuate gender stereotyping as are the children. A wealth of research demonstrates that teachers treat students differently based on gender and that these differences perpetuate exactly the problems many of us hope to address. Sadker and Sadker (1995), for example, find that boys are six times more likely than girls to be called on in group situations in school. They are far more likely to be asked high-quality questions and to be praised and critiqued for the quality of their work. Girls, who receive far less of the teachers' attention, are more likely to be credited for good behavior and following the rules. Walkerdine (1989) found that teachers are more likely to attribute rationality and true understanding to boys' mathematical work—a subject area that is typically understood as "a boys' thing"—than to girls' mathematical work. Newkirk (2002), meanwhile, suggests that teachers are more likely to praise and support girls as readers and writers.

While the Sadkers took note of the effect of socializing girls to low expectations, they didn't observe that this excess of attention paid to boys also means that boys are much more likely to be noticed when not complying and to be disciplined. Boys are far more likely to be sent to special education for behavioral nonconformity (United States Department of Education 2003). My own third- and fourth-grade students had no difficulty when I asked them to identify ways that various teachers treated boys and girls differently. They suggested that boys got in more trouble in my class than girls did and that I did not tend to notice when the girls were "messing around."

I read the Sadker and Sadker (1995) book when I was a teacher. One of the most striking things about their research is that it was often done in classrooms of teachers who were very conscious of gender issues and who identified themselves as practicing gender equity. The authors' point was that our expectations about gender differences are so engrained in us that they have become invisible. I took this as a challenge and decided to conduct a bit of research in my own class. First, I blacked out all the names and pronouns from the narrative reports I had written for the children at the end of the quarter. I then gave these to another teacher and asked him to predict whether each report was about a girl or a boy. Much to my horror, he had no trouble doing this with complete accuracy. I was talking about the children differently. Just as the Sadker and Sadker research would have predicted, I was assigning the boys active descriptions about their accomplishments while predominantly writing about the girls' personalities. I began to realize that tough talk about gender had to begin with me—with my own practices as a teacher.

I began talking with the children about the informal research I was conducting. I talked with them about what the Sadkers found, what I was finding, and about how difficult it was to recognize my own complicity in gender stereotyping. I talked about what it was like when I was a child. I talked about efforts I was making to do better. And I invited them to talk. I asked them to tell me what they noticed about gender in the classroom and at home. I asked them to participate in helping me think about it. I tried to make this a conversation not about "getting it right," but rather about trying to understand how complex it is. One girl talked about how her father treated her and her brother differently. She talked about how much it bothered her and about the kind of pleasures it gave her. This gave us an opportunity to discuss the rewards and penalties associated with "acting like a girl" and "acting like a boy." We talked about how that happened at school. We tried to figure out when it was and was not a big problem. It opened up important discussions.

This does not mean that the children in my class were suddenly transformed into perfect, gender-equitable beings. But it does mean that the first of my two suggestions—that we research our own gender biases in the classroom and include the children in the discussion—led to the second of my suggestions: that we offer and invite as many narratives as possible into the classroom to give children a way to legitimize their own gender-bending and that of others. I came to understand that although the social constructions of gender strongly influence what we are like, this cannot and should not be used to explain who we are. When adults or children in the classroom offered gender as an explanation, I was quick to counter it with other stories. A child says, "Girls like cute animal stories," and I invariably reply, "Anyone has the right to like stories about cute animals. Loving and caring for all animals, cute or otherwise, is a wonderful human way to be. I happen to know many boys and men who love animals. I'll bet you can come up with your own examples. Or we could look on the Internet at animal protection groups to see."

In all honesty, the kids rarely wanted to follow through with the "let's see" part of my speech. They knew I was going to be right and they conceded the point. They didn't want to go to the effort of proving themselves wrong. I also knew that many of the kids continued to feel that they were right in spirit, that cute animal stories were a girls' thing, and that boys ought not to read or write animal stories unless they involved dragons or dogs. But an important part of my goal had become not so much to change every person's mind but to legitimatize competing narratives and to create a structure wherein kids could successfully challenge the exclusion of gender.

As an example, I recall the day a small group of my third- and fourth-grade girls came in after recess very upset and reported to me that a group of boys in our class would not allow them to play basketball. In the class argument that ensued, a girl suggested as an alternative that there be a rotation drawn up that allowed all the kids to take turns being in charge of different sports equipment and different areas of the playground. Several boys howled in protest. Three of the boys in particular responded with comments like, "But the girls just waste the sports equipment because they're no good at it. They don't use it right. We have the right to that stuff because we're stronger and better at sports. We're bigger and faster than the girls. We play better. It's wasted on the girls."

In making this argument, these boys invoked a version of sports prowess that positioned them most favorably—that is, that sports are important and that truly worthwhile engagement in sports was the special province of males, because the sports performances that count are those predicated on being the biggest, strongest, and fastest. In making this argument, the boys appealed to a powerful American narrative. The sports that are most highly valued, that carry the highest financial rewards and rewards of celebrity, do, indeed, value strength and speed. In the argument, the boys made a proposition about what constitutes worthwhile athleticism, about who they were as boys, and who the girls were, relative to a conception of sports that supported their dominance and their exclusion of the girls as well as the boys they considered to be less athletic.

In the ensuing discussion, the girls ended up responding with two lines of argument. First, they asserted that there are many great women athletes, including a girl in the class who was faster and a better soccer player than any of the boys. This argument was of some help. That is, the increasing popularity of women's athletics gives girls a plausible narrative to validate their interests in sports, and it did force the boys to concede that one of their own female classmates was an outstanding athlete. But that wasn't enough. The boys maintained the ability to define what counted in sports by simply asserting that most male athletes could beat most female athletes any day. Thus, sports were once again defined as those things that were contests of size and strength. To support the argument that these were the sports that counted, they appealed to professional sports, pointing out the greater amount of money made by male athletes in comparison with female athletes, the greater popularity of men's sports, and the number of professional men's sports and teams in comparison with women's sports and teams. As for the girl in the class who was a good soccer player, they noted that they were not talking about soccer but about basketball.

The second tack the girls took was to argue that at school, things are supposed to be fair. This was a much more successful strategy because it appealed to discourses about schooling and morality that often came up in their daily lives in our ongoing discussions about gender in the classroom—that school is a place where we were working hard for everyone to have fair chances if they wanted them. In fact, after the girls shifted to fairness, most of the boys seemed to recognize that they weren't going to carry the argument and turned to another tactic. When one of the boys continued to argue that it was fair for the boys to get the equipment and not the girls, one of his male classmates, who seemed to want to cut their losses, said to him in an urgent tone, "No, no, don't say that. Say something else, like, 'It's fair for the girls to get it some of the time.'"

CONCLUSION

As an elementary school teacher, I turned to Judith Butler's writing to try to make sense of my own questions about what children were saying and doing about gender in my classroom. I had two questions. First, how could I understand and respond to the experiences of children in my class whose enactments of gender were not gender normative?— for example, a boy whose behavior was stereotypically understood as "effeminate" or a girl who was seen to have the role of "tomboy." This is a question that I had addressed elsewhere (Boldt 1996), examining the reactions of classmates and myself to gender-bending children in my classroom. The second question, the question I focused on here, has been: Why, in spite of my insistence that there were no such things as

boys' things and no such things as girls' things, in spite of my efforts
to create equal opportunities in the classroom, in spite of my critical
attention to stereotypes in literature and daily life, did the children in
my class continue to express preferences, attitudes, and behaviors that
seemed so clearly delineated by gender? Why did most of the girls continue to refuse to use the classroom computers when offered? Why did
so many of them so persistently play "cheerleader" during recess and
populate their creative writing with bunnies, ponies, and fairy prin-
cesses? Why did so many of the boys write stories full of explosions, car
crashes, and death? Why did they feel the need to express such vocal
disdain for "girls' things"? Why did even the nonathletic boys so often
refuse to take up the criticism of the role of sports prowess in establishing their popularity ranking in the class and school? And what could I
do? What was my responsibility?

I came to understand, then, that most of us, gender bending and
gender conforming alike, experience the confines of gender identity as
both positive and negative. It is the deal we make, whether that prom-
ises a sense of "being true to ourselves" or the possibility of meaning,
community, and pleasure. The children in my classes, like the adults
around them, were compelled to, and at the same time often wanted to,
enact gendered roles.

As a teacher, I came to believe that an important first step to talking
about gender and equity in my classroom was to be honest about all the
pleasure I get from my own gendered identity and all the ways I understand the world through the organizational tool of gender. I needed to
examine the ways I "did gender" (Moss 1989) with the kids in my class.
This felt intellectually honest. In using my own struggles, discoveries,
and mistakes as the material of class research, I hoped to demonstrate
that everyone—not just children—struggles with these issues. I hoped
to show that sometimes it was hard to admit that my pleasure involved
excluding others because part of the pleasure was in the sharing of a
sense of community, and I hoped that we could at least at times expand
what counted as community. Most realistically, perhaps, I believed that
gender would always be used in ways that were troubling, but that we
were developing a bank of stories and images that would allow any of us
to contest exclusions and to experience our own gender performances as
legitimate.

What should the teacher in the kindergarten scenario that opened
this paper have done? I think she did what could be done. She allowed
the children's fun. She accepted and recorded the girl's assertion that

she, too, could join in this fun—she, too, could eat one hundred hot dogs. She accepted and recorded the other girl's assertion that one hundred Froot Loops was an appropriate response. I was an occasional visitor to this classroom and thus was not privy to other things the teacher may have said or done in the larger class context that supported or challenged the implied gender exclusivity of the event.

In my own classroom, I believe the exchange would have taken place in an environment in which those kinds of exchanges were sometimes noticed and commented upon, where perhaps another child could have acknowledged the assertion that it was okay for a girl to eat one hundred hot dogs or for a boy to prefer one hundred Nerds, even if the other boys did not choose Nerds. I know that neither the children nor I would challenge this all the time. I didn't want to risk eradicating pleasure from the classroom by constantly critiquing and correcting, by insisting that everything has to apply equally to everyone all the time. I hoped that the children would come to have enough experience with these conversations that, if it mattered to them, they could stand up for themselves or for each other, or they could retort silently to themselves or with significant looks to others. I think often this would be enough—to know that exclusions could be challenged if it was important to do so at that moment. It is enough if we are able to help the children feel supported by us and by some of their classmates, to experience an authentic and safe sense of gendered self in the classroom.

These goals—that together we (teachers and children) explore the workings of gender in the classroom and in the world beyond, that we admit our struggles and foibles, that we tell many kinds of stories—are modest goals; they are not about grand gender revolutions. They are things that we all can do and they allow change to proceed in an environment that is, I hope, characterized by a sense of intellectual curiosity, active inquiry, and interpersonal care.

Notes

1. An important issue in naming gender as "femininity" or "masculinity" that I do not address in this chapter is that it fails to account for the increasing visibility of intersexed adults and children who pose new challenges to traditional notions of gender. For a discussion of these issues, see Dreger 1999 and 2000; Fausto-Sterling 2000; Kessler 1998; Preves 2003.

2. There are, of course, exceptions to any of these descriptions. Individual boys took nontraditional positions and escaped serious social sanction. Classes

varied in the rigidity of the norms they upheld and the intensity of the policing
they practiced. In the final section of this chapter, I offer two suggestions for
how to make it more likely that kids will take nontraditional positions.

3. All this becomes more complex when other identity factors are brought
into the analysis. Children are not simply "girls" or "boys." Rather, their tastes,
desires, interests, and behaviors are determined in a complicated mix of gender,
race, sexuality, social class, and personal experience. In my class, for example,
certain activities embraced by girls (such as hula) or boys (such as pig hunting)
marked not just gender, but ethnicity—in this case, Hawaiian-ness.

REFERENCES

Boldt, G. 1996. Sexist and heterosexist response to gender bending in an
    elementary classroom. *Curriculum Inquiry* 26 (2): 113–32.

———. 2002. Oedipal and other conflicts. *Contemporary Issues in Early Child-
    hood* 3, (3: 365–82. http://www.triangle.co.uk/ciec/content/pdfs/3/
    issue3_3.asp#5.

Burnham, D., and M. Harris. 1992. Effects of real gender and labeled gender
    on adults' perceptions of infants. *The Journal of Genetic Psychology* 153,
    (2): 165–83.

Butler, J. 1990. *Gender trouble: Feminism and the subversion of identity.* New
    York: Routledge.

———. 1993. *Bodies that matter: On the discursive limits of "sex."* New York:
    Routledge.

Connell, R. W. 2000. *The men and the boys.* Cambridge, UK: Polity Press.

Connolly, P. 1995. Boys will be boys? Racism, sexuality, and the construc-
    tion of masculine identities amongst infant boys. In *Debates and issues in
    feminist research and pedagogy,* ed. J. Holland, M. Blair, and S. Sheldon,
    169–95. Clevedon, UK: Multilingual Matters.

Connor-Greene, P. 1988. The effect of gender on adult perceptions of infant
    behavior. Paper presented at the American Psychological Association,
    96th meeting, Atlanta.

Dreger, A. D., ed. 1999. *Intersex in the age of ethics.* Hagerstown, MD: Univer-
    sity Publishing Group.

———. 2000. *Hermaphrodites and the medical invention of sex.* Cambridge,
    MA: Harvard University Press.

Fausto-Sterling, A. 2000. *Sexing the body: Gender politics and the construction of
    sexuality.* New York: Basic Books.

Ferguson, A. A. 2001. *Bad boys: Public schools in the making of black masculinity.* Ann Arbor: University of Michigan Press.

Kessler, S. 1998. *Lessons from the Intersexed.* Piscataway, NJ: Rutgers University Press.

Kindlon, D., and M. Thompson. 2000. *Raising Cain: Protecting the emotional life of boys.* New York: Ballantine Books.

Mondschein, E. R., K. E. Adolph, and C. S. Tamis-LeMonda. 2000. Gender bias in mothers' expectations about infant crawling. *Journal of Experimental Child Psychology* 77, (4): 304–16.

Moss, G. 1989. *Un/popular fictions.* London: Virago Press.

Newkirk, T. 2002. *Misreading masculinity: Boys, literacy, and popular culture.* New York: Heinemann.

Pollack, W. 1999. *Real boys: Rescuing our sons from the myths of boyhood.* New York: Random House.

Preves, S. E. 2003. *Intersex and identity: The contested self.* Piscataway, NJ: Rutgers University Press.

Sadker, M., and D. Sadker. 1995. *Failing at fairness: How America's schools cheat girls.* New York: Scribner.

Serriere, S. C. 2008. The making of "masculinity": The impact of symbolic and physical violence on students, pre-k and beyond. *Democracy and Education* 18, (1): 21–27.

United States Department of Education. 2003. *Twenty-fifth annual report to Congress on the implementation of the Individuals with Disabilities Education Act.* http://www.ed.gov/about/reports/annual/osep/2003/index.html.

Walkerdine, V. 1989. Femininity as performance. *Oxford Review of Education* 15, (3): 267–79.

FIVE

Encouraging Men in Their Conversations with Children

— Josh Thompson and Stephen Garretson —

Words work. We use them all the time to do things. Children know this. They are listening, copying, experimenting, approximating, trying every which way to communicate. In our early childhood classrooms, educators make a difference in how children learn to communicate; but our offering of language in the classroom is meager compared to the experiences in a child's home, his or her own primary Language Learning Laboratory. The child is first a native of a home—in most cultures, children take on their parents' name, for example. However, what educators do and say in the classroom, and in communicating with parents and family members, can aid and strengthen the language the child learns in the home. In particular, educators can do things that encourage men in their conversations with the children in their lives. However, early childhood educators, who are predominantly female, need to consider three areas of inquiry: how men communicate with children in general, what early childhood professionals can do to encourage the communication that occurs between men and their children, and how educators can improve the classroom experience for young children by learning about the language of men in the lives of their children.

In this chapter, we examine what men are doing and saying, and how they use language. The children are watching and listening to the men in their lives, all the while learning how men use language. A dialogue between Ben and his dad is a helpful example here. Three-year-old Ben has just walked into the living room with a strawberry.

DAD: Did you find a strawberry, Ben? Did you wash it? Ask Daddy next time. I'll wash it for you.

BEN: I want more strawberries. [repeats his demand, because his dad is busy talking to his little sister] I want more strawberries.

DAD: We are all out of strawberries. Do you want cookies and milk?

BEN: What kind of cookies?

DAD: Chocolate chip cookies.

BEN: I don't like 'em.

DAD: Okay, do you want some crackers? [looks in the kitchen for crackers] Ben, do you want some apple?

BEN: [nods]

DAD: Do you want to cut it?

BEN: Yeah!

DAD [steps to the table and hands a knife to Ben]: Saw it like this, Ben. Is this a safety knife? Is this the kind that kids can use? [apple opens in halves] What did we do? Did we do that?

BEN: Yeah.

DAD: Do you want to eat that?

BEN: [nods]

DAD: Look at that! You did it yourself. Take a bite, Ben.

BEN: I did it.

DAD: Did you? Good boy. Now eat that. You sliced a piece, now eat that.

(adapted from Thompson 2001, 135–37)

In this conversation with his child, the dad uses rich vocabulary and engaging syntax (twelve questions in nine lines). This short vignette also reflects the father's multiple intentions, including training his child to manage choices and to use tools to accomplish ends. This pragmatic feature of language use is an interesting contrast between how men and women use language to do things. Pragmatic competence is knowing "when to speak, when not to; what to talk about, and with whom; when, where, and in what manner to interact" (Hymes 1972, 277).

THE HUMAN VOICE

Each voice sounds different and unique. Each of us has a voice print that others can recognize and identify. Gender is one characteristic that comes across through the sound of our voices. Some of what is identified as male speech or female speech differs biologically. Physiologically, the average male has a larger larynx, thicker vocal chords, a bigger chest cavity, and consequently a deeper voice than the average female (Lieberman 2007). Some families describe a calming effect on infants in the father's voice and attribute it to the vocal range, while others see a father's interaction as exciting and invigorating rather than calming. Add the effect of socialization to this physiology and a preferred or predicted pattern for speech production based on gender evolves. Many boys going through the anatomical changes in their voice experience socializing comments, either favorable or derogatory. Boys are expected to develop a deeper vocal range as they travel through adolescence, and most comply, confirming this self-fulfilling prophecy (Sax 2005).

Beyond biology, differences between the genders also exist in vocabulary and syntax (Owens 2008). Baron (1990) described five language functions frequently used in conversations with children—affection, control, information, pedagogy, and social exchange. Using this set of language functions to analyze a case study of one mother and father talking to their children, Thompson (2001) counted twice as many instances of language of affection by the male than the female, and half again as much language of control by the mother than the father (at least in the presence of the researcher).

Men's Use of Language

Men use language to do things differently than women. Tannen (2007) proposed that the differences between male and female speakers come from a difference in motives and intent. Male speakers often use language for power, both to exert control and to influence others. Female speakers frequently use language to demonstrate solidarity and closeness. Tannen's multidimensional continuum of power and solidarity positioned these different emphases into a tandem unit. Tannen writes, "In studying interaction, we need to understand power (or hierarchy, or control) not as separate from or opposite to solidarity (or connection, or intimacy) but as inseparable from and intertwined with it. Because relationships among family members are fundamentally hierarchical and also intensely connected, family interaction is an ideal site for exploring the complex interrelationship between power and solidarity" (28).

Understanding this complex relationship between language of power and language of solidarity can help early childhood educators as they find ways to encourage men in their conversations with children. The earlier example showed how Ben and his dad talked about managing choices and using tools. Now let's examine a classroom experience where the language of power and the language of solidarity intertwine in a complex dance of multiple meanings.

After many years in the early childhood classroom, Josh moved into teacher preparation, including supervising interns and residents in field placements in public school classrooms. He reports on one conversation with some young students.

One fine spring day, I went into a first grade classroom to share lunch with the mentor teacher and a resident I was supervising. I brought my sack lunch in and sat down next to the resident, across from three boys, six- or seven-year-old first graders. These boys had seen me occasionally come in and out of this classroom, but we had not talked before. When they saw my lunch sack, one boy asked, "Where did you get your lunch?"

I answered, "Out in my car."

A second boy inquired, "What kind of car do you drive?"

The third boy added, "Yeah! Is it a Trans Am?"

"No," I answered. "I drive a red minivan."

The third retorted, "When I get my Trans Am, I'm going to get up on two wheels and drive right between the trucks."

"Is it fun to drive?" the second boy interjected.

I recognized that I was now in "guy talk" and that I needed to talk strong and tough to participate in this conversation. I deepened my voice just a bit, "Yeah! I like driving around trucks, and when you go way up high, on the overpass that flies over as you are turning, that's cool!"

An even more abrupt interruption came from the first child, "Who's your hero?"

I noted that he didn't ask if I had a hero. "Oh, I have a few," I offered, scrambling to keep up with these interlocutors. "I guess my sons are quite my heroes right now. One of them has just finished his Eagle Scout award."

"Oh, yeah?" the second boy said. "Well my hero is Booker T."

"Do you mean Booker T. Washington?" I asked, thinking they had just finished a study of African American leaders.

"No, Booker T., the wrestler!"

The third boy jumped up, pulled his pants up high, above his waist, and strutted, left and right, around us, and said, "My hero is Kramer."

These three boys' voices revealed so much about masculine-situated speech. They liked power, heroes, and character. They didn't want to talk about feelings or emotions. They discovered in me a male that they could engage in guy talk. I asked my resident about the interaction, and she reported that she had observed their bond of high-spirited action-oriented language, but that she had not been privy to it. They had never included her in their banter to such a degree.

PATTERNS OF COMMUNICATION

When power and solidarity are turned on their linear axis and cross-perpendicular, the multidimensional aspect puts solidarity across on the x-axis, with closeness on the left and distance on the right. The power axis goes up and down on the y-axis, with hierarchy at the top and equality below. Then the four quadrants posit different aspects of the interrelationship between the two dimensions. A hierarchical relationship that is close would be a grandparent and a grandchild, for example. A hierarchical relation that would be distant would be an employer/employee relationship. Siblings are often close and equal. Neighbors or coworkers are examples of equal relations that are distant.

Multidimensional Pattern of Communication

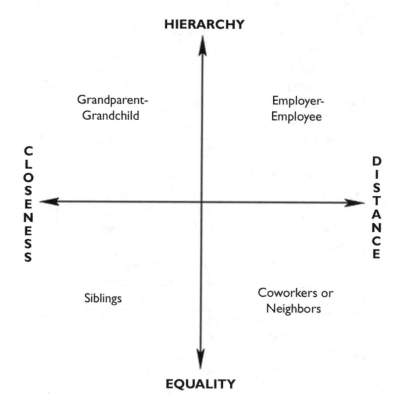

HIERARCHY

Grandparent-
Grandchild

Employer-
Employee

C
L
O
S
E
N
E
S
S

D
I
S
T
A
N
C
E

Siblings

Coworkers or
Neighbors

EQUALITY

(adapted from Tannen 2007, 30)

The multidimensional aspects of solidarity and power appear in the following example of language used between three adult males in the United States. A male customer went to an auto repair shop to pick up his car. Another man was standing at the counter talking with the service manager, who was behind the counter. As the customer approached, the man at the counter moved off to the side and finished his conversation with the service manager: "So, you want to come over tomorrow night and start cooking up that fish?" Now, this was the customer's third visit in six weeks to this same shop, though for different cars and different reasons. Inherent in the social contract between the customer and the service manager is a lot of trust; the customer wanted to trust the mechanic—to trust that the repairs would be reputable and that the charges were fair. Simultaneous with expressing trust, a certain amount of control, along a power axis, is required by both the customer and the service manager. The customer turned aside and, in a friendly manner, asked the man at the counter (not the office manager), "Where d'yall catch all that fish?" "Up on the lake, just north of here," came his reply from the man. Having satisfied a simple exploration into solidarity, the customer turned back to the office manager and assumed the posture and tone of power and control. "Did you get that part installed?"

This example demonstrates the fluidity with which men flow between hierarchy and closeness. The need for closeness was not between the customer and the man at the counter but between the customer and the service manager. But direct confrontation would be inappropriate; it would violate expected norms of closeness, so an alternate took the service manager's place. Then, having accomplished the establishment of closeness by proxy, the two, customer and service manager, could easily handle the complex power conversation—after all, it was a matter of hundreds of dollars being negotiated. Early childhood educators can negotiate complex power relationships with the men in their children's lives if they also negotiate the competing need to balance the right amount of closeness and distance. There is no formula to know the right amount of each element, but it is important to remember the multidimensional aspect of both power and closeness.

Even within the family, these diverse issues of power and solidarity compete. In one couple's recent discussions with a psychologist over the degree and quickness of compliance (they have three young boys), the psychologist told the couple that the reason their children challenged the mother was that women tend to make requests of children, to ask permission, while men tend to command. The difference might be "Will you please get ready for bed?" versus "Get ready for bed!" Understanding these subtle differences in how men and women communicate with children can provide caregivers, teachers, and those involved in the lives of children an insight into gender differences in adult-child interactions.

Many children come from homes where the father is present and active in their lives. The language of these homes is typically robust, generous, and formative (Fagan and Palm 2004). These children speak the native language of their own home. They speak more like their fathers than their teachers. What do schools and teachers, who are mostly female, know about this language of the home? And what do teachers, experts in early childhood language and literacy acquisition, know that can help men become even more potent educators of their own children? The language of the home trumps the language of the school almost every time.

The authors each had times and seasons in early childhood classrooms that influenced their current practice. Our directors and principals, mentors and coteachers—mostly women—helped us find our places in the profession. Our parents, particularly our moms, and our wives supported the development of our voices and our lives among children. Our fathers contributed to our construction of our gendered identity—what it means to be male, even in a world of female early childhood educators.

Josh taught in a Montessori three- to six-year-old classroom for fourteen years. He regularly called the homes of his students, wanting to connect with families, to chat about what he saw going on in the classroom in general and a little about what he saw happening in each child's life. Generally, the approach was well regarded and appreciated. Mostly, he talked with mothers, as they either answered the phone more quickly than the men in their homes, or they were, more often than men, the ones responsible for arranging all things regarding the child and the school. One call reached Michael, the father of two boys in the class—Matthew in kindergarten and John in prekindergarten.

Josh writes:

What amazed me was my lack of preparation for the communication style that this man, a computer engineer by training and trade, presented to me when I called just to chat about his kids.

> MICHAEL: Hello.
>
> JOSH: Hi, this is Josh. I am calling all the families in Matthew's kindergarten just to let parents know how it's going in our class and to listen if you have any concerns.
>
> MICHAEL: No, everything's fine. What can I do for you?

While he never actually used the word "fix," I felt like that was his response to the conversation. "What can I do to help you 'fix' whatever problem or situation you find yourself in?" This insight into male-situated speech clued me in to how "feminized" and nurturing my language and interaction with parents had become. I needed to be prepared to adapt to the families and utilize a greater breadth of communication skills in order to reach the families and truly listen and learn from them.

The continuum aspects of power and solidarity here suggest a dichotomy, an either/or interpretation of this father's interaction with his children's teacher; it sounds like this man is exerting power and control over the conversation and, consequently, the teacher. But Tannen (2007) invites a dualism, a merger of the two dimensions, allowing that the man wants to express power *and* solidarity with his children and the caregivers in his children's lives. Tannen writes, "I explore and argue for what I call the ambiguity and polysemy of power and solidarity—or, in different terms, of status or hierarchy on one hand and of connection or intimacy on the other. By 'ambiguity' I mean that any utterance can reflect and create either power or solidarity. By 'polysemy' I mean that any utterance can reflect or create both at once" (29).

Josh continues the description of this interaction with Michael:

A few weeks later, I saw Michael at a school function. He came up to me enthusiastically.

> MICHAEL: Hi, Josh. I've been meaning to call you. I appreciated your call the other night. It really clued me in to needing to know more about Matthew's time in kindergarten. So, I've been talking with him about how his days are going at school and all.

Exploring conversations with children starts with listening to what men are already doing and saying. But it cannot end there. As educators we must step outside the box and see the potential for what could be, always keeping in mind that fathers do not mother (Popenoe 1996). Men and women see the world through different lenses. If early childhood educators, who are predominantly female, assume fathers should participate in the same types of activities or the same way as mothers do, we will push fathers away (Hall, 2008). So, how can educators reach men and encourage them to be a part of the conversation with their children on their terms? The next section will feature tips on how to encourage men to participate in those conversations. Whether in a newsletter or during a family night or through some other form of teacher/parent communication, educators can model and provide suggestions on how fathers can interact and take part in their children's everyday lives.

COMMUNICATION STRATEGIES

Communication involves listening and talking. Encourage fathers to model good listening skills for their children. The educator can do this by modeling good listening skills when talking with fathers. Make good eye contact. Repeat key pieces of what the speaker said to affirm that the speaker was heard. Ask questions to clarify.

Encourage fathers to listen for opportunities to talk with children. They should listen for their children's interests no matter how small and capitalize on the opportunity to build communication skills. Advise fathers to find a quiet space away from distractions (TV, cell phones, work) to hold conversations with their children.

Talk with Children

- Use mistakes as learning opportunities. Encourage fathers to take a mistake a child might make and talk through what should have happened.
- Use the kitchen as a great location for active learning through exploration. This is an opportunity for fathers to share what they know with their children. Stephen writes: "My oldest was studying volcanoes and we would talk about the differences in lava and magma. We built our own volcano experiment with baking soda and vinegar. His eyes lit up with excitement, and he wanted to do the experiment again and again. This provided an opportunity for me to share a love of learning with my child." Knowing what a child is interested in can make a world of difference.
- Encourage fathers to talk with children during drive time. The ride to and from school or sporting events or other family trips can be a powerful time for interacting with children. Stephen writes: "As a father of three sons, I look forward to the strange stories my four-year-old tells about the day's lessons. The excitement builds as his stories become more elaborate with each passing word." Encourage the fathers of the children in your school or center to hold these rich conversations with their children in the car. Give them conversation starters and show them how to extend conversations. Josh writes: "As the regular carpool driver to and from school, I watched my kids grow up in the rearview mirror. I was able to capitalize on the captive audience to discuss the topics of the day, the sports scores from the previous night, and the projects

due in class that day." These repetitive, predictable patterns are much more powerful than a single formal encounter.

- Encourage fathers to talk to their kids about sportsmanship. When fathers are involved and encouraging, children tend to enjoy sports activities more. Fredricks and Eccles (2005) report that families who supported children emotionally and as a role model have an impact on how the child views the activities in general. There have been many instances where very young children are criticized and torn down from the sidelines of a sporting event. A father who understands how this impacts children later in life can provide a strong model for what should occur. Fathers can teach their children to play with dignity and respect for others. Children are not automatically bad sports; they learn this behavior from someone. Fathers can encourage children to encourage others and to make the most out of inappropriate situations. Teach children to win and lose with respect.
- Encourage fathers to share their passions. Have you ever been so passionate about an activity it was contagious? That contagion rubs off onto others around you, especially children. Fathers can use their love and passion for an activity to promote and encourage their children. Built into this encouragement to express one's passion is a caution. Help fathers see that their passions may be different from their children's passions. Forcing one's own passions on children can actually turn children off of particular activities.

Tell Stories and Read

- When fathers and children are working together, opportunities for storytelling emerge. This can be a time to encourage fathers to talk about their own childhood. Storytelling can be a powerful tool. While it is not sitting down and reading a book, storytelling increases oral language skills and listening comprehension.
- Encourage fathers to read to their children. Fathers can play a crucial role in helping young children develop early literacy and life skills. From story time to socialization skills, stories can play a part in every aspect of children's lives. Some fathers read a wide assortment of materials to their children, such as nursery rhymes and chapter books, newspapers, and even instruction manuals (yes, some men do read instruction manuals). In this way, fathers provide children with a view into the world of technical reading.

Let fathers know how important this is to their child's language and comprehension development.

Spend Time Together

- Encourage participation at mealtimes. What happened to the family gathering at mealtime? Today's families are on the move. Picking up food at the drive-through is an easier choice than a meal at home with everyone sitting together. Mealtimes can have a profound impact on children (Blum-Kulka 1997; Thompson 2008). Fathers can be encouraged to help set that tone. Like any aspect of children's lives, routines help build a sense of character and responsibility. Fathers can demonstrate these skills in a number of ways.

  - Fathers can include their children in the meal preparation and make cooking a family experience. Everyone can be involved in some way. Children can help measure ingredients, pour, and stir, all the time conversing with their families about their experiences. Fathers can talk about safety when grilling outdoors or cooking on the stove and the consequences for not following those safety rules. Help fathers see the importance of accepting mistakes and spills, and encouraging their children to try again. Encourage fathers to be present for mealtime without distractions. This can be a time for families to talk about the day's events, laugh together, and make plans as a family. Encourage fathers to turn off the TV, radio, MP3 player, and phone and be present in mind and spirit. Have the family set boundaries to avoid gloom and doom time. Make this a time when the family can enjoy each other.
  - Encourage the family to clean up together after mealtime. This does not necessarily speed up the process; it may take longer, but it allows for more family time afterwards. Encourage men to ask questions such as, "What can we do first?" "Where does this go?"

- Have a father/child workday at school or a local park. Provide opportunities for fathers to participate in activities that may not be typically attended by mothers. Not only are they spending time with their children but this also provides a stepping stone for later conversations about the experience.

- Encourage fathers to be involved with their children in activities. Camping, fishing, Scouting, boating, baseball, soccer, football, and basketball are all great ways to interact and communicate with children. Fathers play a crucial role in teaching their children how to be good at sports, play games, and develop their abilities. Children watch the adults around them. They pick up gestures, language, and actions.

PARTNER WITH FAMILIES

In addition to promoting the language interaction between a man and his children, professional early childhood educators must cultivate a dynamic partnership with the families. Actively listening to children and their families will aid any early childhood educator in creating an optimal learning environment for young children. In such a space, the training, experience, and insight of the teacher are recognized and appreciated, and matched with responsive attention to what the child brings from home—the child's family literacy or "funds of knowledge" (Sampson, Rasinski, and Sampson 2001). Educators can improve the classroom experience by incorporating elements from the home. In describing many effective classroom teachers, Lawrence-Lightfoot (2003) characterizes teachers as learners of families: "They see parents as the first educators, are respectful of their experience and perspective, and listen carefully to their observations and insights about their children, which will help them be better teachers for these children" (228). Such sensitivity and responsiveness must include understanding how men are already communicating with the children in their lives, and that we, early childhood professionals, can scaffold the dynamic relationship between school and home so that we all learn from each other.

We know much about children and the conversations in their homes. Dads are talking. Children are listening. How they speak to one another in the home and throughout their lives together colors the early childhood classrooms, because the children take their words to heart, and out of the heart the mouth speaks.

Teachers have clues about language and literacy, about development and learning. Early childhood educators can collaborate and cooperate with the teaching and learning that goes on in homes, particularly with the men in children's lives. To do so, teachers must learn to listen—to the multiple meanings of language of power and language of solidarity.

Teachers do not have to change the father into a teacher, or even a "nurturer"; just lend him a hand and offer some tips to encourage his conversations with young children. Let him be real, let him be a man. In his use of language, power is useful in his relationship with his child. As he cultivates intimacy, closeness does not deny that power.

Fathers can help establish good habits, routines, and language for their children. Working on a deficit model with fathers tends to push them away more (Hall 2008). Instead of looking at what fathers are not doing, focus on what fathers are already doing and build on those strengths. This may mean that as caregivers, teachers, and a society as a whole, we involve fathers in new ways. This may mean rethinking what fathers are and how we see them in the lives of their children.

Stephen reflects on the meaning of a man's conversation on his own development as a man, an early childhood professional, and a father: "I look to my own father and see how he used his power as I grew up. He was not a man of many words but of actions. He was honest, hardworking, and demanding. What he did not say verbally he made up for in actions. Many fathers were raised to not express emotion, show feelings, or to communicate; this was a sign of weakness."

We believe fathers can be powerful and still show emotion and feelings with their children. This can happen when we encourage men in their conversations with children.

REFERENCES

Baron, N. 1990. *Pigeon-birds and rhyming words: The role of parents in language learning.* Englewood Cliffs, NY: Prentice Hall.

Blum-Kulka, S. 1997. *Dinner talk: Cultural patterns of sociability and socialization in family discourse.* Mahwah, NJ: Lawrence Erlbaum Associates.

Fagan, J., and G. Palm. 2004. *Fathers and early childhood programs.* Clifton Park, NY: Delmar Learning.

Fredricks, J. A., and J. S. Eccles. 2005. Family socialization, gender, and sport motivation and involvement. *Journal of Sport and Exercise Psychology* 27 (1): 3–32.

Hall, J. Michael. 2008. Life on Mars: Understanding the culture of fathers. *Our Children: National Magazine of the Parent Teacher Association* (February/March): 10-11.

Hymes, Dell. 1972. On communicative competence. In Sociolinguistics, eds. J. B. Pride and J. Holmes, 269–93. Harmondsworth, UK: Penguin.

Lawrence-Lightfoot, S. 2003. *The essential conversation: What parents and teachers can learn from each other.* New York: Random House.

Lieberman, M. 2007. The Barry White effect. Language Log. September 29. http://itre.cis.upenn.edu/~myl/languagelog/archives/004974.html (accessed February 24, 2009).

Owens, R. E., Jr. 2008. *Language development: An introduction.* 7th ed. Boston: Pearson.

Popenoe, D. 1996. *Life without father: Compelling new evidence that fatherhood and marriage are indispensable for the good of children and society.* New York: The Free Press.

Sampson, M. B., T. V. Rasinski, and M. R. Sampson. 2003. *Total literacy: Reading, writing, and learning.* 3rd ed. Belmont, CA: Wadsworth.

Sax, L. 2005. *Why gender matters: What parents and teachers need to know about the emerging science of sex differences.* New York: Doubleday.

Tannen, D. 2007. Power maneuvers and connection maneuvers in family interaction. In *Family talk: Discourse and identity in four American families,* ed. D. Tannen, S. Kendall, and C. Gordon, 27–48. Oxford: Oxford University Press.

Thompson, J. 2001. Adaptations of language functions in caregiver speech: Nurturing the acquisition of pragmatic competence. Unpublished diss., University of Texas–Arlington.

―――. 2008. Table talk: Taking dinner conversation into the classroom. In *Current Issues and Best Practice in Bilingual and ESL Education,* ed. P. Dam and M. T. Cowart, 54–64. Denton, TX: Federation of North Texas Universities.

SIX

Gender Portrayal in Early Childhood Children's Books

— Clarissa M. Uttley and Cynthia A. Roberts —

It is not enough to simply teach children to read; we have to give them something worth reading. Something that will stretch their imaginations—something that will help them make sense of their own lives and encourage them to reach out toward people whose lives are quite different from their own.

(Paterson 1995)

Young children are eager to learn, curious, and, from a developmental perspective, ideally situated to take in information from the world around them. But what messages are they receiving from the world? This chapter will focus on the messages either intentionally or unintentionally transmitted through children's books and the ensuing influence on gender roles and gender typing on young children. The selection of the books children encounter may play a critical role in the development of gender identity as well as self-identity. This chapter will discuss the role of the early childhood educator in a formal setting and the impact of book selection on the development of gender identity in young children.

DEFINITIONS

For the purposes of this chapter, the term "early childhood" refers to children ages birth through eight years old. An "early childhood educator" therefore refers to anyone who works with children birth through age eight. The term "gender" refers to the psychological, social, and cultural aspects of masculinity and femininity (Kessler and McKenna 1978). "Gender identity" is a child's notion of being male or female. The University of Mary Washington (n.d.) describes gender identity as "the internal sense of one's gendered self (for example, as a woman, man, girl, boy, or androgynous person) or of being perceived as a woman, man, girl, boy, and/or androgynous person." It is important to point out that boys and girls are not born with a gender; rather it is something children develop over time (D. M. Newman 2007) as they are socialized to take on the characteristics of what is considered male and female through social interactions. "Gender typing" is the self-fulfilling prophesy of boys and girls taking on the observed roles of "male" or "female" and incorporating those behaviors into their self-concept (Bem 1981). The process of gender typing is self-fulfilling in that culture re-creates this scenario and it gets repeated by the newer generations. Lastly, in the spirit of acknowledging that gender is a status on a spectrum as opposed to a binary state (an either-or category), when possible this chapter will use the expression "all genders" as an alternative to "both genders."

THEORETICAL VIEW OF GENDER

According to Katz (Jalongo 2004), four kinds of learning are indispensable to a young child's development: knowledge, skills, dispositions, and feelings. Children's literature reaches children on each of these levels. Thus, it is incredibly important that the literature to which children are being exposed be selected with care and attention. Cultivation theory (Gerbner et al. 1994) states that the amount of time individuals are exposed to media messages is directly correlated to the level of internalization of the beliefs presented in the media messages. This is particularly troublesome when examining one aspect of media that children are exposed to in a variety of settings: children's books.

The degree to which young children are highly observant in all settings provides an opportunity for early childhood educators to supply children with a wide array of learning experiences and the prospect of exploring and celebrating similarities and differences among people of all genders. The exposure to a variety of experiences provides children with information with which they learn about their world and serves to shape their overall being (Archer 2008). What children see will have an impact on who they become and how they interpret their world. These experiences inform children about the societal norms of their environment, providing cues for behavior expectations and suggesting appropriateness of friendships, relationships, family roles, and even attire. The observations and learning experiences that young children use as their guide to the world take place in every environment: homes, family child care programs, private child care centers, grocery stores, schools, doctors' offices, and so forth. These environments can have a powerful influence over child development.

The U.S. Department of Health and Human Services (2006) estimates that 50 percent of children between the ages of three and four-and-a-half years spend thirty or more hours in child care each week. With the large amount of time children are spending in care outside of the home, more attention is being paid to the quality of care these children are receiving. In fact, many states have programs in place designed to enhance the quality of early childhood settings. The measures used to assess this quality can range from informal to formal assessments; however, the classroom environment is a key component assessed when examining quality in early care settings.

The Environment Rating Scales (ERS) developed through the Frank Porter Graham Child Development Institute and published by Teachers College Press are measures of classroom quality. The ERS include criteria that examine the level, quality, condition, and diversity of the books in the child care setting.

The National Association for the Education of Young Children (NAEYC) has established a set of standards and suggestions for early childhood professionals to use when designing early childhood education programs. The NAEYC has developed a joint position statement with the International Reading Association titled Learning to Read and Write: Developmentally Appropriate Practice for Young Children (1998). This position statement recommends policies and teaching strategies designed to support the acquisition of reading and writing skills of young children. Such recommendations include

- Sufficient resources . . . that include a wide range of high-
  quality children's books . . . at various levels of difficulty and

reflecting various cultural and family backgrounds

(IRA and NAEYC 1998, 10)

- Adults daily reading of high-quality books to individual children and small groups including books that positively reflect children's identity, home language, and culture

(IRA and NAEYC 1998, 9)

- Selecting materials that expand children's knowledge

(IRA and NAEYC 1998, 15)

THEORETICAL FOUNDATION OF GENDER PORTRAYAL IN CHILDREN'S BOOKS

To contemplate the magnitude of the impact of gender on our lives, consider the first question one asks about a newborn baby: "Is it a girl or a boy?" Gender, often viewed as the first label that children receive (Archer 2008), continues to have an impact on individuals throughout their lives and is considered one of the predominant foundations of one's everyday life (D. M. Newman 2007). Children between the ages of three and eight are beginning to create and expand developmental attributes that relate to visual representations. Typical child development for this age group includes an increased interpretation of the seriousness of words heard by children, an increase in noticing differences and similarities that are then verbally discussed with others, and amplified exhibitions of societal norms that have been transmitted to them through a variety of means (Couch 1995). In fact, by the age of five, some children have already developed ideas about gender and cultural identities (Roberts, Dean, and Holland 2005).

A book that tests children's assumptions of cultural and gender identities is *The Ugly Vegetables* by Grace Lin (1999). In this book, a young Chinese American girl and her mother plant a garden of Chinese vegetables. These vegetables are not as pretty as the flowers grown in their neighbors' gardens, but the vegetables serve to bring people from different cultural backgrounds together. The work necessary for preparing the garden and harvesting the vegetables is physically arduous, and the book portrays the work being done competently by capable female mother and daughter characters.

Raag and Rackliff (1998) have found evidence of gender-based social expectations in the selection of toys among preschoolers, while Coplan, Closson, and Arbeau (2007) found gender differences among kindergarteners, especially regarding loneliness and social dissatisfaction. The availability of toys and books that expose children to a balance in gender roles, as opposed to a selection of books that are more male or female stereotypic, encourages children to broaden their views of gender roles and thus extend their circle of friends, thereby decreasing the potential of loneliness and social dissatisfaction. *William's Doll* by Charlotte Zolotow (1972) is an example of a children's book that depicts a boy who wants a doll despite the strong negative and gender-stereotyped reactions he gets from most of the people around him. Ultimately his grandmother gives him the doll and explains to William's father that having the doll will help William learn to be a good father one day.

But there may also be a cognitive purpose for developing stereotypes. Some cognitive psychologists have shown that children develop stereotypes in an effort to conserve mental resources used for organizing and recalling information (Sheldon 2004).

Several well-respected theories have been associated with the discussion of gender typing in early childhood development, and while these theories differ on various dimensions, when considered together they paint a holistic view of how gender typing in children may develop. These theories include gender-schema theory, cognitive-developmental theory, and social cognitive theory.

Gender-schema theory suggests that young children are building a gender schema, a cognitive structure that guides the way an individual perceives behavior and thus learns to unconsciously label it as "male" or "female" behavior (Bem 1981). Children use gender schemas to make sense out of information related to gender (Trepanier-Street and Romatowski 1999). Cognitive-developmental theory emphasizes the concept of gender constancy. Gender constancy is a concept that children grasp in stages, and it encompasses the notion that children not only learn that they are male or female, but they also eventually learn that this label is a constant (Martin, Ruble, and Szkrybalo 2002). Social cognitive theory asserts that children as well as adults learn through observing, and then utilize that observational data to establish behaviors, assumptions, and expectations of themselves and the world in which they live (Bandura 1986; Bussey and Bandura 1999). The book about William's doll provides children with an example of a child who breaks out of traditional gender norms in order to live life more fully.

Social learning theory highlights the specific rewards and punishments for behaving in ways that are deemed appropriate for one's sex.

In *Boy, Can He Dance!* by Eileen Spinelli and Paul Yalowitz (1993), the main character and his father have strong disagreements about the activities in which the son should participate. The son is interested in dancing, but his father wishes he would follow the family tradition and become a chef. Additionally, Newman and Newman (2007) reiterate that people learn from observing others and that this learning guides future actions. Although children acquire a gender identity by about the age of three (Kohlberg 1966), at this age children are still not able to explain their gendered behavior verbally.

EXAMINING GENDER IN CHILDREN'S BOOKS

Adults often use children's books to share perspectives about experiences children are going through. Parents may use books to entertain or educate their children on a particular topic. Pediatricians often have children's books readily available in their waiting rooms to provide families with a means to pass the time while waiting for an appointment.

In early childhood settings books serve several functions, including voluntary and recreational use by children, daily story time, book-related activities, classroom management, and teaching functions (Twardosz 2001). Books can often be found in numerous settings in early childhood classrooms, including dedicated library centers and meeting or circle time space, as well as in specific learning or activity centers where books are used as supplemental supports for learning. Early childhood educators may also use children's books to discuss special events in the children's lives or to support specific classroom projects. Reading aloud to children, according to Chakraborty and Stone (2008), increases motivation for children to return to books independently, thus increasing the amount of time children spend absorbing the messages presented in the books. This reading may take place in either large or small groups.

What kind of learning can picture books, specifically, promote? Jalongo (2004) lists numerous educational and developmental benefits to children, including developing visual literacy skills, understanding relationships and feelings, and thinking more broadly about the world. It follows that if children's literature has such power to educate children and shape their views and understanding of the world, then educators must be mindful of the messages they are consciously and unconsciously sending to children.

Gender has also played a role in teacher education with the continuation of the belief that boys and girls develop differently cognitively (Mercurio 2003). The varying rates that boys and girls develop cognitive skills such as mathematical reasoning, language skills, gross- and fine-motor skills, as well as memory and social cognition (Hanlon, Thatcher, and Cline 1999) has long been a topic discussed in early childhood education, developmental psychology, and educational psychology courses. The idea that boys and girls develop attributes and skills at varying rates, and sometimes not at all, is also evidenced in children's books through the role of main and supporting characters. For example, Anderson and Hamilton (2005) found that male characters, specifically fathers, were significantly less likely to be portrayed as affectionate or to express any emotion, thus not developing a sense of caring for others.

Examining gender in children's books is not a new endeavor, and research findings have been presented by a number of researchers (Oskamp, Kaufman, and Wolterbeck 1996; Patt and McBride 1993; Tepper and Cassidy 1999; Tsao 2008). Gooden and Gooden (2001) presented a study on gender representation in prominent children's books, and Hamilton et al. (2006) reviewed two hundred popular children's books through the lens of gender representation. Indeed, both Singh (1998) and Archer (2008) presented a historical context on the number of male and female characters in children's books and the roles the characters were presenting in the books. Several researchers have identified males in children's books as having stronger roles, being adventurous, more capable, and more independent than the female characters in the books (Ernst 1995; Jett-Simpson and Masland 1993). Female characters, according to Singh's research (1998), are more often the caretakers in the stories or the characters needing assistance from the main male character. Male characters are more often presented with motor vehicles or transportation, engaged in outdoor activities, or in a workplace setting (Monk-Turner 2001).

Monk-Turner's research also exemplifies a significant difference in how male and female characters are depicted in children's books. In this study, Monk-Turner found that this difference is highly evident through the lack of male characters engaged in household activities. Additionally, the majority of female characters who did achieve something positive in the story did so only with the assistance of others, most often male characters. In the few cases where female characters have been portrayed with strong personalities, these personalities have shifted throughout the storyline and leave the reader with a female character who is much more passive than at the beginning of the story. This phenomenon occurs in a wide selection of children's books, including Caldecott award-winning books (Archer 2008). Examples of Caldecott titles that use this storyline include *Mirette on the High Wire* (McCully 1992) and *Rapunzel* (Brothers Grimm 1997). Many of the Caldecott medal books maintain a strong and independent male character and a female character as either insignificant or in a supporting role for the male character (Archer 2008).

WHY WE SHOULD LOOK AT GENDER IN CHILDREN'S BOOKS

Perhaps the major problem with the way children's books portray gender to young children is not found when examining how gender is portrayed but in the fact that young children are receiving messages that do not necessarily present the genders equitably. Since children are in the midst of developing their gender schemas, an obvious danger is that children will develop inaccurate gender schemas that can limit their growing understanding of the world, and equally important, the expectations of their own nature and capabilities (Trepanier-Street and Romatowski 1999). For a sample list of books that equitably portray gender in children's books, please see Table 1 (page 121). For suggestions on how to select children's books that represent gender roles in a fair manner, please refer to Table 2 (page 123). Significant changes have occurred in recent years in the ways that gender is portrayed in children's books (Archer 2008). Changes include expanding children's views of traditional career roles. Boster (2005) presents a table listing several books featuring nontraditional career roles such as a male choreographer, female doctors and police officers, and a male secretary. However, there is still a visible lack of respect toward males and females (Singh 1998), with a slight expansion of gender roles being presented for girls but not for boys (Cahill and Adams 1997).

This is a special concern for young children who have limited access to examples of lifestyle differences at home, in their extended family, or in their neighborhoods. Many young children spend a great deal of their day with females, either family members or educators. The field of early childhood education has an overwhelming number of female teachers compared to male teachers. The MenTeach Web site (www.menteach .org) cites a 2007 report from the U.S. Bureau of Labor Statistics noting the percentage of male educators in various educational settings. Male teachers accounted for 5.4 percent of the workforce in child care settings. In preschool and kindergarten settings, male teachers represented 2.7 percent of the total number of people employed, while male teacher assistants were reported at 8.5 percent. Considerably more male teachers were found in elementary and middle schools, as well as in secondary classrooms (19.1 and 43.1 percent, respectively).

In sharp contrast to the number of male early childhood educators in the classroom is the number of male children enrolled in early care and education settings. According to the U.S. Department of Education (as reported by Planty et al. 2008), during the 2005–6 school year 58 percent of male children were reported as attending center-based care compared with 56.9 percent of female children, while just over 20.5 percent of all children attended home-based care during the same school year.

The discrepancy in the ratio of male children to male teachers has many detrimental effects on all young children. With men constituting less than 5 percent of the child-care work force (Galley 2000) and an overwhelming majority (75 percent) of early childhood teachers being female (Chakraborty and Stone 2008), male children are not often presented with male role models in early childhood settings (Scelfo, 2007). Please note that the previous two studies differentiate between the child care workforce, which includes teacher aides, and early childhood teachers who are certified educators. If children do not see males in the classroom, they begin to believe teaching is only for females, causing the percentages not to add up to 100 percent of the entire early childhood educator field. Add to this the amount of gender stereotyping presented in the children's books in early childhood classrooms, the developmental aspect of young children to begin identifying gender differences (Egan and Perry 2001), the research stating that picture books affect early gender role socialization (Couch 1995), and the understanding that readers, even young readers, identify with characters of their own gender (Singh 1998). Therefore early childhood educators and parents should show a great deal of concern and vigilance in selecting the books to which their children are exposed.

Books may be one of the few places some children can see a variety of male roles that show both women and men in various gender roles. It is equally important to share books that show differences and commonalities between the characters in the books and the children in the classroom.

PRACTICAL IMPLICATIONS FOR TEACHERS

Teachers can have great influence on how children develop and on family relationships. The choices that early childhood educators make in establishing classroom environments not only reflects their beliefs but also impacts the development of the values and beliefs of the young children in their care. Cahill and Adams (1997) found that teachers' beliefs and attitudes can shape children's perceptions of gender, gender roles, and gender stereotypes. Early childhood educators are in a unique position to educate families on such issues and to establish the physical environment of the classroom, including the selection of books, to increase the variety of gender roles children experience through the books presented in early childhood settings.

Teachers need to be aware that the choices they make in selecting children's books for the early childhood classroom can influence the values and beliefs of the classroom as a whole. It is just as important to recognize that text and illustrations present an overall view of the values and attitudes of a given society. Promoting an awareness of gender similarities and differences and discussing both feminine and masculine viewpoints in the children's book stories will present a more complete, diverse, and realistic image to children, providing children of all genders with a wide range of possibilities for future exploration and a global view of gender roles and identities (Moore and Derman-Sparks 2003).

It is also important for teachers to take a step back and reflect on their own values and beliefs about gender. Cahill and Adams (1997) state that teacher attitudes and behaviors are highly influential in shaping the gender perceptions of young children. Early childhood educators should periodically assess their own beliefs and attitudes and look critically at the messages they are sending through their classroom environment and behaviors. The goal of redefining how gender roles are represented in children's books will not be reached overnight. Instead, it is a long-term commitment educators must make to benefit children in their care as well as society as a whole.

The types of books in the early childhood classroom convey the values of both the teacher and the program and can serve to represent a welcoming environment for children and families—or quite the opposite. Children's books can significantly influence gender role socialization (Couch 1995), and families are becoming increasingly sensitive to the messages promoted through children's books. Teachers and environments transmit values and attitudes through storytelling (Monk-

Turner 2001), and the selection of classroom books speaks loudly about the values promoted in the classroom. Selecting a wide variety of children's books that offer alternative views of gender roles (Singh 1998), that break gender stereotypes (see Roberts and Hill 2003 for a list of recommended books), and provide both girls and boys with positive role models (Archer 2008) will provide all children with a supportive environment in which they can thrive socially, cognitively, and emotionally; in essence, supporting children in developing healthy identities.

Table 1: A Sampling of Children's Books Portraying Gender Roles Equitably

Examples of books that challenge gender stereotypes (Roberts and Hill 2003)	*Boy, Can He Dance!* (Spinelli and Yalowitz 1993): A little boy would rather be a dancer than a chef like his father. *Anna Banana and Me* (Blegvad 1999): A brave girl and a timid boy become friends. *The Paper Bag Princess* (Munsch 1988): A princess rescues a prince from a dragon.
Examples of nonsexist literature (Pirofski n.d.)	*The Long Red Scarf* (Hilton 1980): Grandpa can't find a woman to knit him a scarf, so he knits his own. *Daddy Makes the Best Spaghetti* (Grossnickle Hiness 1989): A father picks up his son from child care and takes him to the supermarket to buy food for dinner. *Amazing Grace* (Hoffman 1991): You can be anything you want.

Table 1 (continued)

	Frida Maria: A Story of the Old Southwest (Nourse Lattimore 1997): Frida Maria is an independent girl in the old Southwest.
	The Story of Ferdinand (Leaf 1936): Ferdinand the sweet-natured bull prefers peace to fighting.
	Jess Was the Brave One (Little 1991): Girls are brave.
Examples of folktales that break gender stereotypes (Creany 1995)	*Lon Po Po: A Red Riding Hood Story from China* (Young 1989): Three sisters outwit the wolf instead of the woodcutter who rescues the grandmother and child in the traditional Little Red Riding Hood.
	Mufaro's Beautiful Daughters (Steptoe 1988): Two daughters are beautiful, but the daughter with the kind temperament wins her father's heart.
	The Talking Eggs (San Souci 1989): There are no male characters, and kindness and courage are rewarded with riches.
Example of a fiction book that treats gender fairly (Creany 1995)	*Tar Beach* (Ringgold 1991): Cassie flies through the air and possesses the Brooklyn Bridge.

Table 2: Tips for Selecting Children's Books with Fair Gender Role Representation

Choose books emphasizing the characters as individuals with unique personalities.
Characters' occupations should be gender-neutral.
Females should not always be weaker, smaller, and more delicate than males; consider selecting books where females are depicted in a positive manner and are active.
The message of respect for all genders should be subtle.
Avoid books that have preachy messages on gender equity, as children tend to reject books with such overtly moralistic messages.

(Creany 1995; Singh 1998)

REFERENCES

Anderson, D. A., and M. Hamilton. 2005. Gender role stereotyping of parents in children's picture books: The invisible father. *Sex Roles* 52, (3/4): 145–51.

Archer, M. 2008. The appearance of gender in award-winning children's books. EzineArticles.com. http://ezinearticles.com/?Gender-Stereotypes&id=1115363.

Bandura, A. 1986. *Social foundations of thought and action: A social cognitive theory.* Englewood Cliffs, NJ: Prentice-Hall.

Bem, S. L. 1981. Gender schema theory: A cognitive account of sex typing. *Psychological Bulletin* 88, (4): 354–64.

Boster, M. A. 2005. Gender equity of traditional and non-traditional career roles in Newbery Award-winning and Honor books. Liberty University Dissertation.

Brothers Grimm. 1997. *Rapunzel.* New York: Dutton Children's Books.

Bussey, K., and A. Bandura. 1999. Social cognitive theory of development and differentiation. *Psychological Review* 106, (4): 676–713.

Cahill, B., and E. Adams. 1997. An exploratory study of early childhood teachers; attitudes toward gender roles. *Sex Roles* 36, (7/8): 517–29.

Chakraborty, B., and S. Stone. 2008. Teaching tolerance and reaching diverse students through the use of children's books. *Children's Education* 85 (2): 106–09.

Coplan, R. J., L. M. Closson, and K. A. Arbeau. 2007. Gender differences in the behavioral associates of loneliness and social dissatisfaction in kindergarten. *Journal of Child Psychology and Psychiatry* 48, (10): 988–95.

Couch, R. A. 1995. Gender equity and visual literacy: Schools can help change perceptions. Paper presented at the Annual Conference of the International Visual Literacy Association, Chicago, IL.

Creany, A. D. 1995. The appearance of gender in award-winning children's books. Paper presented at the Annual Conference of the International Visual Literacy Association, Chicago, IL.

Egan, S. K., and D. G. Perry. 2001. Gender identity: A multidimensional analysis with implications for psychosocial adjustment. *Developmental Psychology* 37, (4): 451–63.

Ernst, S. B. 1995. Gender issues in books for children and young adults. In *Battling dragons: Issues and controversy in children's literature,* ed. S. Lehr, 66–78. Portsmouth, NH: Heinemann.

Galley, M. 2000. Man's work? *Teacher Magazine* 11, (6): 17–18.

Gerbner, G., L. Gross, M. Morgan, and N. Signorielli. 1994. Growing up with television: The cultivation perspective. In *Media effects: Advances in theory and research,* ed. J. Bryant and D. Zillman, 43–68. Hillsdale, NJ: Erlbaum.

Gooden, A. M., and M. A. Gooden. 2001. Gender representation in notable children's picture books: 1995–1999. *Sex Roles* 45, (1/2): 89–101.

Hamilton, M. C., D. Anderson, M. Broaddus, and K. Young. 2006. Gender stereotyping and under-representation of female characters in 200 popular children's picture books: A twenty-first century update. *Sex Roles* 55 (11/12): 757–65.

Hanlon, H., R. Thatcher, and M. Cline. 1999. Gender differences in the development of EEG coherence in normal children. *Developmental Neuropsychology* 16 (3): 479–506.

Jalongo, M. R. 2004. *Young children and picture books.* 2nd ed. Washington, DC: NAEYC.

Jett-Simpson, M., and S. Masland. 1993. Girls are not dodo birds! Exploring gender equity issues in the language arts classrooms. *Language Arts* 70 (2): 104–8.

Kessler, S., and W. McKenna. 1978. *Gender: An ethnomethodological approach.* New York: John Wiley and Sons.

Kohlberg, L. 1966. A cognitive-developmental analysis of children's sex-role concepts and attitudes. In *The development of sex differences,* ed. E. E. Maccoby, 82–173. Stanford, CA: Stanford University Press.

Lin, G. 1999. *The ugly vegetables.* Watertown, MA: Charlesbridge.

Martin, C. L., D. N. Ruble, and J. Szkrybalo. 2002. Cognitive theories of early gender development. *Psychological Bulletin* 128, (6): 903–33.

McCully, E. A. 1992. *Mirette on the high wire.* New York: Putnam Books.

MenTeach. 2007. Data about men teachers. http://www.menteach.org/resources/data_about_men_teachers.

Mercurio, C. M. 2003. Guiding boys in the early years to lead healthy emotional lives. *Early Childhood Education Journal* 30, (4): 255–58.

Monk-Turner, E. 2001. Gender roles in children's literature: A review of non-award-winning "easy-to-read" books. *Journal of Research in Childhood Education* 16, (1): 70–76.

Moore, T., and L. Derman-Sparks. 2003. Giving children global views. *Early Childhood Today* 18, (3): 40.

National Association for the Education of Young Children and International Reading Association. 1998. Learning to read and write: Developmentally appropriate practices for young children. Joint position statement. *Young Children* 53, (4): 30–46.

Newman, B. M., and P. R. Newman. 2007. *Theories of human development.* Mahwah, NJ: Lawrence Erlbaum.

Newman, D. M. 2007. *Identities and inequalities: Exploring the intersections of race, class, gender, and sexuality.* Boston: McGraw Hill.

Oskamp, S., K. Kaufman, and L. A. Wolterbeck. 1996. Gender role portrayals in preschool picture books. *Journal of Social Behavior and Personality* 11 (5): 27–39

Paterson, Katherine. 1995. *A sense of wonder: On reading and writing books for children.* New York: Plume.

Patt, M. B., and B. A. McBride. 1993. Gender equity in picture books in preschool classrooms: An exploratory study. Paper presented at the Annual Meeting of the American Educational Research Association, Atlanta, GA.

Pirofski, K. I. n.d. Race, gender, and disability in today's children's literature. Research Room: EdChange Multicultural Pavilion. http://www.edchange.org/multicultural/papers/literature2.html.

Planty, M., W. Hussar, T. Snyder, S. Provasnik, G. Kena, R. Dinkes, A. KewalRamani, and J. Kemp. 2008. *The Condition of Education 2008.* Washington DC: National Center for Education Statistics, U.S. Department of Education. http://nces.ed.gov/pubsearch/pubsinfo.asp?pubid=2008031 (retrieved January 15, 2009).

Raag, T., and C. L. Rackliff. 1998. Preschoolers' awareness of social expectations of gender: Relationships to toy choices. *Sex Roles* 38, (9/10):
685–700.

Roberts, L., E. Dean, and M. Holland. 2005. Contemporary American Indian
cultures in children's picture books. *Young Children* 60 (6): 6.

Roberts, L. C., and T. H. Hill. 2003. Children's books that break gender role
stereotypes. *Beyond the Journal Young Children* (March).

Scelfo, J. 2007. Come back, Mr. Chips: Stereotyping, low pay, lack of role
models. Why the number of men teaching in schools is at a 40-year low.
Newsweek. September 17.

Sheldon, J. P. 2004. Gender stereotypes in educational software for young
children. *Sex Roles* 51, (7/8): 433–44.

Singh, M. 1998. *Gender issues in children's literature*. Bloomington, IN: ERIC
Clearinghouse on Reading, English, and Communication, Indiana
University.

Spinelli, E., and P. Yalowitz. 1993. *Boy, can he dance!* New York: Four Winds.

Tepper, C. A., and K. W. Cassidy. 1999. Gender differences in emotional
language in children's picture books. *Sex Roles* 40, (3/4): 265–80.

Trepanier-Street, M. L., and J. A. Romatowski. 1999. The influence of children's literature on gender role perceptions: A reexamination. *Early
Childhood Education Journal* 26, (3): 155–59.

Tsao, Y. 2008. Gender issues in young children's literature. *Reading Improvement* 45, (3): 108–14.

Twardosz, S. 2001. Children's books in child care classrooms: Quality, acces-
sibility, and reasons for teachers' choices. *Journal of Research in Childhood
Education* 16, (1): 53–69.

United States Department of Health and Human Services. 2006. *NICHD
Study of Early Child Care and Youth Development: Findings for children up to
age 4½ years*. Washington DC: United States Department of Health and
Human Services. http://www.nichd.nih.gov/publications/pubs/upload/
seccyd_051206.pdf.

U.S. Bureau of Labor Statistics. 2007. *Occupational outlook handbook, 2006–
07 edition: Teachers—preschool, kindergarten, elementary, middle, and
secondary*. Washington DC: United States Department of Labor. http://
www.bls.gov/oco/ocos069.htm.

University of Mary Washington. n.d. Related terms and definitions. http://
www.umw.edu/bias/terms/default.php.

Zolotow, C., and W. P. Du Bois. 1972. *William's doll*. New York: Harper
Collins.

SEVEN

Using Picture Books and Literary Experiences to Help Boys and Girls Develop Literacy and Socio-Emotional Skills

— Debby Zambo —

This chapter is dedicated to helping early childhood professionals and others working with young children understand

- emotions, their importance, and development
- emotional literacy and emotional intelligence
- gender differences in emotional expression, development, and regulation
- gender differences in language, emotional literacy, and emotional intelligence
- ways to use picture books to help children understand their emotions and how others feel

Emotions are the physiological and psychological feelings children experience in response to events in their world. Even though some emotions, like anger and fear, may be uncomfortable, all emotions are important because they help children survive. Emotions focus children's attention on matters of importance, help them remember, and energize their bodies for action (Campos, Frankel, and Camras 2004; Izard and Ackerman 2000). Emotions affect interpersonal skills. When children understand their feelings they are better able to relate to how others feel.

This understanding builds empathy and forms the basis of relationships (Greenspan and Shanker 2004; Stamm 2007). Emotional understanding is so vital that Daniel Goleman (1995) contends it to be a type of intelligence. However, being emotionally smart is not always easy for young children. When things do not go their way, two-year-olds throw tantrums with little consideration for who will be hurt. Young children say and do mean things because they think concretely. Instead of considering others' feelings, they act impulsively. Young children lack self-regulation—the ability to manage their emotions and thoughts— because it develops over time. With experience, most children fit into a routine and learn to put their immediate feelings aside. Regulating one's emotions is important but it can be hampered by a lack of ability to express and understand how one feels. Emotional literacy, or knowing how to read and label emotions in oneself and others, grows with language skills. Young children learn the literacy of emotions, develop self-regulation, and achieve emotional intelligence when the adults around them offer support and guidance (Shonkoff and Phillips 2000).

Unfortunately, promoting cognitive intelligence at the expense of emotional intelligence is currently the focus in many homes and schools. Instead of recognizing the importance of emotional intelligence and spending time each day developing it, it is being pushed aside (Hirsh-Pasek and Golinkoff 2003; Siegel 1999). There is no doubt young children need to get off to a good start academically. The early years are the learning years and children need experiences to help them understand their world. However, forgetting the effect of emotions on learning is a grave mistake. The way young children experience, learn about, and learn how to manage or regulate their emotions lays the foundation for their cognitive skills and social competence. Children with emotional intelligence bond with their teachers, have more friends, and learn more easily in school (Stamm 2007).

EMOTIONAL DEVELOPMENT

Most cultures recognize nine basic emotions: anger, anxiety, disgust, fear, happiness, pride, sadness, guilt, and shame (Ekman 2004). Infants communicate their emotions with their cries, giggles, gestures, and movements, but all nine emotions do not appear at the same time. Newborns begin life programmed with fear, anger, and joy because these emotions help them survive. Fear is shown within the first six months and helps infants become aware of their surroundings and alert to harmful things. Fear is a strong and uncomfortable emotion for young children because they lack the cognitive maturity and language skills to reason their fears away. They look to the adults in their lives to interpret uneasy situations. In new settings adults help young children soothe their fears and calm down (Campos, Frankel, and Camras 2004; Feinman 1992).

As they develop, children begin to figure out ways to comfort themselves. They replace human soothing with items like blankets or teddy bears and with behaviors like thumb sucking. Learning how to soothe one's self matters because the human brain is most impressionable at this time (Zambo and Hansen 2007). The brains of young children are immersed in a world full of strange sights, sounds, and smells and they must learn how to handle these new stimuli. Children who are capable of self-soothing become self-reliant and cope with new challenges effectively. Instead of being fearful of new experiences or constantly in need of encouragement to go out and explore the world, they follow their inquisitiveness. In contrast, children who do not soothe themselves often become fearful and withdrawn. This does not mean there is something terribly wrong. These children just need child care professionals to be in tune with their emotions. They need assistance with managing times of fear. Responsive care sets children on the path to healthy emotional lives (Jacobson 2008; Perry and Szalavitz 2006; Siegel 1999).

Self-conscious emotions appear later, when children develop self-awareness. By two years of age most children recognize themselves in a mirror and know that they are individual beings. With this new knowledge children use external standards to evaluate their behavior, and self-conscious emotions like guilt, embarrassment, and pride appear. Toddlers feel proud when they accomplish a task that once seemed insurmountable and feel guilty and shameful when they violate a social norm. Guilt arises from one's awareness of hurting others and shame comes from knowing someone else has seen a forbidden act (Saarni 2000; Wellman et al. 1995). Anxieties are also displayed during the early years, especially when adults are out of sight. As children grow they experience new situations and unfamiliar people. These little challenges help children grow stronger emotionally. Children learn independence and become mentally healthy when they conquer little hurdles and fears (Perry 2005).

As children develop and enter the early school years they bond with individuals outside their family like teachers, coaches, and friends.

Emotions are key to these relationships and key to their success in school. The emotions children bring to social settings like classrooms accelerate or hinder the friendships they form and the social and academic success they achieve. Children perform better when they feel a sense of belonging and security. Children are hampered when they feel uncared for and detached (Izard and Ackerman 2000). Children whose minds are cluttered with anxiety find it difficult to focus their attention and complete their work. Some emotional distractions (like a passing argument with a friend) are temporary, but others (like a child custody battle) require intervention and support. Table 1 contains a summary of this information on emotional development.

Table 1: Milestones in Emotional Development

Age	Emotional Milestones
birth–6 months	• signs of basic emotions (fear, anger, and happiness) present • increasing repertoire for communicating emotions (crying, smiling, hand gestures) • social smiles appear • happiness is expressed when familiar people are near • attachment behaviors begin to form • attunement to those around; child fits into daily routines • ability to soothe self (sucking thumb, clutching blanket) beginning to emerge
7–12 months	• social referencing develops—look to adults in their world to know how to react and feel • anger and fear get shown more intensely • attachment continues to grow—adults continue to be a secure base • can detect emotional signals • self-regulation begins to bud

Table 1 (continued)

1–2 years	• with crawling and walking child ventures into a wider emotional world • self-conscious emotions appear • vocabulary expands and labels for feelings are made • empathetic responding is shown sometimes
3–6 years	• increasing number of bonds with those outside the family (for example, peers, early childhood professionals) • cognitive and behavioral strategies for emotional regulation begin to bud and grow • ability to understand emotional cues of others expands • understanding of emotional reactions and behaviors grows • empathic and sympathetic responses increase • self-reflection begins

(Adapted from McDevitt and Ormrod 2002)

Children need early childhood professionals to help them understand and regulate the emotions they feel. But just as important as helping children learn about emotions is recognizing individual strengths and needs. The next section uses gender as a framework to understand the emotional development of boys and girls. Later in this chapter I will explain how to use picture books to help boys and girls develop socially and emotionally.

GENDER DIFFERENCES IN EMOTIONAL DEVELOPMENT AND EXPRESSION

In the picture book *When Sophie Gets Angry—Really, Really Angry . . .* (Bang 1999), Sophie gets mad at her sister and loses self-control. She

kicks and screams. She is so angry she wants to smash the world to smith-
ereens. Sophie's extreme anger is shown in the illustrations. Pictures of
Sophie illustrate her furrowed brow, frowning mouth, and kicking feet.
Words like "roar," "explode," "smash," and "pabam" surround Sophie,
and fire shoots out of her mouth. But, with a turn of the page, things
change. Sophie begins to run and cry. Sophie is embarrassed because she
lost self-control and let her anger get the best of her.

Boys and girls feel the same emotions, but their reactions vary
because of their culture and family. Halpern (2004) captures this idea
nicely in her psychobiosocial view of gender and learning. From her
standpoint, variability between the sexes occurs because nature and
nurture alter each other in sequentially interacting ways. What boys
and girls learn influences the structure (branching and size) of their
neurons and the architecture of their brains. Brain architecture, in turn,
supports certain skills, perceptions, and abilities that lead to certain
behaviors. Extrapolating this idea to emotions shows that both biology
and the environment shape emotional development. Basic feelings get
enacted then reinforced or punished by childhood professionals, and
this gets built into how their brains think. From the moment they are
born children get treated differently based on whether they are a boy
or a girl. In the opening scenario from *When Sophie Gets Angry*, Sophie
was embarrassed by the anger she felt. Gender differences in emotional
expression are formed by society and culture. Ideas about emotions and
oneself get built early and remain throughout childhood, as the following points reveal.

Boys

- Young boys typically show more anger than girls. They are more
  likely to hit, kick, and bite, and this behavior seems to peak in
  kindergarten. It declines between the ages of six and fifteen (Sax
  2007).
- Boys are better able to tolerate feeling scared. When given a choice
  of stories to hear, boys as young as two years old will pick violent
  and scary fairy tales as opposed to flowery tales (Sax 2007).
- Competition is part of boys' make up and they are not as dis-
  turbed by anger and aggression because they have more testosterone in their brains (Gurian and Stevens 2005).
- Boys and girls process emotions in different parts of their brain.
  The brains of boys use the amygdala, the center for reaction. They

do not use as much of the cerebral cortex, the reasoning/reflective part, as girls do (Brizendine 2006).

- When boys are feeling emotionally distressed they tend to distract themselves (Gurian and Stevens 2005).
- When boys are feeling emotionally distressed they want to be left alone (Gurian and Stevens 2005).

Girls

- When girls react aggressively or with strong emotions they tend to be rejected by their peers and experience shame (Gilligan 1982).
- When girls react aggressively they experience shame and guilt (Brizendine 2006).
- All babies are born with the need for social interaction, but for girls it is more critical (Brizendine 2006).
- Areas in the female brain devoted to observing emotions and the hormone estrogen cause girls to be more attuned to feelings (Sax 2005).
- Girls are better at detecting subtle emotions in another's voice (Gilligan 1982).
- Girls react more negatively to failures (Brizendine 2006).
- Girls report feeling sad, fearful, and guilty more often than boys do (Brizendine 2006).
- Girls tend to ruminate about their problems rather than taking action or distracting themselves (Sax 2005).

Implications

Responsive professionals who model positive emotions and soothe unpleasant ones literally shape brain systems and influence the way young brains react to the world (LeDoux 1996; Perry 2005; Stamm 2007). Early childhood professionals attuned to children's emotions help them find comfort in times of distress; this, in turn, helps them become cognitively and socially adept. Children with emotional confidence explore the environment without reservation, interact with others in positive ways, and make friends because they trust the world is safe. Young children need these skills to become self-reliant as they grow (Stamm 2007).

Young children need to develop emotional understanding, and they do this when they connect with others. As children interact with their family, early childhood professionals, and peers they begin to connect with how they feel. Empathy (the ability to understand others' feelings) and sympathy (the ability to identify with others' feelings) are talents that develop the same as any intelligence. Children learn to be empathetic and sympathetic when they work with others and when others depend on them.

Responsive educators recognize there are gender differences. They know girls like Sophie can get so angry they explode. Yet, in real life girls are often shamed when they feel this way. Children are biologically programmed to feel emotions, and childhood professionals, within the context of their society and culture, shape the way children are allowed to express anger, sadness, or fear. The points above indicate that boys and girls have unique emotional strengths and needs. Later I explain how to use picture books to help boys and girls learn about the emotions they feel.

GENDER DIFFERENCES IN LABELING AND UNDERSTANDING EMOTIONS

In the book *Yo! Yes?* (Raschka 1993) two boys become friends with very few words between them. Their short sentences and body postures help the reader understand the emotions they have as they move from being strangers to becoming best friends.

Children's first forms of communication are performed with their faces and bodies. They cry when they are unhappy and giggle with delight when those who care for them are near. But these forms of communication become more inappropriate as they develop. Children need to develop language to express and manage the emotions they feel. A two-year-old wanting her best friend's toy can use words to negotiate that toy away or she can throw a tantrum to scare the child away. The early years can be a time of conflict for children or they can become teachable moments. Emotional outbursts can be frustrating, but they can offer opportunities to talk with children about their feelings and help them learn labels for how they feel.

Language is the tool children can use to develop emotional intelligence. However, language is not developed uniformly; it is influenced by biology and culture. Boys and girls develop language differently due to the input they receive (Eisenberg, Martin, and Fabes 1996). Early childhood professionals often talk more about emotions and encourage more emotional expression in girls than in boys. Boys are expected to keep their fears, anxiety, and sadness bottled inside. However, when it comes to anger and pride, boys have much more leeway than girls have

(Eisenberg, Martin, and Fabes 1996; Sax 2007). Biology and the way children are treated matter to their emotional literacy. The following points reveal gender differences in emotional language skills.

Boys

- Testosterone and the way their brains are built cause boys to be less communicative in general (Sax 2005).
- Many boys do not have the opportunity to talk about their emotions. This causes them to keep emotions bottled up and become distant from how they really feel (Gurian and Stevens 2005).
- Boys are more likely to express their feelings when they are standing side by side or doing something. They are less willing to discuss their feelings when they are face-to-face (Gurian and Stevens 2005).
- Boys will ignore suggestions about their vulnerability, brag, and threaten (Sax 2007).

Girls

- Girls have 11 percent more neurons in brain centers devoted to language and hearing than boys. Girls speak earlier, speak more clearly, and form longer sentences than boys (Sax 2005).
- More neurons devoted to hearing allow girls to perceive subtle emotional differences in voices (Brizendine 2006).
- Young girls acquire words faster and have vocabularies two times larger than boys (Brizendine 2006).
- Girls are better at using words to communicate (Sax 2005).
- Because of the way their brains are built, to girls emotional expression and relationships are important. Conversation is central to girls' emotional well-being (Brizendine 2006).
- Girls develop their sense of self through relationships. They want friends they can talk with, and they want to keep social harmony between themselves and their friends (Gilligan 1982).
- As girls grow older they often hide their true feelings in order to keep their friends (Gilligan 1982).

Implications

It is important to help young children develop the language they need to understand, express, and manage the emotions they feel. Self-regulation with language is much better than regulation with tantrums and fists. Early childhood professionals who encourage young children to talk about their feelings in gender-comfortable ways foster emotional literacy. Words help children sort out and label their feelings, and one of the best ways to develop this emotional language is reading stories aloud (Tompkins 2003). Stories offer children opportunities to vicariously experience the emotions of others. Encouraging children to talk about a character's emotions builds emotional literacy and intelligence (Zambo and Brem 2004; Zambo and Hansen 2007).

Learning about emotions through language is important, but it is also important to recognize differences. Boys and girls develop and use emotional language in a different sequence, at a varied pace, and with diverse interaction styles. Boys are slower at language development and like to talk side by side instead of face-to-face. Understanding biological differences and interactional style is important (Gurian and Stevens 2005). Boys learn about emotions more readily with few words and from male characters just as girls learn from female protagonists (Brozo 2002; Sprague and Keeling 2007). Early childhood professionals can use these differences to foster individual emotional needs.

EMOTIONS, SELF-REGULATION, AND GENDER DIFFERENCES

In the book *Ronald Morgan Goes to Bat* (Giff 1990), Ronald Morgan is able to manage his behaviors but not his emotions. Ronald practices batting every day despite the fact that he is afraid of the ball. Ronald's positive attitude changes when he realizes he is the worst hitter on the team. He wants to give up baseball, but his father steps in to help. He tells Ronald that he too once was the worst player on his team. Instead of letting Ronald give up baseball, his father helps him control his fears, focus his attention, and regulate his thinking long enough to hit the ball. With this help, Ronald gains self-respect and the respect of his teammates.

Like Ronald Morgan, children encounter a range of emotions and express their emotions in their behaviors and words. Children cry when they are sad, laugh when they are happy, and close their eyes when they are afraid. Emotions serve a survival purpose, but they can become a liability if they are not regulated or controlled. Had Ronald Morgan let his fear of the ball get the best of him he never would have practiced and hit a home run. Shonkoff and Phillips (2000) define self-regulation as the ability to gain control of one's bodily functions, manage powerful emotions, and maintain focus and attention when distractions arise. Emotional regulation is likely to be *the* most challenging aspect of childhood that children face. Infants who cry for long periods and toddlers who hit, bite, or scratch seem out of control because they are not regulating themselves. Young children learn self-regulation when they conquer manageable challenges (Perry 2005; Perry and Szalavitz 2006). With support and encouragement children develop self-regulation. Allowing little challenges with moderation and guidance is a component of responsive care (Campos, Frankel, and Camras 2004; Shonkoff and Phillips 2000). However, children do not develop self-regulation all at once or in a uniform way.

Self-regulation is the ability to control one's behaviors, emotions, and thinking, and there are gender differences in this ability (Shonkoff and Phillips 2000). Boys and girls are expected to manage the emotions they feel in different ways. Boys are expected to regulate their sadness, as the expression "big boys don't cry" attests. Girls are allowed to display more emotions overtly but are discouraged to show some emotions, like anger and pride (Sax 2005). Gender differences are seen in children because of innate differences and because of the way they are treated (Eisenberg, Martin, and Fabes 1996). Gender differences in self-regulation are evident, as the following points reveal.

Boys

- Boys are taught not to show vulnerable emotions like sadness and anxiety. In preschool and beyond boys who cry are called "sissies" and are less popular (Gurian and Stevens 2005).
- Boys will put on self-confident airs even when they feel vulnerable (Sax 2007).

Girls

- Girls receive more input. Mothers tend to display a greater variety of emotions and show more intense facial expression of emotions to their daughters than to their sons (Eisenberg, Martin, and Fabes 1996).
- Girls who act aggressively and don't inhibit their anger have lower status among their peers (Brizendine 2006).
- Because relationships are so important to girls, they display relational aggression more often than overt anger (Brizendine 2006).

- Girls tend to learn how to regulate their emotions earlier than boys. However, with societal changes this is beginning to change (Brizendine 2006).

Implications

When children do not adapt to a routine or when they display the wrong emotion at the wrong time or with the wrong intensity, they are displaying a lack of self-regulation. Children who are emotionally out of sync experience great difficulty at home and in school. Early childhood professionals find them difficult to manage, and peers reject them because their emotions are too intense. Young children learn self-regulation when early childhood professionals understand individual strengths and needs. To help children develop self-regulation Bronson (2000) offers individualized strategies. Adapting Bronson's strategies for boys and girls provides the following ideas.

- Observe closely. Young children send cues that reveal how they feel. These cues can help early childhood professionals understand when a child is feeling strong emotions and when they may need to offer support. Watch for differences between boys and girls.
- Respond. Be alert to individual differences. Boys and girls have varied needs for regularity, support, and interaction.
- Provide structure and be predictable. Young children need consistent routines that make them feel safe. These needs may vary by gender and temperament.
- Set age-appropriate limits. Help children feel safe by using boundaries. Boys and girls need individual, appropriate limits to learn how to regulate their emotions and behaviors.
- Be empathetic and show care. Assist children in developing empathy by modeling empathetic behaviors. Empathy is an ability that depends on cognitive, social, and moral development. Recognize and respond to individual needs. Let girls and boys show empathy and care.

The above ideas offer insight to help children learn to regulate the emotions they feel. The remainder of this chapter is dedicated to putting these important ideas into action with picture books chosen for girls and boys.

USING PICTURE BOOKS
TO ENCOURAGE EMOTIONAL INTELLIGENCE
AND EMOTIONAL LITERACY

It is the first day of preschool and the children in Sonjia Hernandez's classroom are gathered around her listening to her read *Wemberly Worried* (Henkes 2000). Sonjia uses a calm and soothing voice, and all eyes and ears are on her as she reads about a mouse named Wemberly. Like the children listening, Wemberly is attending her first day at school and she's worried. Will the children like me? Will they make fun of me? Will my teacher be mean? As Sonjia reads about these worries a few of her students move closer, especially when she shows the illustration of Wemberly rubbing her stuffed rabbit's ears. One child stops the story to show the class his "Teddy bear with soft brown fur" and another discusses the "silky blanket" she has in her lap. Sonjia smiles at these words because she knows her students are connecting the story to their experience. Sonjia listens respectfully because she knows that expressing and labeling emotions is helping her students relieve their anxiety and fears.

After the children have had a turn sharing, Sonjia tells them about her first day at school. She tells them that she too was worried like Wemberly. As the children hear this, their bodies begin to relax, and Sonjia knows they are ready for the next activity. To make this transition easier, Sonjia sings a song as the children move to the art area. There they find easels, paint, brushes, and smocks. The children don the smocks and are ready to begin their next task: to paint a picture of their first day at school. As the children work, Sonjia talks to each child and writes a few words each child says on their picture. One boy paints himself standing next to Wemberly and says, "This is me and my friend Wemberly." Another boy paints a smiley school building with a happy teacher reading a book. The caption on his paper reads, "I go to a happy school." The students' pictures and words will be revisited tomorrow and used to remind them of their first happy day at school.

This story shows the power of picture books. Picture books are a practicable way to teach children because they are easily accessible. School and public libraries typically have a bounty of picture books, and many children are accustomed to hearing books read to them before bed (Tompkins 2003). Picture books are practical and they are also cognitively, socially, and emotionally beneficial. Children find the stories and illustrations in picture books exciting and interesting. When properly selected, picture books capture children's attention and help them learn. Picture books teach important concepts with both text and imagery (Sadoski and Paivio 2001). Children experience emotions through stories, and they see emotions in the illustrations that accompany the words they hear. The narratives in picture books represent the world by describing characters' experiences within the context of events (Graesser, Golding, and Long 1991).

Research in psychology reveals that narratives appeal to the natural attributes of human memory (McCauley 2000). As children hear a story, they automatically search their memories to locate a similar story. A deep level of comprehension is built as children mix what they hear with what they know (Schank 1995). The work of Sipe (2001) suggests that when children hear and discuss stories they become transparent with their ideas and feelings and more analytical and creative in their thoughts. Through narratives children enter characters' lives and experience the emotions vicariously. This is important for young children, because through stories they experience small challenges and learn how others conquer them. This is especially true when children have favorite characters. Roser et al. (2007) discovered that children become attached to certain characters. They know their stories intimately and see the dilemmas they face and experience the emotions they feel. Experiencing a character's feelings helps young children learn labels for their own feelings and helps them realize they are not alone in the challenges they face. Good characters help children understand how an emotion looks, sounds, and feels. This understanding encourages emotional intelligence, regulation, and social development. Children attuned to the feelings of others as well as their own get along with their teachers, family, and peers. The story from Sonjia's classroom is testament to the power of story on young children's lives.

In addition to the value of story, picture books also provide a visual representation of the emotions characters feel (Evans 1998). The illustrations in picture books depict facial expressions and body language that reveal feelings openly. These visuals encourage young children to look at people to understand them. In many ways this is a natural process, because young children use their eyes before they use words. Young children look at the faces and body language of the adults in their world to learn about emotions; as they grow they develop the ability to learn from symbols and images (Feinman 1992). This is especially important for reading the complex emotions that children often feel but cannot label. Reading to children about a broad array of emotions helps them build the language they need to label their own feelings. Picture books with both boys and girls displaying and learning about a variety of emotions help children build their emotional intelligence. Table 2 provides a list of picture books in which boys and girls display a broad array of emotions.

Table 2: Books for Readalouds That Contain Both Genders Displaying a Broad Array of Emotions

Feelings (Aliki 1986)

The Story of My Feelings (Berkner 2007)

ABC I Like Me! (Carlson 1999)

Today I Feel Silly: And Other Moods That Make My Day (Curtis 1998)

Glad Monster, Sad Monster (Emberly 1997)

Feelings A to Z (Masteller 1988)

The Feelings Book (Parr 2005)

Lots of Feelings (Rotner 2003)

Feelings to Share from A to Z (Snow and Snow 2007)

Feet Are Not for Kicking (Verdick 2004)

Words Are Not for Hurting (Verdick 2004)

Feeling Happy (Weiss 2006)

Reading books matters to children, but it is not only the reading that matters. Early childhood professionals and the environments they create matter most. Helping children learn about emotions with picture books takes planning and care. To help accomplish this, Table 3 offers a comprehensive list of strategies to foster emotional intelligence. The following sections break down this information for boys and girls.

Table 3: Specific Strategies to Foster Emotional Literacy, Intelligence, and Regulation

Help children recognize, express, and label their emotions	• Prior to reading a book do a walk-through. Help children gain perspective by predicting how they think characters are feeling. Point out and define emotional words and use the illustrations. Talk about visual clues (for example, smiles, frowns, tears) to understand feelings.
	• Occasionally pause during stories and have children predict how characters might be feeling at that point—scaffold talk to extend ideas.
	• Confirm and reward appropriate responses. Be open and accepting of answers. Remember, children do not think like adults. Guide and redirect inappropriate replies.
	• Have children role-play characters and show how they feel with their faces and bodies.
	• If the child is developmentally ready, after the story has been read ask him or her to retell the story from another point of view.
	• Talk about what characters could have done better.
	• Model your emotional reactions to characters' actions. Use self-reflective language (for example, "I really felt sad when . . ." and "I really felt happy when . . .").
	• Model ways to be caring and considerate. Provide opportunities for children to experience these actions.
	• Model empathy and supply sympathetic replies throughout the day. Reward and praise positive behaviors when they are displayed.
	• Talk about your own emotions. When you do, exaggerate your facial and body language to match those emotions (for example, show what your face looked like when you heard the happy news).

Table 3 (continued)

	• Talk about your reactions to emotional situations and explain how you dealt with them. • Model appropriate ways to deal with negative emotions. • Help children understand that emotional eruptions, although embarrassing, can be learning experiences. Provide training in conflict resolution and problem solving. • When children express an emotional reaction, take time to talk with them. Don't dictate, lecture, or make them think their feelings are unimportant. • Provide opportunities for children to act in positive ways so they experience the good feelings these behaviors provide.
Help children read and identify emotions in others	• Use specific words to describe emotions—words children are unlikely to hear every day. • To help children get their message across, extend their comments into more descriptive, grammatically mature statements. • Create a chart of emotional pictures and words. Have children use this when they do not know what to say about how they feel.
Help children develop the language of emotions	• Discuss and label both positive and negative emotional reactions. • Help children gain emotional language with "I" statements; for example "I feel angry when . . ." • Model and talk about how you handle disappointment or sadness. • Use puppets to model emotional reactions. • Supply stuffed animals or other soft familiar items for comfort. • Be open and caring—listen and respond to what children have to say. Listen more than you speak.

USING PICTURE BOOKS WITH YOUNG BOYS

To help clarify ideas about boys that are presented above, I revisit and place them within a classroom context that is designed to highlight gender differences, strengths, and needs.

José Hernandez is a second grade teacher. He is concerned about several boys because they are getting into heated arguments and showing a disregard for how others feel. The boys lack emotional self-regulation and are not very good at explaining how they feel. Also, they are often unaware of how their behaviors make others feel. Although José understands the unique characteristics of boys and the influence he has on them, he wonders what he should do. To figure out a solution José begins mulling over the things he knows about boys.

Table 4: Characteristics of Boys and Implications for Teachers

Boys	Implications
• are more reactive than reflective about feelings	• provide insight and guidance to help boys regulate, tolerate, and manage their emotions
• are allowed to show anger more openly and are not disturbed by aggression	• offer age-appropriate outlets for emotional expression
• are competitive and daring, like excitement, and learn from male role models	• provide action stories with positive male characters who can teach them about emotions
• are taught not to show vulnerable emotions	• help boys learn emotional literacy—how to read and label their emotions and the emotions of others
• are taught not to talk about their feelings	• encourage boys to express their feelings instead of brushing them off
• sometimes lack emotional literacy—have trouble labeling and articulating how they and others feel	• help boys develop their emotional intelligence
• display an uncaring demeanor even when they feel emotions	• use illustrations in books to help boys learn how to read faces

Table 4 (continued)

• distract themselves when emotionally distressed	• read stories with expression so boys hear emotional tones in voices
• when emotional, they do not want to talk—they want to be left alone	• provide age-appropriate opportunities for boys to express their emotions
• don't like discussing their feelings face-to-face—they prefer talking side by side	• provide opportunities for boys to express their feelings side by side rather than face-to-face

Given these characteristics José decides to form a Boys' Only Book Club. For thirty minutes each day, he and the boys in his classroom will meet, read, and discuss a book. José will choose these books carefully. Books will contain a male protagonist, and their story and illustrations will help the boys understand emotions and how their behaviors make others feel. José decides the first book will be *For You Are a Kenyan Child* (Cunnane 2006), one of his favorites because it has a substantive plot and contains informative illustrations. The facial expressions and body language of the characters show pro-social behaviors and positive ways to express feelings. José wants his students to look at people's faces and body language to understand how they feel. He is hoping this insight will help the boys learn labels for their feelings and develop emotional control.

During the first Boys Only Book Club the boys sit side by side and engage in a family-like conversation. The structure of the conversation is relaxed and cordial. Turn taking is expected and put-downs are not allowed. The discussion is focused on the book's plot and setting and really delves into the characters' qualities. To spark this discussion José asks authentic, open-ended questions like these:

- What challenges did the Kenyan boy face?
- What positive emotions did he feel? Think about what you heard. How did what you heard sound or feel? Thinking about the illustrations, how do they look?
- How do you feel when you display these emotions?
- How do others feel when you act this way?

- What negative emotions did the Kenyan boy feel? Think about what you heard. How did it sound or feel? Thinking about the illustrations, how do they look?
- How do you feel when you display these emotions?
- How do others feel when you act this way?

This conversation helps the boys gain insight into the positive feelings they get when they cooperate and how guilty and sad they feel when they fail to act responsibly. Table 5 lists *For You Are a Kenyan Child* and other books early childhood professionals can read with boys. The suggested titles are categorized by emotions, so specific needs can be targeted. These books can be used as a starting point to individualize instruction for boys and girls. The books listed in Table 5 feature a male protagonist, a substantive story, and interesting illustrations that can help boys understand the emotions they and others feel.

Table 5: Picture Books for Boys Organized by Emotion

anger	• *On Monday When It Rained* (Kachenmeister 2001) • *Franklin's Bad Day* (Bourgeois 1997)
anxiety	• *Parts* (Arnold 1997) • *Arthur's First Sleepover* (Brown 1996) • *Owen* (Henkes 1993)
disgust	• *Once Upon a Potty* (Frankel 1979) • *Everyone Poops* (Gomi and Stinchecum 1993) • *That's Disgusting!* (Pittau and Gervais 2004)
fear	• *What's That Noise?* (Edwards and Root 2002) • *Hooway for Wodney Wat* (Lester 1999) • *There's a Nightmare in My Closet* (Mayer 1968)
guilt	• *It Wasn't My Fault* (Lester 1985) • *David Goes to School* (Shannon 1999)
happiness	• *Wilfred Gordon McDonald Partridge* (Fox 1985) • *William's Doll* (Zolotow and Du Bois 1985)

Table 5 (continued)

pride	• *For You Are a Kenyan Child* (Cunnane 2006) • *Mike Fink* (Kellogg 1992) • *Quick as a Cricket* (Wood 1982)
sadness	• *Tough Boris* (Fox 1994) • *Oscar Wilde's the Happy Prince* (Grodin 2006)
shame	• *The Sissy Duckling* (Fierstein 2002) • *Leo the Late Bloomer* (Kraus 1971) • *Ira Sleeps Over* (Waber 1972)

USING PICTURE BOOKS WITH YOUNG GIRLS

The following revisits information presented above about girls and places it within a classroom context designed to highlight gender differences, strengths, and needs.

Roxanne teaches second grade in a large urban district in the United States. Her class is composed of twenty-nine students, of which nineteen are girls. Roxanne uses literature to promote gender equity and help her female students develop a positive vision. Roxanne is aware of the social and emotional needs of girls as she considers the following list:

Table 6: Characteristics of Girls and Implications for Teachers

Girls	Implications
• tend to be rejected and feel ashamed when they show strong emotions • react more negatively to failure—they display more sadness, fear, and guilt • ruminate about their feelings • begin to hide their true feelings as they grow	• provide encouragement and support for self-regulation • help girls respond positively to failures • provide opportunities to enrich girls' emotional literacy and develop their emotional intelligence • provide opportunities for girls to display a broad array of emotions

Table 6 (continued)

• tend to regulate their emotions earlier	• supply guidance and support to help girls manage strong emotions
• thrive on social interactions	• provide opportunities for girls to connect and bond
• value relationships and develop their sense of self through relationships	• provide opportunities for girls to connect and bond
• value conversation between friends	• use girls' strengths—their observation and communication skills
• display relational aggression rather than overt aggression	• help girls learn how to manage relational aggression
	• provide opportunities for girls to display a broad array of emotions
• strive to keep social harmony so much they hide their own feelings	• provide stories with positive female characters
• learn from female role models	• use girls' strengths—their observation and communication skills
• are good at observing and being attuned to emotions	• provide opportunities to enrich girls' emotional literacy and develop their emotional intelligence
• are good at using words to communicate	
• have better emotional literacy skills	• provide opportunities to enrich girls' emotional literacy and develop their emotional intelligence

Roxanne understands these unique qualities and decides to use Readers Theater (RT) as a strategy to help her girl students learn about the emotions they and others feel. RT is similar to old-time radio plays. The scripts for RT performances can be taken from short stories, and Roxanne has targeted several stories she will use. The beauty of RT for early childhood professionals is that it does not demand fancy scenery or props. Performers are not concerned with overt appearances but with acting and voice (Campbell and Cleland 2003). Roxanne believes this is important for the young girls in her classroom because it will help them express their feelings openly. The first RT script Roxanne develops comes from *Mary Smith* (U'Ren 2003).

As Roxanne prepares the girls, she comes to recognize how uneasy some of them feel in their roles. Even though they are young, some of the girls have begun to hide their feelings and hold them inside. One of these girls is Maya, the tallest girl in the classroom. Maya is mature beyond her years, and because of this the other girls make fun of her. Maya tries to put on a brave exterior but deep down inside she is very sad. To help Maya manage these emotions Roxanne assigns her the lead role. Maya will play the strong and bold Mary Smith, a woman with an unusual occupation who is not afraid of voicing how she feels. After several rehearsals Maya is ready to perform. The class next door is invited, and everyone at the performance is amazed by what they see. Maya reads her part confidently, with eloquence and charm. The other girls are so taken by her performance that they begin to look at her in a new light. Maya has shown her true self. This small start has revealed what a strong and friendly person she can be when others give her a chance.

In the following week Roxanne will have Maya read two nonfiction books, *Officer Brown Keeps Neighborhoods Safe* (Flanagan 1998) and *My Mother Is a Doctor* (Simon 2006). Roxanne wants Maya to read them because they contain more examples of strong women in nontraditional roles. These books and others like them that can be used with girls are listed in Table 7.

Table 7: Picture Books for Girls Organized by Emotion

anger	• *If You're Angry and You Know It!* (Kaiser 2004) • *When I Feel Angry* (Spelman 2000) • *Sometimes I'm Bombaloo* (Vail 2002)
anxiety	• *Wemberly Worried* (Henkes 2000) • *Knuffle Bunny: A Cautionary Tale* (Willems 2004)
disgust	• *Once Upon a Potty* (Frankel 1979) • *Everyone Poops* (Gomi 1993) • *That's Disgusting!* (Pittau 2004)
fear	• *Sheila Rae, the Brave* (Henkes 2003) • *The Recess Queen* (O'Neill 2002)

Table 7 (continued)

guilt	• *Jamaica's Find* (Havill 1990) • *Lilly's Purple Plastic Purse* (Henkes 1996)
happiness	• *Olivia* (Falconer 2000) • *Chrysanthemum* (Henkes 1991)
pride	• *My Mother Is a Doctor* (Simon 2006) • *Officer Brown Keeps Neighborhoods Safe* (Flanagan 1998) • *Stand Tall, Molly Lou Melon* (Lovell 2001) • *Mary Smith* (U'Ren 2003)
sadness	• *Koala Lou* (Fox 1988)
shame	• *The Brand New Kid* (Couric 2000) • *Chrysanthemum* (Henkes 1991) • *Something Beautiful* (Wyeth 1998)

GIVING TO EACH CHILD

In this chapter you have learned about emotions, their importance, and how the stories and illustrations in picture books can be used to help children develop emotional literacy and regulation. Unfortunately, the importance of emotions is not being recognized. In homes and schools cognitive skills are taking precedence, and this is a grave oversight (Hirsh-Pasek and Golinkoff 2003; Siegel 1999). Becoming emotionally smart is not easy nor is it a small part of what children need to learn. Goleman (1995) contends that emotional intelligence is as important as any construct. Emotional intelligence grows with unyielding love and responsive care that recognizes individual strengths and needs. Boys and girls have varied emotional needs and they have varied emotional strengths. Biology, society, and culture influence and affect the way children think, act, and feel (Halpern 2004).

This chapter has focused on strategies to help young children develop emotional literacy, intelligence, and regulation. The main strategy offered has been the stories and illustrations in picture books.

The stories help children build an emotional vocabulary and teach them about the emotions they and others feel. The illustrations show young children how emotions look within the context of a scene. However, it is not only the books that make a difference—it is you, as educators, who matter most. When classrooms are places of comfort and care, children know that they are loved, and they grow emotionally (Zambo and Hanson 2007). Bruce Perry (2005) speaks of the emotional memory templates children form from their experiences. There is little denying how important positive stories and images can be for supporting these emotional memory templates.

In her book *"Don't Get so Upset!"* (2008), Tamar Jacobson notes that children need love and kindness as much as they need air to breathe. As an early childhood professional you can either help children develop positive emotional experiences or you can stifle their development with sarcasm and cruel words. The behaviors of children can exasperate at times, but you must never forget that you are the model children look toward to understand the emotions they feel. As a professional, you are called on to model positive emotions even when you feel drained or empty inside. You have an enormous and important task. So, I end this chapter with one more story designed to help you understand just how important you really are to young children.

In *Oscar Wilde's The Happy Prince* (Grodin 2006) a swallow comes to rest on the base of the Happy Prince's statue. The bird notices the Prince is crying and through his questions learns the Prince lived his life in luxury and never ventured beyond the castle walls. However, now that he is a statue perched high above the town, the Prince is able to see all the hardships of the people below. Given this new insight the Prince decides to help them and asks the swallow for his assistance. The swallow complies and begins to remove the Prince's outward treasures one by one. He takes the ruby from the crown atop his head, the gold leaf from his clothing, and the emeralds that sparkle in his eyes and gives them to the townspeople. The Prince gives everything he has until there is nothing left and he becomes a dull statue. The little swallow, once so eager to leave, now becomes reluctant to fly south even though winter is approaching. This is a fatal mistake, for on a cold night at the stroke of midnight the swallow freezes to death and the Prince's heart breaks. Bare and no longer beautiful, the Prince is melted down. Fortunately, the men at the furnace notice his broken heart and place it in a box with the dead swallow. The box is set in a place of honor to remind the townspeople of the kindness and compassion of the pair.

As early childhood professionals you are called on every day to be like the Happy Prince. You are asked to give your time, resources, and love with unending generosity. The love you show and the stories you read will matter to young children for a very, very long time.

REFERENCES

Bang, M. 1999. *When Sophie gets angry—Really, really angry.* New York: Blue Sky/Scholastic.

Brizendine, L. 2006. *The female brain.* New York: Morgan Road Books.

Bronson, M. B. 2000. *Self-regulation in early childhood: Nature and nurture.* New York: Guliford Press.

Brozo, W. G. 2002. *To be a boy, to be a reader: Engaging teen and preteen boys in active literacy.* Newark, DE: International Reading Association.

Campbell, M., and J. V. Cleland. 2003. *Readers theater in the classroom: A manual for teachers of children and adults.* New York: iUniverse, Inc.

Campos, J. J., C. B. Frankel, and L. Camras. 2004. On the nature of emotion regulation. *Child Development* 75 (2): 377–94.

Charnan, M. 2006. *My mother is a doctor.* New York: Child's World.

Cunnane, K. 2006. *For you are a Kenyan child.* New York: Atheneum/Anne Schwartz.

Eisenberg. N., C. L. Martin, and R. A. Fabes. 1996. Gender development and gender effects. In *Handbook of educational psychology,* ed. D. C. Berliner and R. C. Calfee, 358–96. New York: Macmillian.

Ekman, P. 2004. *Emotions revealed: Recognizing faces and feelings to improve communication and emotional life.* New York: Henry Holt and Company.

Evans, J. 1998. *What's in the picture? Responding to illustrations in picture books.* London: Paul Chapman Publishing Ltd.

Feinman, S. 1992. *Social referencing and the social construction of reality in infancy.* New York: Plenum Press.

Giff, P. R. 1990. *Ronald Morgan goes to bat.* New York: Puffin.

Gilligan, C. 1982. *In a different voice: Psychological theory and women's development.* Cambridge, MA: Harvard University Press.

Goleman, D. 1995. *Emotional intelligence.* New York: Bantam.

Graesser, A., J. M. Golding, and D. L. Long. 1991. Narrative representation and comprehension. In Vol. 2 of *Handbook of reading research,* ed. R. Barr, M. L. Kamil, P. B. Mosenthal, and P. D. Pearson, 171–205. White Plains, NY: Longman.

Greenspan, S. I., and S. G Shanker. 2004. *The first idea: How symbols, language, and intelligence evolved from our primate ancestors to modern humans.* Cambridge, MA: Da Capo Press.

Grodin, E. 2006. *Oscar Wilde's The happy prince.* Farmington Hills, MI: Sleeping Bear Press.

Gurian, M., and K. Stevens. 2005. *The minds of boys: Saving our sons from falling behind in school and life.* San Francisco: Jossey-Bass.

Halpern, D. F. 2004. A cognitive-process taxonomy for sex differences in cognitive abilities. *Current Directions in Psychological Science* 13, (4): 135–39.

Henkes, K. 2000. *Wemberly worried.* New York: Scholastic.

Hirsh-Pasek, K., and R. M. Golinkoff. 2003. *Einstein never used flashcards: How our children REALLY learn and why they need to play more and memorize less.* New York: Rodale.

Izard, C. E., and B. P. Ackerman. 2000. Motivational, organizational, and regulatory functions of discrete emotions. In *Handbook of emotions.* 2nd ed., ed. M. Lewis and Haviland-Jones, 523–64. New York: Guilford Press.

Jacobson, T. 2008. *Don't get so upset! Help young children manage their feelings by understanding your own.* St. Paul, MN: Redleaf Press.

LeDoux, J. 1996. *The emotional brain: The mysterious underpinnings of emotional life.* New York: Touchstone.

McCauley, R. N. 2000. The naturalness of religion and the unnaturalness of science. In *Explanation and cognition,* eds. F. C. Keil and R. A. Wilson, 61–85. Cambridge, MA: MIT Press.

McDevitt, T. M., and J. E. Ormrod. 2002. *Child development and education,* 4th ed. Upper Saddle River, NJ: Merrill.

Perry, B. D. 2005. Self-regulation: The second core strength. http://teacher .scholastic.com/professional/bruceperry/self_regulation.htm.

Perry B. D., and M. Szalavitz. 2006. *The boy who was raised as a dog and other stories from a child psychiatrist's notebook: What traumatized children can teach us about loss, love, and healing.* New York: Basic Books.

Raschka, C. 1993. *Yo! Yes?* New York: Orchard.

Roser, N., M. Martinez, C. Fuhrken, and K. McDonnold. 2007. Characters as guides to meaning. *The Reading Teacher* 60, (6): 548–59.

Saarni, C. 2000. The social context of emotional development. In *Handbook of emotions.* 2nd ed., ed. M. Lewis, and J. M. Haviland-Jones, 306–22. New York: Guilford Press.

Sadoski, M., and A. Paivio. 2001. *Imagery and text: A dual coding theory of reading and writing.* Mahwah, NJ: Erlbaum.

Sax, L. 2005. *Why gender matters: What parents and teachers need to know about the emerging science of sex differences.* New York: Doubleday.

———. 2007. *Boys adrift: The five factors driving the growing epidemic of unmotivated boys and underachieving young men.* New York: Basic Books.

Schank, R. C. 1995. *Tell me a story: Narrative and intelligence.* Evanston, IL: Northwestern University Press.

Shonkoff, J. P., and D. A. Phillips, ed. 2000. *From neurons to neighborhoods: The science of early childhood development.* Washington, DC: National Academy Press.

Siegel, D. J. 1999. *The developing mind: Toward a neurobiology of interpersonal experience.* New York: Guilford Press.

Sipe, L. R. 2001. Picturebooks as aesthetic objects. *Literacy Teaching and Learning* 6, (1): 23–42.

Sprague, M. M., and K. K. Keeling. 2007. *Discovering their voices: Engaging adolescent girls with young adult literature.* Newark, DE: International Reading Association.

Stamm, J. 2007. *Bright from the start: The simple science-backed way to nurture your child's developing mind from birth to age 3.* New York: Gotham Books.

Tompkins, G. E. 2003. *Literacy for the 21st century.* 3rd ed. Upper Saddle River, NJ: Merrill Prentice Hall.

U'Ren, A. 2003. *Mary Smith.* New York: Farrar, Straus and Giroux.

Wellman, H. M., P. L. Harris, M. Banerjee, and A. Sinclair. 1995. Early understanding of emotion: Evidence from natural language. *Cognition and Emotion* 9 (2/3): 117–49.

Zambo, D., and S. K. Brem. 2004. Emotion and cognition in students who struggle to read: New insights and ideas. *Reading Psychology an International Quarterly* 25, (3): 189–204.

Zambo, D., and C. C. Hansen. 2007. Love, language, and emergent literacy: Pathways to emotional development of the very young. *Young Children* 62, (3): 32–37.

EIGHT

The Role of Early Childhood
in Gender Differences in Mathematics

— Sylvia Bulgar —

As a college student majoring in education and mathematics some forty years ago, I was one of fewer than five females in this dual major, even though I attended a school in a very large city. Today, as a university advisor of mathematics majors at a small private university, working with students who are planning to teach, I find that approximately 73 percent (43 out of 59) of the math students I am currently advising are female. However, when students change their majors from mathematics, they are more likely to be female. Mathematically speaking, if there are more females initially, it is more likely that more of them will change their majors, so this is not a significant issue. Of course, teaching has been and still is a profession that consistently attracts more women, but nonetheless, this data does indicate somewhat of a shift in gender participation in the field of mathematics from just four decades ago. This provides the impetus for an investigation of larger-scale statistics and an examination of the role of early childhood mathematics in the creation of what appears to be, at least on the surface, a more equitable situation. But, to effectively do so, one needs to first scrutinize the status of gender issues in mathematics, from both the historical and contemporary perspectives, as well as other related issues such as the movement toward more extensive testing and the linkage between performance on these tests to federal funding for education.

A HISTORICAL PERSPECTIVE ON GENDER INEQUITY IN MATHEMATICS

Historically, many studies have documented gender inequities in mathematics (cf. Armstrong 1981; Fennema and Sherman 1978; Sadker and Sadker 1994; Stipek and Granlinski 1991; Tate 1997). Nevertheless, girls did perform as well or better than boys when it came to solving problems that involved just using a rule (Bokhove 1994). This result was confirmed in the Willingham and Cole studies completed by researchers from Educational Testing Service (Latham 1997/1998). When students are taught to use rules to perform procedures, they approach mathematics in a very mechanistic way. They often memorize the rule or procedure with little understanding of the concept behind it or why it works. Many students then use the rule successfully by applying procedural knowledge of how to "plug in" numbers in place of variables. This requires little mathematical competence and insight. Therefore, the fact that girls do as well as boys in this area of mathematics says very little about a comparison between the genders in their actual mathematical ability. One very common example of such a situation is the rule for division of fractions. When being taught to "invert and multiply," we do not need to know why it works or in fact whether it is always true. What is also true, based on research, is that when boys and girls perform at similar levels, boys indicate that they expended less effort to do well than the girls did and that they had greater expectations for continued success (Eccles et al. 1985).

Yun Xie (2008), a PhD student with a bachelor of science degree in chemistry and biochemistry from the University of Michigan, points out that past inequities between the genders in mathematics were caused by the social inequities that existed. Yet, other researchers attribute these discrepancies to other factors such as differences between the way boys and girls generally think, differences in goal orientation, the influence of parents and counselors, and student-teacher interactions.

It is assumed that many things, including personal beliefs, motivation, and affect, influence the development of the thought system and that related skills are gender-specific (Fennema and Peterson 1985; Eccles et al. 1985). Generally, boys approach mathematical tasks in a more positive way than girls do. The way students think about themselves indicates how they feel about themselves in terms of attitudes, feelings, and knowledge about their own abilities and skills (Seegers and Boekaerts 1996).

Goal orientation also affects a student's achievement and participation in mathematics. Goal orientation is a description of what the basic goal of an activity would be. This includes several components and comparisons, which have been defined by researchers and have been studied. For example, one pair of opposing goal orientations examined is task orientation versus ego orientation. Goal orientation focuses on the mathematical task itself as the significant issue in problem solving, whereas ego orientation focuses on the learner and how he views *himself* as a problem solver (Nicholls 1984). In this kind of situation, whether the student is focused on himself as a learner or on the problem being solved affects the outcome of the problem-solving situation. Another example of a pair of opposing orientations is performance orientation (Dweck and Elliott 1983) versus mastery (Ames and Archer 1988). Basically, the difference exists between students who can demonstrate to others how they excel and those who want to actually increase their own knowledge and improve their skills. Studies have shown that greater gender differences emerge when ego orientation (the desire to show others how well you solve a problem) is encouraged (Ames 1992; Meece, Blumenfeld, and Hoyle 1988). Additionally, males tend to be more competitive than females and thus are more successful in the mathematics classroom that encourages competition. Therefore, since most mathematics classrooms of the past fostered an ego-oriented attitude, boys were at an advantage (Peterson and Fennema 1985).

The influence of parents and counselors also has played a role in widening the gender gap. Specifically, parental attitude has been shown to stifle girls' performances in mathematics. However, parents, with the guidance and support of teachers, can help their daughters to be more successful in mathematics. Teachers can encourage parents to talk about mathematics to their daughters. Parents should stress the importance of mathematics, the usefulness of mathematics, and the need to be proficient in mathematics in order to enter various professions (Campbell 1992). In 1994, 34 percent of females as opposed to only 26 percent of males reported being discouraged from taking senior mathematics courses (NSF 1994).

Other concerns surrounding gender issues in mathematics are the nature of mathematics itself, mathematics curriculum and pedagogy, and the philosophical and cultural factors surrounding mathematics classrooms. Mathematics had been alleged to be male-centered in content and process because of its abstract nature. This has further led to a belief that mathematics is a subject that is austere and absolute. To believe this is to deny the social nature of mathematics and to separate mathematics from its social settings (Noddings 1996). Men have dominated the history of mathematics—perhaps this has also contributed to this line of thinking. At my university, the full-time faculty of the mathematics department is 100 percent male.

While curriculum and pedagogy seem to evolve simultaneously, it is important to recognize that each, independently, must be addressed to meet the needs of both genders. Textbook publishers and test makers have attempted to address content inequities with respect to all groups, but the pedagogy needs to be addressed as well. While many mathematics classrooms have begun to use cooperative learning groups for problem solving, which had previously been experienced in other domains such as language arts and social studies, an examination of *how* the collaboration of students is encouraged and what is expected of the students must be called upon as well.

The philosophical and cultural aspects of equity need to be examined so that educators can be helped to encourage all students. All students need to know about the political and practical importance of mathematics. Students should be encouraged to study biographical, historical, and literary issues related to mathematics to develop their cultural literacy. This would also serve to help students keep from becoming segregated from mathematics and from mathematics being an isolated domain. Thereby, it would help students see the social nature of mathematics and its usefulness and significance to them as individuals. Mathematics would more likely become a part of students' lives, regardless of their gender. Thus, students of both genders would feel more connected to the practical use of mathematics. Teachers can also foster this enculturation of the mathematics domain while showing appreciation for students as individuals. When teachers respect students for themselves rather than solely for their achievements, they may achieve more success in mathematics (Noddings 1996).

THE ROLE OF EXPANDED TESTING

One goal of large-scale testing has been to improve teaching as teachers attempt to "teach to the test" (Schorr and Bulgar 2002, 2003; Schorr et al. 2004). One of the reasons that opponents indicate their resistance to testing is that they believe extensive testing will encourage measurement of less relevant skills and reinforce traditional approaches to teaching (McNeil 2000). There are also those who believe that this has been exaggerated and that any modest changes in teaching exist alongside what has been conventional practice (Wilson and Floden 2001). Regardless of the format, the evidence that testing promotes instructional change remains unconvincing or inconclusive at best (Newmann, Bryk, and Nagaoka 2001; Smith 1996).

While teachers reported important and substantial changes and were genuinely trying to reform their practice to include changes in line with those developed by the profession (National Council of Teachers of Mathematics 2000; National Research Council 1996; AAAS 1993) and more general governmental entities (United States Department of Labor 1987; National Commission on Mathematics and Science Teaching for the 21st Century 2000), observation data from our study (Schorr et. al. 2004; Schorr and Bulgar 2003; Schorr, Bulgar, and Firestone 2002; Schorr et. al. 2002; Schorr and Bulgar 2002)[1] suggested that instructional practice fell far short of what these standards called for. The New Jersey third and fourth grade teachers in self-contained classrooms that we visited as part of a two-year study of the effects of testing on teaching practice adopted the surface characteristics of state and national standards without fundamentally changing their approaches to teaching and learning mathematics. The characteristics or strategies that they adopted included small group instruction, use of manipulatives or other hands-on objects, and a focus on what was termed "problem solving," especially problems involving real-world situations or applications. However, these new strategies were modified to fit within older, more traditional patterns of practice. The observed teachers did not substantively refine, revise, or extend practices to create more challenging learning opportunities for children. Thus we saw small groups of children seated near each other with little or no mathematical communication taking place. We also saw children using manipulatives with little or no opportunity to explore mathematical ideas. While 90 percent of the observed teachers were using manipulative materials, only 10 percent of those used them in ways that promoted conceptual understanding of mathematical ideas. This is precisely the type of skill that girls have traditionally demonstrated greater weakness in and is needed for them to build the knowledge and skills that can help them to develop into stronger mathematics students in the future. Additionally, we saw children working on problems activities, but with little or no chance to build, represent, test, defend, or justify their solutions.

We concluded that while tests did sensitize teachers to using new strategies and methods (ones that would be advantageous to the building of conceptual knowledge for both genders) and oftentimes motivated them to start changing their style of teaching, tests alone did not get teachers to change the more fundamental aspects of their classroom practice (Schorr and Bulgar 2002, 2003; Schorr et al. 2004). How, for example, can tests alone get teachers to understand more fully the notion of fractions or subtraction with "regrouping" and guide them to present these subject matters in ways that would make them more accessible to children of both genders? These are just two examples of the many topics that teachers in the United States tend not to know about in a way that goes beyond the execution of rote procedures and, therefore, they do not understand in ways that are sufficiently meaningful to provide thorough, equitable instruction (Ma 1999). Questions remain about how school districts can continue to work to improve teachers' understanding to go beyond the surface aspects of the mathematics that they guide children through so they can promote conceptual learning and understanding for all students, which would enhance the level of success for both genders and foster equity.

In our study, we also found that teachers, principals, and supervisors often would correlate the surface aspects of these new practices—that is, the presence of manipulatives, physically putting students into groups—with the reforms themselves. We found that many of the people we surveyed and interviewed actually *believed* that the strategies cited above, among others, were what the standards are all about. While the teaching practices we observed were not focused on the more conceptually oriented aspects of instruction, teachers were, at least in principle, moving closer to understanding that students need more than the seatwork on procedures and algorithms that had been used so often in the past. With increased opportunities for professional development surrounding the teaching of mathematics, these attributes can be expected to continue to improve and move further toward developing deeper understanding of the underlying features of mathematical topics, thereby helping teachers to promote the opportunities for gender equity (Schorr and Bulgar 2002, 2003; Schorr et al. 2004).

The teachers repeatedly emphasized that these types of problems encouraged them to rethink their methods of teaching so that students would be more adept at answering these kinds of questions. The modest, though explicit, surface changes in instruction that we documented (Schorr, Bulgar, and Firestone, 2002; Schorr and Fire-stone, 2004) may be part of a process that can lead to more substantial improvement. In the meantime, the current instructional changes seem unlikely to help students develop a deeper understanding of mathematical ideas. On the bright side, however, many teachers noted that these new strategies do help to make the classroom atmosphere more interesting and appealing. The risk is that by making these changes without fully implementing the intent of such practices, teachers, administrators, and supervisors may be deluded into believing that the standards are "being implemented" and so "mission accomplished."

While the general pattern of instruction we observed in our study was the introduction of new practices that did not make use of them in ways that fully carried out the larger intent of those practices—that is, to have children think more deeply about mathematical ideas—the specific response to the state tests was mixed. We did find a great deal of "teaching to the test," which took two forms. One of these forms was fundamentally what critics of high-stakes testing would expect. In this form, teachers adopted strategies like "test-besting," which included drilling students on test mechanics. Teachers made use of multiple choice items and practice tests taken from commercial test preparation materials. These strategies emphasize a procedural approach to solving problems that match to known test items. Teaching test mechanics and setting aside time to practice on commercial test materials and examples from the state Web site were more closely related with conventional didactic teaching—that is, providing students with routines to follow and plenty of opportunity to practice. Such teaching to the test is troubling for both genders. It tends to invalidate the test data itself, since any increases in test scores may reflect the preparation activity rather than changes in the underlying concept being measured: students' understanding of mathematics content. What is more important, it tends to lead to classroom instructional practices that are focused on having children repeat, often with little or no understanding, the procedures, rules, or routines most likely to appear on the test. This type of teaching can be quite disheartening both for children and for their teachers.

The second form of teaching to the test was identified as teachers who were incorporating strategies that challenged children to think more deeply about the mathematics they were learning as part of everyday instruction. When these types of strategies were fostered, teachers used tasks they believed to be consistent with the newer and more challenging parts of the test that resemble the open-ended items and used different types of instructional designs (for example, small group instruction that encourages students to talk about their solutions, and the use of manipulatives or other hands-on materials and equipment in ways that foster students' understanding of mathematical concepts). Teachers also told us they felt that testing prompted them to have their students explain their reasoning more often. As stated above, this is critical for developing deeper understanding of mathematics for both genders. While teachers using this second form of teaching to the test may not have moved as far in this direction as they reported to us, our observations do suggest that they were at least trying to ask more probing questions (Schorr and Bulgar 2002, 2003; Schorr, Bulgar, and Firestone 2002; Schorr et al. 2004). Perhaps with appropriate support and professional development, they will enhance their practice by learning how to better facilitate this type of discourse. Overall, however, the professional development teachers described featured short-term learning opportunities that touched on issues related to mathematics education but rarely provided the depth and follow-through needed to help teachers change practice.

In some settings, principals proved to be a key source of support. Supportive principals preferred a less authority-based approach to instructional leadership than their less supportive peers. Moreover, their understanding of new standards and the more challenging approaches to instruction that could be triggered by the tests were uneven. When principals observed teachers, they evaluated them using criteria that often emphasized *both* traditional instruction and more inquiry-oriented strategies, with significantly less emphasis on actual content. Teachers should be encouraged to build their own communities in their schools to support each other as they develop their practices to include approaches that will build deeper understanding of the underlying features of the mathematics so that they can provide instruction that offers maximum opportunity for learning and valuing mathematics in their classes for both genders. Many principals did not personally spend much time directly with the state standards, but they did provide teachers access to resources that would expose them to these standards.

While many early childhood educators and teacher educators are not fond of the extensive testing that has been a hallmark of the No

Child Left Behind legislation, the fact remains that this testing is a reality of our national educational life. When federal funding is tied to success on these tests, it is quite understandable that the testing would provide a strong drive toward teaching to the test. Our study indicates that it is possible to do so and still provide quality instruction for all students.

THE ROLE OF NCTM

In September 2007, the National Council of Teachers of Mathematics (NCTM 2007) issued the following position statement regarding early childhood mathematics education: "The National Council of Teachers of Mathematics affirms that a high-quality, challenging, and accessible mathematics education provides early childhood learners with a vital foundation for future understanding of mathematics. Young children in every setting should experience effective, research-based curricula and teaching practices. Such practices in turn require policies, organizational support, and resources that enable teachers to do this challenging and important work."

NCTM has recognized that a growing number of young children are educated in environments where mathematics can be learned developmentally, with activities building upon each other and encompassing children's real-world experiences. However, the organization stresses the need for teachers and caregivers of young children to acquire more professional development in a form that supports their efforts to build a strong knowledge base for the mathematics that the children will continue to experience. This type of professional development needs to be embedded in a strong understanding of the pedagogy that is most developmentally appropriate for young children. Such commitments to early childhood mathematics development can only exist with the support of administrators and policy makers.

NCTM has noted that several obstacles exist that hinder the building of communities of practice where teachers and caregivers can provide a wide range of high-quality experiences for young children. Such initiatives involve a great deal of collaboration and planning.

NCTM also stresses the importance of providing guidance regarding early childhood mathematics in teacher education programs. In my own methods of teaching mathematics courses, as students create a Big Idea Module, they trace the development of a mathematical idea from kindergarten through middle school. Interestingly, these students often critique the project by indicating that they never realized just how significant the work of early childhood mathematics is in the development of mathematical competence in the upper grades. A by-product of this realization is that students take the work they do in their early childhood internship classrooms in mathematics much more seriously; they plan more carefully and reflect more substantively on the skills that children have acquired.

The NCTM principles and standards for school mathematics are steered by six guiding principles: equity, curriculum, teaching, learning, assessment, and technology. Standards are divided into two categories, content and process standards, and children in grades kindergarten through two are now expected to meet those specified standards. Recognizing the significance of early childhood mathematics in developing skills for older students, some states (such as New Jersey) are expanding and specifying their standards (Rosenstein, Caldwell, and Crown 1996) to more specifically delineate standards and cumulative progress indicators to include preschool, kindergarten, and first and second grades, whereas previous iterations included one category for the range kindergarten through second grade.

In sum, the National Council of Teachers of Mathematics, in its early childhood position statement (2007), addresses the issue of gender through a general call for equity among all young children. Because matters concerning gender equity are often very subtle, it is debatable as to whether this is sufficient.

THE ROLE OF NAEYC

In 2002, the National Association for the Education of Young Children (NAEYC) issued a position statement jointly with the National Council of Teachers of Mathematics (NCTM). In 2007, the NCTM issued a statement that was nearly identical. It was followed by the articulation of several challenges faced in attempting to implement the ideals found in this statement. Among these is the concern as to whether the mathematical skills developed in early childhood will prepare these youngsters for a future that is constantly changing in terms of the needs for mathematical competence. This concern is echoed in the report by the National Commission on Mathematics and Science Teaching for the 21st Century (also known as the Glenn Commission) that states: "As our children move toward the day when *their* decisions will be the ones shaping a new America, will they be equipped with the mathematical and scientific tools needed to meet those challenges and capitalize on those opportunities?" (2000, 6).

There is concern as to how the United States will continue to compete in a global society because of continuing poor performance in mathematics on international assessments. This has led to an increased emphasis on standards, both at the national and state levels. Results from this widespread standardization of mathematical skills vary widely among the states and even at the district level, as some have more enthusiastically embraced the reforms needed at the early childhood levels for positive outcomes. The mere fact that NAEYC has issued this statement jointly with NCTM would seem to indicate a conviction that the experiences children have in the first eight years of their lives have an effect on future development of mathematical outcomes.

NAEYC refers to the growing number of young children who are in child care and to the growing body of research indicating that mathematical development begins very early on. In fact, research conducted at New York University has contributed to a video called *Surprises in Mind* (Harvard-Smithsonian Center for Astrophysics 2001), designed by Annenberg Media to be a documentary for professional development for teachers and administrators and part of which deals with a study highlighting a child eighteen months old who is showing a sense of number and beginning numeracy skills.

Some states have recognized just how significant the early years are in developing skills needed to be successful adults in the second quarter of the twenty-first century and beyond. Among these states is New Jersey, where offering preschool education became a requirement in September 2009. Though no doubt very costly, the governor and supporters believe it is a worthwhile investment in our future. The forerunner to this mandate may have been the creation of an initiative called Good Start, Grow Smart by President George W. Bush's administration, which was designed to work with states to enhance early childhood education and the Head Start Program in particular. The initiative was based on the belief that there is a strong connection between the development a child undergoes early in life and the level of achievement he acquires as an adult.

As support for the joint position statement with NCTM, NAEYC has come up with a series of recommendations for both classroom practitioners and policymakers based on research indicating the significance of the early years in mathematics education in developing gender equity. There are ten recommendations for teachers and other practitioners:

1. Young children's natural interests and dispositions regarding mathematics must be compatible with what makes sense to them in their physical and social environments.
2. Young children's formal and informal knowledge of their culture, community, family, and so on should be a basis for their learning of mathematics.
3. Cognitive development of young children should be a basis for curriculum design in early childhood mathematics education.
4. Curriculum and pedagogy that reinforces problem solving and reasoning should be implemented in early childhood mathematics classrooms, as well as making use of activities that reinforce the use of representations, communication, and making connections among mathematical ideas.
5. Classroom practitioners should develop a cohesive curriculum that encourages the development of associations and progressions of mathematical ideas.
6. Classroom practitioners should create opportunities for young children to develop profound and persistent interface with key mathematical ideas.
7. Mathematics should be embedded in other domains and other domains should be embedded in mathematics.
8. Children should be given adequate time to explore mathematical ideas through play as teachers obtain support, materials, and time to sustain this.
9. Suitable mathematical concepts, methods, and language should be introduced by using varied activities and teaching tactics.
10. Young children's learning of mathematics should be maintained through the use of thoughtful and frequent assessment of their skills and knowledge.

(NAEYC and NCTM 2002)

Some of these recommendations require very sophisticated pedagogical and content knowledge on the part of all teachers. It follows then, that substantive professional development should be a part of any plan to enhance young children's knowledge of mathematics in a manner that fosters equity.

NAEYC and NCTM have also come up with four suggestions for the implementation of these recommendations by institutions, program developers, and policy makers:

1. In addition to encouraging professional development, these ten recommendations should be embedded in all teacher preparation programs.
2. Standards, curriculum, and assessment should be aligned and created by collaborative processes.
3. The support of teachers' continuous learning, collaboration, and planning must be an integral part of institutional frameworks and policies.
4. Resources needed to facilitate young children's mathematical aptitude must be made available at all levels, ranging from the classroom level to the entire system of education.

(NAEYC and NCTM 2002)

For details about each of these recommendations, see www.naeyc .org/files/naeyc/file/positions/psmath.pdf.

NAEYC concludes its document by articulating an optimistic vision for developing a strong foundation for the learning of mathematics that takes place in early childhood and is essential for the development of the skills that citizens of the world will need in the future. Based on research, the organization calls for the collaborative support of educators, administrators, policymakers, and families. Part of this vision is to create equitable opportunities for all children.

THE EVOLUTION OF GENDER ISSUES IN MATHEMATICS

After looking at math scores from the large-scale testing required by the No Child Left Behind mandate to measure accountability, Hyde (2008), a psychology professor at the University of Wisconsin–Madison, concluded that there was no indication of significant gender differences in mathematics performance and that this should stimulate parents and teachers to revise their thinking on this issue to dispel the stereotype of boys being more successful in mathematics. However, an Associated Press article (2008) reported that the study also noted it is common for teachers to work diligently to prepare their students for the testing that has become a significant element of our educational culture, and that since these tests have not had a preponderance of complex problem solving, teachers have not focused on preparing students for this type of thinking. We know from other research (see Latham 1997/1998; Bokhove 1994; Nicholls 1984 above) that it is precisely this type of problem-solving skill that is needed for both genders to develop into successful students of mathematics.

Since it is accepted that a competitive classroom environment favors boys, it would seem that a mathematics classroom with more emphasis on cooperative learning groups—one that stresses cooperation rather than competition—can help create equity between the genders. Sara Rimer (2008) writes in a *New York Times* article that math skills, in general, in the United States still fall below the international average. Janet E. Mertz is quoted saying, "We are living in a culture that is telling girls you can't do math—that's telling everybody that only Asians and nerds do math." The article reports on the first study to look at international competitions in mathematics, rather than merely SAT scores, and reports that the most successful mathematics students in the United States are either immigrants or the children of immigrants from countries that place a high value on mathematical knowledge— and until 1998 were exclusively boys. This would suggest that educators in the United States need to instill in children the notion of valuing mathematics.

Elizabeth Fennema of the Wisconsin Center for Educational Research has been well known for her studies on gender issues in mathematics for several decades. In 2000, she prepared a summative report for the fifth annual Forum of the National Institute for Science Education (Fennema 2000). In the lengthy paper, she reports on one study wherein she and other renowned researchers looked at children, and their teachers, as they advanced from grades one to three. The focus of the study was on strategies used by these children. The researchers found a significant difference in the strategies used by boys and girls during each of the years. The boys' approaches to solving problems tended to be more abstract, which reflects stronger conceptual understanding, while the girls' approaches were more concrete. This led the researchers to conclude that even at this early age, there were differences between boys and girls in solution strategies that they chose to use. By the end of the third grade, girls tended to rely on rules and procedures more than boys. At this stage, in the case of both boys and girls, students who had invented their own strategies were able to use more flexible thinking and also were able to solve more problems that relied on applications of the skills they learned. For example, a familiar problem in early childhood classrooms is the following: In an ice cream store that sells vanilla and chocolate ice cream with the choice of whipped cream, cherries, and hot fudge as toppings, how many different ice cream sundaes can I make? After solving and examining the solution to this problem, an extension might be, What would happen if I added walnuts as an extra topping?

Thus, the ability to develop one's own strategies is a factor in being able to apply and extend one's knowledge to future success in mathematics. Since it is boys who display more abstract thinking early on, this could be a factor in more delineated evidence of boys' greater success in mathematics by the time they get to high school. Therefore, while it may be possible to demonstrate success in mathematics without deep conceptual understanding at very early grades, the groundwork for flexible thinking that is developed at the level of early childhood education in mathematics is essential for future successes. This would also explain why the differences between the genders appears to be nonexistent at a very young age. Both boys and girls are solving problems, but the boys are doing so using more abstract thinking. This also emphasizes the need to focus less on the ultimate solution and more on the process used to arrive at that solution. When children listen to each others' explanations, they acquire knowledge from each other, so encouraging discourse related to mathematical work would help to "level the playing field" at a more conceptual stage for both boys and girls.

The teachers who were involved in the above-mentioned study all were applying reform math teaching (which involves teaching through inquiry, using manipulatives, and encouraging discourse) and were taking part in a professional development project wherein issues related to gender differences were discussed. The National Council of Teachers of Mathematics (2000) suggests that gender inequity will be dispelled by major curricular reform. Yet, despite the efforts of the teachers in this study to comply with that supposition, inequities still emerged. Fennema (2000) suggests that because these children had a great deal of freedom in how they chose to solve problems, they chose solution strategies that perpetuated the stereotypical gender roles in mathematics. Additionally, the strategies were self-reported by the children, so they were selective in what they reported. Hyde and Jaffee (1998) propose that girls are more socially aware of the responses of others and tend to be more compliant. This may be in part responsible for girls' decision to use more concrete solutions, having more of a desire to explain their solutions clearly to others. A concrete model or representation enables a student to explain a solution to a problem without relying on more abstract thinking, which is characteristic of boys' thinking. Thus using a concrete model helps girls satisfy their eagerness to share their ideas.

A LOOK AT EARLY CHILDHOOD MATHEMATICS CLASSROOMS

Because my students serve as interns in K–3 classrooms, I have the opportunity to visit these classrooms and hear reports of the mathematics being taught in two New Jersey school districts. These districts are purported to have very high standards, and students there tend to be proficient in all areas of instruction. We can learn a lot from exemplars of success by discerning what characterizes their achievement and then emulating it in less successful districts.

I also have been supervising first-grade student teachers in one of these districts. As I have become familiar with the faculty in the participating schools, I have also been permitted to sit in on math lessons being taught by the regular classroom teachers. After each visit, teachers were asked to answer the following questions:

1. Based on your experience, would you say there are gender differences during math centers? Please explain.
2. Based on your experience, would you say there are gender differences when math is not taught in centers? Please explain.
3. What, if anything, do you do to promote gender impartiality?
4. Is there anything additional you think I should know about the lesson I observed?

Most of the classes I visited used "centers" during the mathematics lesson. A center involves a series of four to five activities set up in different areas of the classroom. The children spend fifteen to twenty minutes at a center and then they all rotate to the next one, eventually experiencing all of the activities at each center. Mostly, each center involves an application of a different mathematics skill, but sometimes each one is another form of reinforcing the same skill. Essentially, the use of centers provides children with an experience in small group instruction where collaboration and discourse among the children is encouraged. Though children at many centers create individual work products, they are encouraged to work in partnerships and discuss the work they are doing. These early grades often have assistant teachers, paraprofessionals, and interns present so that an adult is available for approximately every two centers. At times the teacher was observed working with children at one particular center, usually the one that involved one of the more newly learned skills, and at other times the teacher was observed following specific children as they rotated through all of the centers. In the observed situations where the lesson itself was not conducted in centers, children completed the follow-up or practice part of the lesson in small groups, thus providing opportunities for collaboration and substantive discourse.

Most of the observed centers involved the use of some form of manipulative material that children used to solve problems. As noted above, research indicates that using concrete objects provides instruction in a way that enhances girls' understanding, even though it is not indicative of a deeper conceptual understanding of the mathematics, which would be demonstrated through more abstract applications. Though all of the children seemed to perform equally well on this task, there was minimal evidence of transitioning the children from the concrete examples to a more abstract generalization. While this kind of shift may not take place until subsequent years of instruction, it might explain why there appears to be equity among the genders in mathematical performance at this young level. However, we have learned from research (see NAEYC Position Statement; Fenema 2000 above) that skills students need later on to flexibly solve complex problems are rooted in their development of these skills early on. If boys seem to move more seamlessly to an abstract understanding of "big ideas" about the mathematics they are experiencing, perhaps we need to more explicitly require all children to make the progression of ability from concrete understanding to more abstract notions. This can be done when the whole class comes together to talk about the activities at each center. Failure to extend the concrete experience of the center to a discussion involving abstract thinking and generalizations appeared to be the shortcoming of all of the classroom settings observed.

Some of the observed centers included games. Since research has shown that boys do better when competition is involved, this would appear to support their learning styles better than those of the girls. There are ways to create games having no individual "winners" and "losers," which would have the by-product of enhancing equity between the genders.

Teachers generally decided the makeup of the groups, but one teacher indicated that she allows children to self-select their groups. Interestingly, there was only one observed classroom where each of the groups consisted of one gender only, and it was not the classroom where the teacher allowed the children to self-select their groups. For the most part, when children sat in mixed-gender groups, they collaborated seamlessly, as if ignoring the gender differences. Another item of interest noted during the observations was that as children stood up at their group centers to reach for materials, girls tended to remain standing while boys tended to sit down again as soon as they had retrieved what they needed. When discussing this phenomenon with one of the teachers, she remarked that she found this very surprising, since she would have expected the boys to be generally more physically active.

Some of the differences between the genders reported by the observed teachers were that boys tended to need more reminding of the directions, that girls seemed to create more esoterically attractive patterns with manipulatives and/or drawings, and that boys had a greater tendency to "misuse" manipulative materials—throwing them or playing with them in nonmathematical ways. However, all teachers indicated that they did not see a great difference in performance between boys and girls, and they made a deliberate effort to foster equity between the genders by calling on them equally and treating them equally. However, as noted above, perhaps the lack of observation of differences between the genders at the early childhood stage of development results from differences between boys and girls at this early stage of education that are masked because the activities do not necessarily permit or encourage children to demonstrate their abstract thinking.

CONCLUSIONS

While test results and anecdotal information support that a wide gap in upper grade mathematics performance still exists, the gap seems to be narrowing. In spite of this ongoing discrepancy, there is an accepted notion that the gap does not begin until somewhere around the time children enter middle school. What happens between early childhood mathematics education and middle school to cause that change?

While what happens in early childhood classes in mathematics may not lead to observable inequity of the genders, the development of flexible mathematical skills—or lack thereof—is subtle and may have an effect on future years of mathematical study. Researchers have noted that from middle school on boys demonstrate their mathematical success—which tends to be greater than that of girls—by being able to apply their knowledge more flexibly, which is necessary for solving the more complex problems that are part of the curriculum beginning in middle school. Girls' inability to overcome the disadvantage that they may have at this level can lead to lowered self-esteem regarding mathematics and to shifting the focus from the mathematical task itself as the significant issue in problem solving to a focus on the learner herself as being significant. This may also lead to a need for girls to more explicitly demonstrate to others how they excel rather than a need to actually increase their knowledge and improve their skills. This type of reallocation toward an ego orientation has been shown to contribute to inequity between the genders.

Therefore, it is necessary that at the early childhood levels, teachers foster experiences that will help all children develop abstract notions of the mathematics in which they are engaged. While it is appropriate and even desirable to begin with concrete representations of the mathematical ideas, smooth, effective transitions to abstractions must be included in the curriculum regularly. Though this may not cause a significant difference in explicit demonstration of understanding of mathematics during these early years, it is essential for the development of the natural trajectory of understanding that will be called upon when these students enter the upper grades.

Things have changed quite a bit since 1992 when Mattel introduced a Barbie doll who said, "Math class is tough"; the American Association of University Women immediately attacked the comment as offensive, leading to an alteration of the computer chip that had randomly selected four phrases from a possible 270 (this phrase was deleted, as noted in a *New York Times* article on October 26, 1992). Nonetheless, many of us just nodded in agreement with the phrase. If such a doll were introduced today, most of us would either smile with nostalgia, laugh at the stereotypical representation of women, or be outraged at the limitations that this kind of thinking can place on the women who will help carry us all through the twenty-first century.

Note

1. The work on this study was supported by two grants from the National Science Foundation (NSF) awarded to the Center for Educational Policy Analysis (CEPA) at Rutgers University in New Jersey. The opinions presented here are solely those of the author and are not necessarily shared by NSF, Rider University, or Rutgers University.

REFERENCES

American Association for the Advancement of Science Project 2061. 1993. *Benchmarks for science literacy.* New York: Oxford University Press.

Ames, C. 1992. Achievement goals and the classroom motivational climate. In *Student perceptions in the classroom,* ed. D. H. Schunk and J. L. Meece, 327–43. Hillsdale, NJ: Erlbaum.

Ames, C., and J. Archer. 1988. Achievement goals in the classroom: students' learning strategies and motivation processes. *Journal of Educational Psychology* 80 (3): 260–67.

Armstrong, J. 1981. Achievement and participation of women in mathematics: Results of two national surveys. *Journal for Research in Mathematics Education* 12 (5): 356–72.

Associated Press. 2008. Study: No gender differences in math performance. http://esciencenews.com/articles/2008/07/24/study.no.gender .differences.math.performance.

Bokhove, J. 1994. Eerste Resultaten Van Het 1993 Periodiek Peilingsonderzoek van het Onderwijs in Nederland (PPON) (group 8). First Results of the 1993 Dutch National Assessment Program in Education (grade 8). Paper presented at the Panama Conference, Noordwijkerhout, The Netherlands, November 1994.

Campbell, P. B. 1992. *Math, science and your daughter: What can parents do?* Encouraging Girls in Math and Science Series. Washington, DC: U.S. Department of Education.

Dweck, C., and E. Elliot. 1983. Achievement motivation. In Vol. 4 of *Socialization, personality, and social development,* ed. P. H. Mussen, and E. M. Hetherington, 644–91. New York: Wiley.

Eccles, J., T. F. Adler, R. Futterman, S. B. Goff, C. M. Kaczala, J. L. Meece, and C. Midgley. 1985. Self-perceptions, task perceptions, socializing influences, and the decision to enroll in mathematics. In *Women and mathematics: Balancing the equation,* eds. S. F. Chipman, L. R. Brush, and D. M. Wilson, 95–122. Hillsdale, NJ: Erlbaum.

Fennema, E. 2000. Gender and mathematics: What is known and what do I wish was known? Paper presented at the fifth annual Forum of the National Institute for Science Education, Detroit, MI.

Fennema, E., and P. L. Peterson. 1985. Autonomous learning behavior: A possible explanation of gender-related difference in mathematics. In *Gender influences in classroom interactions,* eds. L. C. Wilkinson and C. B. Marrett. Orlando: Academic Press.

Fennema, E., and J. A. Sherman. 1978. Sex-related differences in mathematics achievement, spatial visualization, and related factors: A further study. *Journal for Research in Mathematics Education* 9 (3): 189–203.

Harvard-Smithsonian Center for Astrophysics. 2001. *Surprises in mind.* Video. Washington, DC: Annenberg Media.

Hyde, J. 2008. Boys = girls in math? Not really. http://motls.blogspot .com/2008/07/janet-hyde-boys-girls-in-math-not.html.

Hyde, J. S., and S. Jaffee. 1998. Perspectives from social and feminist psychology. *Educational Researcher* 27, (5): 14–16.

Latham, A. 1997/1998. Gender differences on assessments. *Educational Leadership* 55, (4): 88–89.

Ma, L. 1999. *Knowing and teaching elementary mathematics: Teachers' understanding of fundamental mathematics in China and the United States.* Mahwah, NJ: Lawrence Erlbaum Associates.

McNeil, L. M. 2000. *Contradictions of school reform: Educational costs of standardized testing.* New York: Routledge.

Meece, J. L., P. C. Blumenfeld, and R. Hoyle. 1988. Students' goal orientations and cognitive engagement in classroom activities. *Journal of Educational Psychology* 80 (4): 514–23.

National Association for the Education of Young Children (NAEYC). Early childhood mathematics: Promoting good beginnings. Position Statement. http://www.naeyc.org/files/naeyc/file/positions/psmath.pdf.

National Commission on Mathematics and Science Teaching for the 21st Century. 2000. *Before it's too late: A report to the nation from the National Commission on Mathematics and Science Teaching for the 21st century.* Publication number EE0449P. Washington, DC: U.S. Department of Education.

National Council of Teachers of Mathematics. 2000. *Principles and standards for school mathematics.* Reston, VA: National Council of Teachers of Mathematics.

———. 2007. What is important in early childhood mathematics? Position statement. Reston, VA: The National Council of Teachers of Mathematics. http://www.nctm.org/about/content.aspx?id=12590.

National Research Council. 1996. *National Science Education Standards: Observe, interact, change, learn.* Washington, DC: National Academy Press.

National Science Foundation. 1994. *Women, minorities, and persons with disabilities in science and engineering.* Arlington, VA: National Science Foundation. http://purl.access.gpo.gov/GPO/LPS40632.

Newmann, F. M., A. S. Bryk, and J. K. Nagaoka. 2001. *Authentic intellectual work and standardized tests: Conflict or coexistence?* Chicago: Consortium on Chicago School Research.

Nicholls, J. 1984. *Research on motivation in education,* Conceptions of ability and achievement motivation. In Vol. 1, eds. R. Ames and C. Ames. New York: Academic Press.

Noddings, N. 1996. Equity and mathematics: Not a simple issue. *Journal for Research in Mathematics Education* 27 (5): 514–23.

Peterson, P. L., and E. Fennema. 1985. Effective teaching, student engagement in classroom activities, and sex-related differences in learning mathematics. *American Educational Research Journal* 22 (3): 309–35.

Rimer, S. 2008. Math skills suffer in U.S., study finds. *The New York Times,* October 10. http://www.nytimes.com/2008/10/10/education/10math.html.

Rosenstein, J. G., J. H. Caldwell, and W. D. Crown. 1996. *New Jersey mathematics curriculum framework.* New Brunswick: New Jersey Mathematics Coalition.

Sadker, M., and D. Sadker. 1994. *Failing at Fairness: How America's Schools Cheat Girls.* New York: Touchstone.

Schorr, R. Y., and S. Bulgar. 2002. Teaching mathematics and science: Investigating classroom practice. Paper presented at the Annual Meeting of the American Educational Research Association, New Orleans, LA.

———. 2003. The impact of preparing for the test on classroom practice. Paper presented at the twenty-seventh conference of the International Group for the Psychology of Mathematics Education held jointly with the twenty-fifth conference of the North American Chapter of the International Group for the Psychology of Mathematics Education, Honolulu, HI.

Schorr, R.Y., Bulgar, S., Monfils, L., & Firestone, W.A. (2002). Teaching and testing at the fourth grade level: An analysis of a two-year study in New Jersey. In D. S. Mewborn, P. Sztajn, D. Y. White, H. G. Wiegel, R. L. Bryant, and K. Nooney, eds. Twenty-fourth annual meeting of the North American Chapter of the International Group for the Psychology of Mathematics Education, Vol. 2. Linking Research and Practice, 577–88.

Schorr, R. Y., S. Bulgar, and W. A. Firestone. 2002. Testing and fourth grade teaching. Paper presented at the twenty-sixth conference for The Psychology of Mathematics Education, Norwich, UK.

Schorr, R. Y., S. Bulgar, J. Razze, L. Monfils, and W. Firestone. 2004. Teaching mathematics and science. In *The ambiguity of teaching to the test: Standards, assessment, and educational reform,* ed. W. A. Firestone, R. Y. Schorr, and L. Monfils, 19–35. Hillsdale, NJ: Lawrence Erlbaum.

Schorr, R. Y., and W. A. Firestone. 2004. Conclusion. In *The ambiguity of teaching to the test: Standards, assessment, and educational reform,* ed. W. A. Firestone, R. Y. Schorr, and L. Monfils, 143–58. Hillsdale, NJ: Lawrence Erhlbaum.

Seegers, G., and M. Boekaerts. 1996. Gender-related differences in self-referenced cognitions in relation to mathematics. *Journal for Research in Mathematics Education* 27 (2): 215–40.

Smith, M. L. 1996. *Reforming schools by reforming assessment: Consequences of the Arizona student assessment program.* Southwest Educational Policy Studies. Tempe, AZ: Arizona State University.

Stipek, D., and H. Gralinski. 1991. Gender differences in children's achievement-related beliefs and emotional responses to success and failure in mathematics. *Journal of Educational Psychology* 83 (3): 361–71.

Tate, W. F. 1997. Race-ethnicity, SES, gender, and language proficiency trends in mathematics achievement: An update. *Journal for Research in Mathematics Education* 28, (6): 652–79.

United States Department of Labor. 1987. *Workforce 2000.* Washington, DC: U.S. Government Printing Office.

Wilson, S. M., and R. E. Floden. 2001. Hedging bets: Standards-based reform in classrooms. In *From the capitol to the classroom: Standards-based reform in the states,* ed. S. H. Fuhrman, 193-216. Chicago: University of Chicago Press.

Xie, Y. 2008. Math gender gap gone in grade school persists in college. http://arstechnica.com/news.ars/post/20080724thevanishinggendergap inmath.html.

NINE

Block Building in the Primary Classroom as a Gender Equalizer in Math and Science

— Debra Dyer —

There is a general perception that males do better than females in math and science. However, research shows that the gender-related differences in ability and career pathway choices in math and the sciences are not as clearly defined as many researchers and educators previously believed and there are many more subtleties and complexities that need to be further investigated. In 2004, women earned 58 percent of all bachelor's degrees; by field, women earned the following proportions of all degrees: psychology, 78 percent; biological sciences, 62 percent; chemistry, 51 percent; mathematics, 46 percent; computer sciences, 25 percent; physics, 22 percent; and engineering, 21 percent (National Science Foundation 2006a). At the master's level, women earned 59 percent of all master's degrees, with the percentage of graduate degrees granted closely following the same pattern as the undergraduate degrees (National Science Foundation 2006a). In stark contrast, at the doctoral level, women earned 45 percent of all doctoral degrees, but they earned less than one-third of those degrees in chemistry, computer sciences, physics, math, and engineering (National Science Foundation 2006a). The career pathways that women choose are limited due to this decline in the pursuit of terminal degrees in advanced science and math studies. Women make up nearly half of the U.S. workforce, yet they comprise only 26 percent of the science and engineering workforce (National Science Foundation 2006b).

Why are women choosing not to pursue advanced degrees and careers in engineering, computer science, or the physical sciences? The potential reasons for this disparity may lie in the coursework, ability, interests, and beliefs of females (Freeman 2004). Research suggests that children's beliefs about their abilities and the interests that stem from exposure to new learning are pivotal in determining their concentration on and performance in subject areas, course and major study choice, after-school activities, and ultimately, chosen career pathways (Pajares 2006). This chapter will investigate the interests and beliefs concerning math and science that females hold and how their perceptions are important in determining their futures. Fostering girls' greater interest and increased self-confidence in math and science ability through block building in the early childhood classroom is the focus of this chapter.

SPARKING FEMALES' INTEREST AND INSTILLING THEIR CONFIDENCE

Throughout the research on female participation in math and science, students' interest is found to be a strong predictor of long-term performance in and choice of math and science courses, majors, and lifetime careers (Simpkins, Davis-Kean, and Eccles 2006). Gender differences in students' interests have been discovered, with boys usually more interested in activities and future careers involving mathematical, scientific, and engineering endeavors and girls displaying greater interest in activities and careers that entail social and artistic endeavors (Lapan et al. 2000). Long-term interest in a subject is often built on initial curiosity that is a more short-term response to a situation or problem posed. Early childhood teachers are well aware that an effective way to nurture students' long-term interests in math and science is to use their initial curiosity as a hook to engage the students in math and science content material (Hidi and Renninger 2006). Once the student interest is kindled teachers can build on the curiosity by providing frequent student engagement in interesting material and problem-solving scenarios that can transform into long-term interest.

Self-confidence evolves from a sense of achievement, an increased inner control of one's self, and a perceived external control and mastery of one's environment. Wassermann (1990) writes about the sense of "power-to"—what we feel as a result of something important accomplished—that is related to a young child's ego strength, self-confidence, and heightened personal autonomy. Children who have a well-developed sense of power-to often grow into adults who are in charge of their lives—fully functioning adults. These are people who are able to take charge, remain positive, and in tough situations are able to visualize thoughtful and effective solutions. Their confidence in themselves often inspires confidence in those around them.

Researchers have found that generally girls and women have less confidence in their math abilities than males do and that from the onset of adolescence, girls show less interest in math and science careers. As many girls move from elementary grades to secondary education they often underestimate their abilities in mathematics and science. However, research has shown it is more probable that those females and males who have a strong self-concept regarding their math and science abilities will choose and perform well in math and science courses as well as math-related and science-related majors and careers (Simpkins and Davis-Kean 2005). As educators and researchers, it is important that we empower our female students to heighten their sense of power-to—their self-confidence, ego strength, and personal autonomy—which is central in determining their career pathway choices.

How do educators instill this sense of empowerment in young girls? First, educators need to implant in students the belief that abilities can be strengthened through effort and hard work (Halpern et al. 2007). Students who are persistent in attempting to master difficult material enjoy greater success than students who doubt their ability and give up. Teaching girls that knowledge and intellect increase as they persevere through difficult problem solving provides girls with a desire to endure short-term failures in order to enjoy long-term success in math and science. Educators and parents can remind all their students about the "malleability of intelligence when they make progress, pointing out that their brains are actively building new connections as they study" (Halpern et al. 2007, 12).

Second, educators need to provide active learning experiences that genuinely challenge thinking. By encouraging girls to engage in problem-solving situations that require concrete and abstract thought processes, new skills, understanding, and meaning develop. Purposeful engagement in challenging tasks that are neither too easy nor too difficult provides students with multiple opportunities to learn habits of thinking and gain self-confidence as thinkers and problem solvers

(Wassermann 1990). Block building serves as an exemplary venue in which this cognitive scaffolding that builds self-confidence leading to a sense of power-to can flourish.

Third, educators need to provide prescriptive, informational feedback (Halpern et al. 2007). Students usually receive feedback in the form of grades, scores, smiley faces, or general comments from the teacher. However, research shows that timely, specific, and concrete feedback regarding student effort and strategies more positively influences student performance (Mueller and Dweck 1998). When teachers combine positive comments with specific strategies for solving a problem, students become more engaged and self-sufficient in their learning (Halpern et al. 2007). Block building in small groups provides a daily event in which the teacher can provide the specific, positive encouragement and concrete strategic thinking that supports and extends the learning.

Fourth, educators need to allocate large amounts of time for direct instruction, scaffolding, and student practice time in specific spatial skills training. Spatial relationships are central to geometric thinking and to general understanding of how objects are related in space. Spatial skill performance is directly correlated to performance in math and science. For example, research has found that kindergartners' efficacy in perception and discrimination of various geometric shapes and rotations is a strong predictor of math performance in fourth grade. Researchers have found that when standardized test items are spatial in nature, boys are more successful in answering the questions correctly (Halpern et al. 2007). Gender differences in spatial problem-solving strategies begin as early as first grade, with boys using more conceptual spatial strategies—especially those that require visualizing what an object looks like when rotated. Later, this gender disparity becomes glaring, largely due to the fact that geometry items comprise nearly one-third of the math portion of the SAT (Halpern et al. 2007).

Block building provides experiences "that lead to the ability to solve cognitive problems requiring mental rotation and transformation of shape (visualizing how an object will look when it is moved, turns, or altered in some way)" (Wellhousen and Kieff 2001, 145). Halpern et al. recommend that teachers offer girls scaffolded, consistent spatial skills training by

- encouraging young girls to play with toys that require the application of spatial knowledge, such as building toys.

- teaching older girls to mentally imagine and draw mathematics or other assignments so that they become as comfortable with spatially displayed information as they are with visual information.
- requiring answers that use both words and spatial display.
- providing opportunities for specific training in spatial skills, such as mental rotation of images, spatial perspective, and embedded figures. (Halpern et al. 2007, 29)

By providing ample block building materials, time, and problems to be solved, teachers are providing girl students the spatial skills training (for example, mental rotation, spatial perspective) to improve performance on related visual and spatial measures (Halpern et al. 2007). Greater expertise in the concepts and skills that block building engenders results in increased student self-confidence and efficacy.

BLOCK BUILDING AS A TOOL

Perhaps no other material has been more traditionally identified with early childhood settings than blocks. Wooden blocks have been a mainstay in early education for over a hundred years, forming the heart of the block center. Blocks promote learning in math, science, architecture, and engineering. Spatial skills training is specifically targeted in block building. Block building also provides a forum in which young students use investigative play to build their interest and self-confidence in problem solving.

Block building provides a cognitively and socially rich venue in which girls' initial curiosity in math- and engineering-based learning can be sparked and fostered into becoming a lifelong interest. Using curriculum-generated play with innovative tasks in the block center is an effective way to provoke student interest. In an integrated curriculum model set in a centers-based classroom, a block-building project can serve two functions, depending on when it occurs in relation to guided instruction (Johnson, Christie, and Yawkey 1999). Both functions allow inquisitiveness to be ignited.

The first opportunity to play with materials and ideas is prior to instruction: allowing children to use their prior knowledge and experience as they act on those materials and ideas. The teacher provides a problem to solve or a scenario to build that is interesting and engaging.

This preinstructional exploration provides the teacher with an opportunity to determine student prior knowledge and plan for further instruction (Wellhousen and Kieff 2001). For girls who have not come to school with a great deal of block-building experience, this provides a suitable opportunity in which the teacher may assess both the block-building acumen of the student and the content knowledge needed to complete the building scenario.

When the play occurs after the instruction, children are then able to practice newly learned skills. They also have the opportunity to connect new knowledge in meaningful ways to prior knowledge and new contexts. Again, this provides an assessment opportunity for the teacher to evaluate the assimilation and application of the new knowledge and skills. Using block building as both a preinstructional strategy and as a way to consolidate new knowledge can be highly motivating and interesting to all students.

The investigative play scenarios that the teacher designs for the block center can result in a greater understanding of the important concepts and issues embedded in the activity or—as Wassermann (1990) refers to them—the "big ideas." Wassermann developed an investigative play sequence of play-debrief-replay to help students formulate these big ideas. SPEDRA (Dyer 2004) is another model that is both a curriculum delivery system and a philosophy of how children learn.

Based on Wassermann's work, SPEDRA—Set the stage, Play, Explore, Debrief, Revisit, and Assess-Apply—is a recursive planning-learning-assessing system that uses investigative play as its medium. The teacher designs scenarios, problems, or dilemmas that set the stage for student investigation involving essential concepts. The play and explore stages begin as students experiment with materials and ideas, constructing and testing hypotheses intended to resolve the dilemma. In the debriefing session the teacher provides a forum for discussion of student ideas. During the discussion, students are encouraged to respect and consider the ideas of others; the teacher checks for student understanding and clarifies misconceptions. The teacher poses questions that challenge children's thinking and incites an excitement for further investigation. During the revisit stage, children use the same materials or additional materials and dilemmas to carry out more complex investigations leading to more extensive understanding. During the final assess-apply stage, the teacher poses scenarios, questions, and dilemmas related to the concept or skill previously explored but often transported to new contexts. By completing this recursive cycle the teacher is able to assess student learning and plan for new learning.

The thematic unit "The Zoo" offers a wonderful learning opportunity to use the SPEDRA model to teach spatial skills, as well as many other skills, through block building. To set the stage the teacher would use pictures of zoos and zoo animals from all parts of the world and artifacts such as animal models. An assessment of student schema (prior knowledge and experience that create mental files) would then ensue, with the possible use of a graphic organizer such as a KWL chart—a three-column chart on which children record, prior to immersion in a thematic unit, what they know (K) about the topic and what they want to learn (W) about the topic. As a culminating assessment of the learning, the children return to the chart and record what they have learned (L).

Next, the teacher would use a fiction/nonfiction literature pairing for a read-aloud to build student schema. By pairing fiction and nonfiction literature children are engaged at a narrative level and then knowledge is built through the expository text. An example of a pairing appropriate for kindergarten through second grade could be *Zoo-Looking* by Mem Fox and *Who Works at the Zoo?* by Alyse Sweeney. After the read-aloud and discussion the teacher would pose a problem such as "Our neighborhood does not have a zoo. We need to build the zoo and the various animal habitats, transport the animals to the zoo, and invite our neighbors to a grand opening party."

The teacher would then introduce the learning centers that support the activity to solve the posed problem. The block center would have a variety of materials already in place: wooden blocks in various shapes and configurations, small zoo animal and people models, materials to make fences, habitats, and so on. The art center would have materials and patterns to be used in constructing items for the block center zoo. The writing center, containing all kinds of writing and drawing materials, would be where the planning for and advertising of the grand opening would happen. The children would either choose a team to be on or would be assigned to collaborative teams.

Creating the environment for play and exploration is not enough. Teachers must also ensure that all students receive a balance of experiences in that environment. Research shows that boys usually dominate the block centers in early childhood classrooms, while girls spend most of their time in language-rich play, such as the play in the theme or housekeeping center (Wellhousen and Kieff 2001). Knowing that providing experiences with blocks enhances a child's ability in spatial relationship skills, teachers must ensure that all children are provided equal opportunities to play and explore in the block area. To encourage girls' participation in the block center the teacher needs to monitor the collaborative grouping at first to ensure girls' comfort level and self-confidence in their risk-taking as they play, explore, and construct. For example, if the class is divided into three teams who each build, create, and write simultaneously, the teacher needs to be sensitive to the personalities, abilities, and self-motivation of each child to provide optimal learning environments.

As the students reposition blocks and objects, first mentally and then physically, and decide by trial and error how to fit objects together, they are developing spatial relationship skills. As the students develop spatial awareness they move from pure trial and error to mental positioning of the blocks prior to building (Wellhousen and Kieff 2001). In their minds and then in their hands they slide, flip, reverse, or rotate different blocks before putting them together on the floor. At this juncture, students move from two-dimensional thinkers to three-dimensional thinkers and gain the facility for solving problems through mental actions rather than physical actions (Diamond and Hopson 1999). Again, ensuring that girls have plentiful and protracted opportunities to manipulate the blocks and problem solve is paramount to their logico-mathematical skill development.

The debriefing stage is where the teacher encourages the students to share ideas and demonstrate steps they took in problem solving. This is a time when the teacher asks questions and encourages student reflection on their understanding and clarification of ideas. The play episode is used as a basis for increasing students' understanding of "big ideas" in the debriefing. Debriefing may take place in either small or whole group settings. A block-building debriefing event would be highlighted by questions such as "Tell me what you have built. How did that work? What did you do to make it work? Why was that successful? Do you have any other ideas for the building?" Girls spend the majority of their time in language-rich play (Wellhousen and Kieff 2001), so this discussion stage of SPEDRA comfortably lends itself to their strength in language skills. Refined language skills needed for effective communication of ideas allows for higher levels of thinking and comprehending (Wassermann 1990).

Effective debriefing lays the groundwork for the next day's replay. The questions raised during the debriefing often build the framework for new play and investigations. The replay stage is a return to the block center to refine and polish the building-making alterations and additions. During the replay a more complex problem may be posed, such as "The zoo has just received two polar bears. How will you build their zoo habitat? What materials will you need? What do you have to think about?" The replay stage provides the opportunity for higher-level and more focused spatial skill practice as well as higher-level problem solving. Girls are given the chance to both mentally imagine spatial displays and develop spatial skills and perspective (through the mental rotation of images)—both recommendations from the U.S. Department of Education (Halpern et al. 2007).

The replay stage also provides an ideal authentic assessment venue. Truly valuable assessment occurs when students have first had a scaffolded learning experience and then time to practice and test hypotheses, followed by options for demonstrating mastery and extension of the skill or knowledge. When conducted in small group block building, the teacher can concentrate on the students' actual building and justification for the process of construction. In-depth anecdotal records and photography both serve as accurate accounts of student learning.

MAKING THE BLOCK CENTER FEMALE FRIENDLY

Group block building also provides a social development opportunity in which girls can refine their spatial and problem-solving skills using negotiation and collaboration. When children build a structure together they learn to appreciate and understand others' ideas and intentions. This social context allows children to negotiate ideas, building their self-confidence and sense of achievement. Block building provides a bridge between the familiar and comfortable social world of females and the logico-mathematical world in which they may not have as much experience.

Providing equal opportunity for all students, regardless of gender, to build and learn in the block center is most important. Designing and structuring both planned building scenarios and time for free exploration in the block center affords a healthy balance of direct instruction, guided practice, and independent problem solving. Girls should be offered various entrance points to the block building that align with their comfort level.

On the practical side, what can teachers do to ensure that the block-building center and the building scenarios offer a secure learning environment for girls as well as boys? Keeping daily records of where children spend their time during the play-exploration part of SPEDRA will alert teachers to large disparities in gender participation in any center. Changes can then be made to encourage equitable participation in the activities and experiences in the classroom.

Some other suggestions include the following:

1. Expand the size of the block center or set up two block centers.
2. Make sure there is a rotation of children so that no one "over-uses" the block center. Using a planning board and checklist will help the teacher keep track of participation in all the centers.
3. Integrate blocks into other centers. Smaller blocks in the kitchen/housekeeping corner can be used for dolls, cooking, and other activities.
4. Place the block center close to traditionally female-dominated centers and design play scenarios that necessitate all students' participation in all centers.
5. In the block center provide small manipulatives that girls are familiar with such as figures of people and animals.
6. Spend time building with all students, particularly girls, in the block center.
7. Intervene if gender-biased attitudes and language prevent free access and full participation in the block center.
8. Make sure there are pictures of both genders building, and use similar language with boys and girls when debriefing the building. (Wellhousen and Kieff 2001, 146)

Teachers and parents play the primary role in encouraging and supporting block play. Traditionally, it has been the teacher's responsibility to pay attention to the environment and materials made available to the students. It has become increasingly important that the teacher also ensures equal access and opportunity for all children to engage in enriched block-building scenarios. Many of the skills such as spatial skills—in which males have outperformed females—can be developed and strengthened in girls through specific experiences and training in the block center. We owe all our students the leveling of the gender playing field that block building can provide.

REFERENCES

Diamond, M., and J. Hopson. 1999. *Magic trees of the mind: How to nurture your child's intelligence, creativity, and healthy emotions from birth through adolescence.* New York: Plume.

Dyer, D. L. 2004. SPEDRA. A learning/teaching framework that makes all children successful. Unpublished manuscript.

Freeman, C. E. 2004. *Trends in educational equity of girls and women: 2004.* Washington, DC: U.S. Department of Education, Institute of Education Sciences.

Halpern, D. F., J. Aronson, N. Reimer, S. Simpkins, J. R. Star, and K. Wentzel. 2007. *Encouraging girls in math and science.* Washington, DC: U.S. Department of Education.

Hidi, S., and K. A. Renninger. 2006. The four-phase model of interest development. *Educational Psychologist* 41, (2): 111–27.

Johnson, J. F., J. F. Christie, and T. D. Yawkey. 1999. *Play and early childhood development.* 2nd ed. New York: Longman.

Lapan, R. T., A. Adams, S. L. Turner, and J. M. Hinkelman. 2000. Seventh graders' vocational interest and efficacy expectation patterns. *Journal of Career Development* 26 (3): 215–29.

Mueller, C. M., and C. S. Dweck. 1998. Praise for intelligence can undermine children's motivation and performance. *Journal of Personality and Social Psychology* 75 (1): 33–52.

National Science Foundation. 2006a. *Science and engineering degrees: 1966–2004.* Arlington, VA: National Science Foundation. http://nsf.gov/statistics.

National Science Foundation. 2006b. *Science and engineering indicators 2006.* Arlington, VA: National Science Foundation. http://www.nsf.gov/statistics/.

Pajares, F. 2006. Self-efficacy during childhood and adolescence: Implications for teachers and parents. In *Self-efficacy beliefs of adolescents,* eds F. Pajares and T. Urdan, 339–76. Greenwich, CT: Information Age Publishing.

Simpkins, S. D., and P. E. Davis-Kean. 2005. The intersection between self-concept and values: Links between beliefs and choices in high school. *New Directions for Child and Adolescence Development* 110:31–47.

Simpkins, S. D., P. E. Davis-Kean, and J. S. Eccles. 2006. Math and science motivation: A longitudinal examination of the links between choices and beliefs. *Developmental Psychology* 42 (1): 70–83.

Wassermann, S. 1990. *Serious players in the primary classroom: Empowering children through active learning experiences.* New York: Teachers College Press.

Wellhousen, K., and J. Kieff. 2001. *A constructivist approach to block play in early childhood.* Albany, NY: Delmar.

TEN

Healthy Sexuality Development and Gender Roles in Early Childhood

— Donna Couchenour and Kent Chrisman —

This chapter examines the relationship between young children's gender roles and their healthy sexuality development. Although children's understanding of gender is not often specifically linked with sexuality development, it is one of many factors related to conceptions about sexuality (Chrisman and Couchenour 2002). The authors of this chapter present their view of healthy sexuality development as a holistic, integrated approach that considers all processes of child development: physical, cognitive, social, and emotional. Thus, the prevailing view of young children's healthy sexuality development is not based solely on children's curiosity about sex and reproduction, but is also related to positive interactions and relationships with adult caregivers, siblings, and peers that are necessary for all aspects of children's healthy development.

Gender role development is based on children's understanding of themselves and their relationships to significant others in their lives. Typically in developmental studies, gender roles are linked to social and emotional development. A comprehensive framework for examining healthy sexuality development in young children is inclusive of this aspect in that sexuality is as much about caring for others, empathy, and responsibility, as it is about physical behavior.

THE WHOLE CHILD VIEW OF HEALTHY
SEXUALITY DEVELOPMENT

To fully understand any aspect of children's development, a whole child framework is necessary. For example, evidence is clear that children's academic success is related not only to cognition and language, but also to physical and socioemotional health. Healthy sexuality development is no different. To understand how children develop in this realm, one must know about physical, cognitive, social, and emotional development.

Physical

Children's healthy sexuality relates to the physical development domain in a variety of ways. Children are interested in their bodies; they move in new and different ways to accomplish goals such as reaching and grasping, rhythmic dancing, and practicing skills for sports. As children grow and develop, their coordination increases and they gain greater control over bodily functions. In addition, young children are interested in all parts of their bodies, including genitals.

- Children may touch their own (and sometimes others') genitals to explore sensations, to discover, and to try to understand differences (just as they touch hair, noses, hands).
- Children may rub genitals for stimulation and tension release (just as they engage in other physical actions for stimulation and tension release, such as running, singing, shouting, playing in water).

Cognitive

Cognitively, children increase their understanding about all of their body parts and the functions of each part. They are able to label themselves and others as girls or boys, they observe and are curious about similarities and differences in humans (as well as other animals), and they ask questions about biological systems, including growth, nutrition, health and wellness, and reproduction. Curiosity about topics related to genitals, sex differences, and where babies come from emanates from the same source as curiosity about the world at large—children's interactions with their physical and social environments.

- Children name body parts, "pee pee," "wee wee," "weiner," as well as "penis," "vagina," "vulva."

- Children notice and examine differences in their own (and some-times others') body parts: "I'm a girl, I have a vulva; Jimmy is a boy, he has a penis." "My daddy has a penis."
- Children make statements of fact: "Your nose is big." "You have a penis." "My mom feeds the baby with her boobies."

Social

Learning how to get along with others is a process that is initiated when loving adults nurture children. This is the basis for children to form friendships and, later, intimate relationships. Developing assertiveness is important for decision making and self-control. Through interactions with adults and older children, young children begin to understand right and wrong as they establish early notions of morality. Relation-ships with caring adults and early moral conceptions are essential for children to respond to limits that are set by those adults. This social development process is crucial for lifelong reciprocal interactions and respecting appropriate boundaries in those interactions.

- Children may define other children as boys or girls based on their expectations for appearance or activity. "I didn't know that Sam is a girl; there was no barrette in her hair."
- "Dolls are for girls." A teacher responds to a child's comment that her toy is only for girls: "I understand that you believe that Harriet Horse is only for girls, Tiffany. But Tony is thinking that it looks like fun and he'd like to play with your toy."
- A parent responds to children who are playing "doctor" and exam-ining one another's bodies: "Sam, pull your pants up. Bodies are private and not for others to touch. Let's find a game to play."

Emotional

Each young child progressively establishes a sense of self. Managing emotions requires support from adults and practice on the part of chil-dren. Learning about expected or appropriate ways to handle anger, sadness, and joy are achievements that are important in the early child-hood years. Children learn to demonstrate respect by receiving respect. Adults who speak calmly to children—without blaming or threatening—provide a model for children to use in their conversations with others. When adults nurture and provide necessities for children, they, in turn, express affection, caring, and empathy. Children's social, intellectual, and physical competence leads to ego strength and healthy self-esteem. Among other aspects of self, young children develop an awareness of gender identity as well as identities with cultural and ethnic groups.

- Children use words to express feelings: "Sometimes I cry when I'm sad."
- Children explore feelings in different situations: "I'm sad when you go to work." "Shelby (a new puppy) makes me happy."
- "Mommy and Daddy kiss a lot. Ewww. I'm never going to kiss a boy (girl)."
- Children learn to express caring in appropriate ways: A teacher says, "Some of our friends do not like it when you hug them. Let's ask before hugging. Maybe some of you would like to high five instead of hug? Who would like that better?"

Children who learn that their world is a trustworthy place move on to learn to trust themselves (Erikson 1963), developing a sense of autonomy. When caregivers encourage and affirm children's efforts to become autonomous by doing things for themselves, children are helped to build strong self-esteem. Children view their own identities positively when their significant adults accept and celebrate children's interests and abilities. These experiences are the basis for children's development of empathy and caring for others. In a comprehensive understanding about sexuality, caring for others is central.

CHILD AND ADULT SEXUALITY DIFFER

With their curiosity about body parts, sex differences, and reproduction, young children are open and playful (Rothbaum, Grauer, and Rubin 1997). Whereas appropriate adult behaviors related to sexuality are responsibly discreet, children's forthrightness may lead to asking questions or engaging in unexpected behaviors in settings that are awkward for adults to respond to in encouraging ways. However, this openness is an important factor in understanding how children's sexuality differs from adults.

Responsible adult sexuality requires deliberation and privacy. On the other hand, young children are spontaneous in most of their interactions and comments (Rothbaum, Grauer, and Rubin 1997). Not only are children open, but they act in the moment. Spontaneity may lead to discussing body parts or asking questions about where babies come from at inopportune moments.

Although children find topics about sexuality at once disgusting and exciting, they lack the eroticism of adults (Rothbaum, Grauer, and Rubin 1997). As young children develop, they demonstrate interest in body parts and body movements, ask questions about various types of relationships, and even announce that they have girlfriends or boyfriends that they plan to marry. Simultaneously, they make faces or sounds of aversion in response to adults who are kissing or other demonstrations of romance. At all times, young children's attention to bodies, relationships, or information is innocent wonder not marked by sexual desire.

NATURE AND NURTURE INTERACT

All development occurs through both nature (biology and genetics) and nurture (environmental interactions). Earlier beliefs about whether nature or nurture is the dominant force have now been reconceptualized "in a way that emphasizes their inseparability and complementarity, not their distinctiveness: it is not nature *versus* nurture, it is rather nature *through* nurture" (Shonkoff and Phillips 2000, 41). This understanding of children's development addresses the child as an active participant in his or her developing sense of self. Children's abilities and interests stem from their inherent biological base and are infused with environmental inputs.

Biological parents provide the genetic inheritance of their children. All parents (or adults in parenting roles) provide much of the environment in which their children develop. They are children's first and most important teachers about everything, including sexuality, both implicitly and explicitly (Chrisman and Couchenour 2002). When this relationship is built on trust and encouragement, children model parental behavior and make meaning of conversations.

CHILDREN CONSTRUCT MEANING
ABOUT RELATIONSHIPS AND SEXUALITY

Relationships are at the center of children's understanding of social phenomena. Healthy sexuality development is as much about caring for others, empathy, and responsibility as it is about physical behavior.

When children are appropriately nurtured, when they are the recipients of understanding, and when they have expectations for helping others, they gain the foundation for the values and abilities necessary for meaningful and intimate relationships in adulthood.

As parents and other caregivers provide information to answer young children's questions about bodies and where babies come from, children are constructing meaning from these responses, from their observations and interactions, and with their current cognitive capabilities. This is why it is critical to provide honest and suitable information. In *Wally's Stories,* Vivian Paley (1987) writes about kindergarten children who, when presented with information about reproduction, refuse to believe in the existence of the uterus. Instead, based on their observations of pregnant women with expanding abdomens, they insist that the growing baby inside the mother's stomach is at risk of being hit by the food the mother eats. This example of children's meaning making may lead some adults to question the wisdom of offering children factual information that seems too difficult for them to understand. Perhaps this is why stories about storks delivering babies and other such myths have emerged. However, such fantasies do not help children understand the world and should not be shared as learning experiences.

ADULT ACTIONS OR RESPONSES TO CHILDREN

Adult responses to children will vary based on individuals and context. Here are some typical situations for children at three developmental levels (infancy/toddlerhood, preschoolers, and kindergarten/primary age) along with adult recommended practices. Practice recommendations have been culled from *Developmentally Appropriate Practice in Early Childhood Programs* (Copple and Bredekamp 2009).

	Developmental Expectation	Adult Role
Infants/ Toddlers	• Develop attitudes about own body • Develop male or female identity and learn expected behaviors by gender	• Adults communicate healthy, accepting attitudes about children's bodies and their bodily functions. • Adults respect individual children's

		preferences for objects and people without regard to sex typing.
Preschoolers	• Aware of and curious about gender differences and establish firm beliefs that they are male or female	• Adults integrate children's interests into learning experiences.
Kindergarten/Primary Age	• Strong same-sex friendships • Strong interest in stereotyped gender roles • Choose gender-stereotyped activities	• Adults ensure that all children in the class get to know and work with each other. • Adults design all activities so that each child can fully participate. • Adults promote a sense of community and respect diversity in the classroom. Respect and appreciation are shown to all.

CHILDREN'S DEVELOPING GENDER ROLES

"A gender role is a set of expectations that prescribe how females and males should act, think, and feel" (Santrock 2005, 346). Both nature and nurture are influential in establishing each child's developing gender role. Although most children are genetically either male or female, environmental influences are ever present. Even very young children clearly discern environmental cues about expectations for male and female differences in interests and behaviors. "Every known human society has rules and customs concerning gender. Members of every society have expectations and beliefs—sometimes explicit, sometimes unspoken—concerning what boys and girls, or men and women, are supposed to do or not do" (Maccoby 1998, 2). At the same time, children have inherent preferences that may easily be incorporated into expected gender roles or preferences that may be more difficult to express in their various environments. Some environments are open to accepting more fluid gender roles so that both girls and boys are encouraged to play and engage in activities in which they are interested and also are provided with opportunities to try novel experiences. Other environments may limit children to activity that is seen as more appropriate for their gender.

"Gender typing is the process by which children acquire the thoughts, feelings, and behaviors that are considered appropriate for their gender in a particular culture" (Santrock 2005, 346). Stereotypical gender expectations are based on narrow perceptions and limited information about what girls and women are like versus what boys and men are like. Such constricted views base social expectations solely on biology.

Biological differences in boys and girls are, of course, evident from birth. Obstetricians or other health professionals present at birth announce the baby's sex—boy or girl—based on observation of the newborn's genitals. In infancy, this is the prominent observable difference between the sexes. Differences in babies' size, body shape, amount of hair, or activity level are not based on sex. Although not observable, two kinds of sex hormones are known to influence gender. All developing fetuses have both estrogens and androgens. Typically, girls have higher concentrations of estrogens and boys have higher concentrations of androgens. Levels of sex hormones likely affect gender typing in that those with higher concentrations of androgens demonstrate higher levels of aggression (Santrock 2005).

Environmental influences take effect as soon as the baby is identified as a boy or girl. When a baby is dressed in neutral clothing, some observers assume the baby's sex. Those who "see" a girl talk about her cuteness, sweetness, and innocence; those who "see" a boy talk about his toughness and the future trouble he is sure to cause (Santrock 2005). Certainly when infants are dressed in more gender-identifiable clothing, such as a pink dress or a blue baseball cap, even strangers indicate their understanding of gender expectations in the way they speak to the baby.

During the first two years of life, observational studies have found that children do not demonstrate gender preferences in their play and interactions. Toddlers are just as likely to interact with others of the opposite sex as they are to choose same-sex playmates. However, interactions with parents do show some understanding of expected behavioral differences between moms and dads. Both boys and girls are inclined to go to their mothers for comfort and to their dads when seeking fun (Maccoby 1998; Honig 2006). It seems likely that children learn these behaviors based on differences in parental roles, not differences based on the child's sex.

By age three, observational studies report conspicuous changes in children's playmate preferences. Many three-year-olds exhibit preferences for peers of their same gender. Girls appear to make such choices a little earlier than boys, with boys showing preferences for same-sex friends by age four. It is noteworthy, though, that young children also continue to play in groups with both boys and girls (Maccoby 1998).

After age four and into the early school years, gender-segregated play increases. The same-sex preference is often stronger for boys than for girls (Maccoby 1998). There is great apprehension about being called a sissy. One way to avoid the label is to participate in the sports or adventure themes chosen by most boys. Boys who show any interest in the activities of girls are subject to "homophobic slurs" (Honig 2006, 381) and rejection by their peers.

Many adults are reminded of their own childhood play experiences when they watch and listen as boys and girls avoid each other to fend off "cooties." Children's play themes vary tremendously by gender during this period of development, with girls involved in collaborative domestic themes and boys engaged in active competitions (Maccoby 1998; Honig 2006).

As children enter the primary grades, "patterns of gender segregation become more firmly entrenched than they were at younger ages, but only in certain settings" (Maccoby 1998, 23–24). It appears that when children have choices in school settings—such as at lunchtime or recess, they choose to interact in gender-segregated groups. When they are required to participate with children of the opposite gender in school-related assignments, they do so. However, even when there are lulls in these mixed-gender class assignments, children seem to automatically group themselves by gender (Maccoby 1998).

CHILDREN CONSTRUCT MEANING ABOUT GENDER ROLES

The broad range of research completed in Western societies and other cultures supports typical developmental patterns in children's establishment of gender roles, moving from interacting with peers of both sexes in toddlerhood to gender segregation in middle childhood. As with other areas of child development, the construction of gender role understanding is influenced by both nature and nurture.

It is likely that some of children's interests may be related to sex hormones. Boys' generally higher levels of active play, competition, and aggression may well be related to higher levels of androgens. Girls' typical interest in domestic themes, relationships, and cooperative play may have origins in estrogens. And yet, "Nature and nurture are jointly involved in everything human beings do" (Maccoby 1998, 89).

Children's same-sex friendships and play styles are convincingly documented as typical development. While adults provide support and encouragement for such friendships, it is also important that they understand the limiting consequences that may be involved in rigid gender stereotyping (Cyprian 1998). First, gender roles that are too inflexible are likely to limit friendships. When boys or girls are overly concerned about gender-specific behavioral expectations, they may be unwilling to consider befriending a child of the opposite sex. Tiffany, a preschooler, believed so strongly that her new toy horse was only for girls that she refused to allow Tony to pick it up from her table, softly squealing, "Nooo, Tony. Harriet Horse is a girl toy."

A second limitation of beliefs about overly strict gender roles is that they may influence how children feel about themselves (Cyprian 1998). If some toys or activities are seen as only for girls or only for boys, it is likely that a child who holds such views will not only prevent boys from playing with her toys, but she will practice this belief by avoiding experiences she attributes as only for boys. Children who place limits on themselves in this way may not develop a sense of competence necessary for risk taking in learning or for later necessary responsibilities. Four-year-old Didi watched as her preschool peers Raul and Raj built a block structure. After observing Didi's interest in the blocks, Ms. Pam approached her and suggested a way for her to join the block play. Didi responded, "I can't play with boys," and quickly moved to the library center, settling on a book about castles. As a follow-up the next day to encourage her interest in structures, Ms. Pam invited Didi to take the castle book to the block table. As Didi began her construction, Peter walked by and asked if he could join her. "Sure," she replied.

Another limitation regarding stringent gender roles may promote homophobia, and homophobia may promote unbending gender expectations (Cyprian 1998). Although no existing evidence suggests that children's play preferences are related in any way to homosexuality or heterosexuality, many teachers of young children share anecdotes of parents' concerns about children's pretend play and the roles that they take. Sometimes adults indicate their discomfort when preschoolers prefer play partners of the opposite gender. Teachers report that one of the most common situations occurring in early childhood settings is parental complaining about boys' engagement in pretend play centers, particularly dressing in stereotypical female clothing. Of course, traditional male clothing is often not available for dress up. Note, though, that pretend play is just that—pretense. No current indicators link pretend play to later sexual orientation. At the same time, parents and teachers need to understand that warmth, support, and positive guidance for children's interests lead to healthy ego strength and caring for others. These characteristics, as noted throughout this chapter, provide a foundation for healthy sexuality development.

It is not uncommon that a kindergarten boy invites all of the boys in the class and none of the girls to a birthday party. It is far more common for girls to choose "masculine" toys or activities than it is for boys to choose "feminine" ones (Honig 2006). Also, boys are more likely to be chided by peers and corrected by parents for selecting toys or activities that are traditionally female.

ADULT RESPONSES TO CHILDREN

When young children are given options about playmates and activities, they will often choose same-sex friends and stereotypical play. While it is critical that the important adults in children's lives support and encourage friendships and individual interests, it is also their responsibility to ensure that children are not artificially limited by their choices. Adults can provide a sense of balance by introducing young children to a variety of interests through books, media, field trips, and toys. For example, primary age girls may be very interested in adornment themes and imitating Hannah Montana in their play, yet when introduced to a microscope or a story about Sojourner Truth, they are able to expand those interests. Boys who are interested in superhero play have also been known to enjoy helping with dinner or baking brownies. It is often up to adults to offer a variety of activities to stretch children's knowledge, interests, and understanding of themselves and others.

In preschool, kindergarten, and the early grades, teachers can assign projects to groups of children who may not typically spend time together during free choice activities as a way to increase flexibility of gender stereotypes. Also, teachers can ensure that a wide variety of activities—sedate, active; quiet, a little louder; solitary, cooperative; small groups, whole group; language-based, spatial, or kinesthetic— are offered to both boys and girls. Efforts to decrease any grouping by gender, including addressing the class as "boys and girls" or "girls and boys," are helpful in reducing unnecessary segregation. Calling the class to attention with "Friends" or "Second graders" serves as a unifier. Since children segregate themselves by gender, they need adults to create more gender balance in their experiences. When adults avoid sexist comments themselves and challenge existing assumptions about gender, children are provided with critical responses to environments that are strongly influenced by media and commercialism (Levin and Kilbourne 2008). Efforts to support variations in interests and abilities help children feel worthy and accepted. Children are then not constricted to traditional gender roles but are free to express themselves as individuals. Healthy sexuality development requires that one have a positive sense of self in order to authentically care for others.

CONCLUSION

So, how is gender-role development related to healthy sexuality development? Sexuality is, at its essence, about relationships. Children who have a healthy sense of themselves—who they are, what they like, what they don't like—have a good start at developing relationships with others. Respect for self is necessary in order to respect others. Children who have had experiences stretching themselves in terms of interests, activities, and social interactions will have had better opportunities to truly know themselves and possibly to appreciate others.

Having playmates or friends of both genders, as well as of other cultures, ethnicities, and abilities, leads to a broader set of experiences. In turn, children are more likely to have greater understanding of both commonalities and individual differences. Even when children try a new interest or activity and find that it's not for them, their appreciation of others is likely to grow. Didi agreed to allow Peter to join her block building even as she had a stated belief that she could not play with boys. Because of the teacher's observation of her interests and encouragement to engage in construction, Didi was able to bend her perspective about gender roles. Families and teachers have a critical function in supporting children in their understanding of various types of relationships.

Extreme stereotyping leads to a lack of interaction or understanding of differences related to gender. Name-calling and interruption of positive interactions among children lead to divisions in the learning community as well as a lack of respect and tolerance for individual differences.

Healthy sexuality is based on positive human relationships. When flexibility of gender roles is the norm, all children are able to feel a sense of belonging. This early view of acceptance of others and stretching one's self is a foundation for understanding, respect, empathy, and responsibility—all at the heart of sexuality development.

REFERENCES

Chrisman, K., and D. Couchenour. 2002. *Healthy sexuality development: A guide for early childhood educators and families.* Washington, DC: National Association for the Education of Young Children.

Copple, C., and S. Bredekamp, ed. 2009. *Developmentally appropriate practice in early childhood programs serving children from birth through age 8.* 3rd ed. Washington, DC: National Association for the Education of Young Children.

Cyprian, J. 1998. *Teaching human sexuality: A guide for parents and other caregivers.* Washington, DC: Child Welfare League of America.

Erikson, E. H. 1963. *Childhood and Society.* 2nd ed. New York: W. W. Norton & Company.

Honig, A. S. 2006. Sociocultural influences on gender-role behaviors in children's play. In *Play from birth to twelve: Contexts, perspectives, and meanings.* 2nd ed., ed. D. P. Fromberg and D. Bergen, 338–47. New York: Routledge.

Levin, D. E., and J. Kilbourne. 2008. *So sexy so soon: The new sexualized childhood and what parents can do to protect their kids.* New York: Ballantine.

Maccoby, E. 1998. *The two sexes: Growing up apart, coming together.* Cambridge, MA: Harvard University Press.

Paley, V. G. 1987. *Wally's stories: Conversations in the kindergarten.* Cambridge, MA: Harvard University Press.

Rothbaum, F., A. Grauer, and D. J. Rubin. 1997. Becoming sexual: Differences between child and adult sexuality. *Young Children* 52 (6): 22–28.

Santrock, J. W. 2005. *Children*. 8th ed. New York: McGraw-Hill.

Shonkoff, J. P., and D. A. Phillips, ed. 2000. *From neurons to neighborhoods: The science of early childhood development*. Washington, DC: National Academies Press.

ELEVEN

Creating Preschool Classroom Environments That Promote Gender Equity

— Janis Strasser and Lisa Mufson Koeppel —

On a bright April morning, first year teacher Carlotta scans her classroom during center time. She has worked hard to make sure that each center is equipped with lots of materials, and she smiles when she realizes that each of the fifteen preschool students is actively engaged. But as she takes a closer look, she notices a distinct tendency related to gender in the way the children play and where they choose to play. The same three girls always play with the baby dolls and cook dinner in the dramatic play area. Two boys are building together in the block area and a third boy is lining up the trucks, getting ready to race them on a track he has constructed. The other four boys are at the sand and water tables or playing with the manipulatives. In the art area, Cherisse and Adele are happily making collages while Francesca and Lynn are painting flowers at the easels. Carlotta wonders if it is natural for children this age to self-select play roles according to gender. Should she be encouraging boys and girls to play together? How can she involve more girls in the block area and encourage boys to play in the art and dramatic play centers? She makes a mental note to observe their outdoor play to see whether she notices any trends according to gender.

THE DIFFERENT WAYS THAT BOYS AND GIRLS PLAY IN THE PRESCHOOL YEARS

As toddlers, boys and girls often play together. But by the age of three or four, they begin to segregate themselves by gender (Scarlett et al. 2005). Boys as young as two and a half years of age are more physically aggressive than girls are. Girls, on the other hand, are more relationally aggressive (not playing with someone, threatening to do so, excluding them socially, and so on) (Crick et al. 2006). One girl may do something hateful to another girl and then immediately ask, "Are you my friend?" These behaviors were observed most clearly in same-sex peer relationships. So we can see that perhaps girls and boys not only play differently with materials but also with their peers of the same gender.

Children do play differently with their same-sex peers than with peers of the opposing sex according to Lindsey and Mize (2001). Boys initiate more play events and engage in more physical play with other boys while girls engage in more pretend play with other girls. One study showed how boys and girls have varying responses to "vulnerability" in their play situations (pretending that a playmate is sick, babyish, helpless, and so on) (Benenson and Del Bianco 1997). When boys pretend with this type of scenario, they physically dominate the vulnerable player. Boys may be more prone to acting out the aggressive behaviors they observe in their lives (TV and video game violence, spanking, or punishing) in these play scenarios. When girls enact this type of scenario, they act in a caring way toward the vulnerable player, engage in nurturing activities like feeding and bathing the dolls, and want to share their peer's problems. It is interesting to note that although boys and girls may witness the same amount of violent acts in their lives, boys seem to internalize the violence more and represent it through these power-play scenarios.

By three years of age, children are aware of their identity as either a boy or a girl and they begin to self-select same-sex groupings. These same-sex groups appear to facilitate more social interaction than when toddlers play with children of the other sex. Although children prefer to choose playmates that are of the same sex, when teachers positively reinforced playing with children across genders, the children were more willing to cross the gender boundary during play (Fabes, Martin, and Hanish 2004).

Research has shown that preschool boys and girls differ in their toy preferences and activities, where they enjoy playing in the classroom, and themes of play and playmates (McMurray 1993). They clearly tend to segregate themselves during free play time in school according to gender (Hagglund 1993). They even differ in the conscious or unconscious decisions they make about how they are going to play. In general, girls like to play games where they take turns, and they avoid conflicts, but boys prefer games that have flexible rules and that involve negotiation and disagreements. Boys play independently, whereas girls ask for help (Frost, Wortham, and Reifel 2001).

Boys often enjoy play that includes lots of adventure, action, and movement, while girls may prefer gentle, more passive and domestic play activities (MacNaughton 1997). Boys typically play with low levels of talk, while girls' play is much more verbal (Frost, Wortham, and Reifel 2001). It is documented that school-age boys prefer electronic games and play them more than girls do (Frost, Wortham, and Reifel 2001). We have observed this in our preschool classrooms.

There is an anatomical explanation for the phrase "boys being boys." Research on the anatomy of the eyes shows that boys and girls detect location and movement differently. The male eye consists of a greater number of cells that perceive location, direction, and speed. The female eye is wired to distinguish things in the environment (Zambo and Brozo 2009). This information has strong implications on the way boys and girls learn and interact with each other and their environment.

The Struggle for Power

The struggle for power has been identified in the literature as a rationale for understanding children's play (MacNaughton 1999). Sometimes we can see the struggle for power take hold of play as children argue over toys (who gets to be the first one to play with the new puzzle) or try to take over an area of the room for their individual or group play scenario (who gets to make the block area into a train station) or dramatic play roles (who gets to be the mommy). In their dramatic play scenarios, girls give the role of "mother" a tremendous sense of power. She is the one who decides "what to do, who can do it, and she creates the flow, duration and style of the play" (MacNaughton 1993, 13).

Other times, this struggle is less obvious as children compete for the attention of a particular child or adult or take a risk at initiating play with a child they have never played with before. MacNaughton (1999) writes of children who play across gender boundaries as taking great risks. Girls who do this, she says, may want to be superheroes, and play in noisy, physically active ways with the boys. Boys who cross gender boundaries want to join in domestic play with the girls and are quieter and less physically active than many of the boys.

Crossing Gender Boundaries

Crossing these gender boundaries can be difficult for children and needs much support from the adults in the classroom so that these children can be seen by their peers as leaders. This is reminiscent of the heroine of the children's book *Amazing Grace* (Hoffman 1991) who wants to be Peter in the class play *Peter Pan*. At first, the other children make fun of her and tell her she can't be Peter because Peter is a boy. (They also tell her that she can't be Peter because she is African American.) The teacher and Grace's family encourage Grace to follow her dream. The same theme is evident in another children's book, *I Look Like a Girl* (Hamanaka 1999), about a girl who doesn't want to be bound to the traditional passive roles that young girls take on. She wants to be physically active, free, and wild, like the tiger depicted on the cover of the book. Teachers who model activities and jobs stereotypically representative of the opposing sex set a positive example. Female teachers can use power tools, like an electric drill or an electric screwdriver, to fix classroom furniture and toys themselves. Male teachers can perform domestic chores like washing dishes and caring for a baby.

Effects of Society on Children's Gender Play Behaviors

Families, peers, teachers, and the media affect the gender behaviors that preschool children exhibit (McMurray 1993). Of course, many children's play attitudes are already partially shaped before they even enter preschool. It has been shown that fathers play differently with their preschool sons than with their preschool daughters (Lindsey and Mize 2001). Fathers engage in more physical play (playful contact or gross motor activity) with sons and mothers engage in more pretend play (using objects to represent other objects and/or assuming pretend play roles, like "cooking" using Legos as pasta) with both boys and girls. Additionally, parents of preschool children report that they encourage their sons to be more independent. They offer more warnings to their daughters about safety and risk-taking issues and give more physical assistance to their daughters (Little 2006).

Young children perceive that boys are more physically active than girls and they identify social differences in boys and girls (Hyun and

Choi 2004). But, in the same study, children also responded that boys and girls can "bend" a little and play together. The children's book *Horace and Morris but Mostly Dolores* (J. Howe 1999) tells the story of three mouse friends, two boys and a girl, who decide they must go their separate ways because of gender differences. Horace and Morris join the "Mega-mice" (no girls allowed) and Dolores joins the "Cheesepuffs" (no boys allowed). By the end of the story, they come to find that true friendship runs deeper than gender. They ultimately create a clubhouse where "everyone is allowed."

Risk Taking in Play—Superheroes, Bad Guys, and Rough-and-Tumble Play

A review of risk-taking behavior in young children in Australia reported that boys take more risks than girls (Little 2006). Risk taking can have positive and negative consequences. At either extreme, it can enable children to learn new skills and discover new ways of doing things or it can lead to injury. It may also affect the way children utilize outdoor equipment and how they should be supervised in indoor and outdoor classroom settings.

It is well documented that boys engage in more superhero, good versus evil, rough-and-tumble play scenarios than girls (Paley 1984; Benenson and Del Bianco 1997). Rough-and-tumble play is play fighting and includes things like tackling, running and chasing, pushing, and kicking (Johnson, Christie, and Wardle 2005). In rough-and-tumble play, children laugh and smile as they engage in "bad guy" and "good guy" scenarios, often related to superheroes they see on television (Frost, Wortham, and Reifel 2001).

Teachers can use these experiences as opportunities to teach conflict resolution and help children develop constructive ways of problem solving ("Christopher, how can we save Jorge? He's trapped under the table and all we have is this jump rope," or "Amir, you and Stefan both want to play the villain. How can we solve this problem?") (Fromberg 2002).

Research shows that these gender specific ways of playing are deeply ingrained in preschool children (Johnson, Christie, and Wardle 2005). Do we as teachers accept these notions as the way things are or do we try to promote a more gender-integrated way of playing where children will take risks and try new ways of playing?

PRESCHOOL TEACHERS' PERCEPTIONS
OF THE WAY BOYS AND GIRLS PLAY

The subtle gender bias often exhibited by teachers and other adults has been called "the hidden bias." Research exists showing that teachers *do* treat boys and girls differently (Wellhousen 1996). We often have drastically different expectations of children as they work and play that are defined by gender.

In preschool classrooms where a child-centered ("experiential education") approach is observed, boys tend to engage in more play with dolls and participate in more art activities than in classrooms where the teachers are more controlling. Additionally, in the child-centered classrooms, the girls take more initiative (Laevers and Verboven 2000). Teachers who maintain a low-risk classroom environment will see more children taking emotional risks when making play choices. A non-threatening classroom climate helps children remain unintimidated when choosing areas or activities that may be unfamiliar to them.

The gender of the preschool teacher may affect how the teacher perceives the way children in the class play. One small study in Sweden showed that male teachers value "playfulness" and physical development, while female teachers consider calm play and the importance of social development to be important (Sandberg and Pramling-Samuelsson 2005).

Teachers can help to deemphasize gender stereotypes by being conscious of the many small, subtle things we do on a daily basis. We encourage boys' achievements and comment on girls' cooperation (Evans 1998). We interact more with boys than girls, often assign classroom duties according to gender, praise girls according to their appearance, and praise boys for their ability. We promote "learned helplessness" in girls while challenging boys to be independent (Wellhousen 1996). Those types of interactions manifest themselves in the preschool classroom in ways like engaging in creative block-building scenarios with boys; expecting girls to be leaders in cleaning up, while asking the boys to help move heavy objects; telling girls how pretty their dress-up clothes are while telling the boys how strong and brave they are as they dress up as firefighters; reminding boys that they are big enough to be able to put together a large puzzle, while reminding girls not to get their clothing dirty while playing.

As children play in preschool, it is important not to use the pronoun "he" when we refer to inanimate objects or nonspecific gender persons or roles (Wellhousen 1996). When we use male terms, we reinforce the notion that there are more males than females and the stereotypes about male and female roles (Wellhousen 1996). By using gender-free terms such as "police officer," "mail carrier," and "firefighter," we can expand the roles that boys and girls take on in dramatic-play scenarios in the classroom.

Are a teacher's perceptions about where girls and boys play in their own classrooms accurate? One way to really understand where children choose to play is to make an environmental checklist (Gonzalez-Mena 2005) to record this information. Gonzalez-Mena suggests listing the play centers and noting the number of boys and girls who visit each area during free play time in one day. Figure 1 shows a tally mark adaptation of the environmental checklist.

Figure 1: Sample Checklist of Gender-Based Center Play

PLAY CENTER	DAY: _Monday_	
	Boys	Girls
blocks		
dramatic play		
library		
art		
sand table		
water table		

THINKING ABOUT GENDER AND THE OVERALL CLASSROOM ENVIRONMENT

Prior to the 1960s, children's play materials and scenarios often reflected the occupations of men and women (boys were doctors or firefighters and girls were mothers or nurses). Beginning in the 1970s, there was an effort to cross these gender stereotypical lines (Van Hoorn et al. 2003). However, companies still target vehicles and building toys specifically to boys and pretend play and dress-up merchandise to girls through advertising and packaging techniques. Often, only girls are depicted playing with pretend-play toys, while only boys are seen zooming around with motorized cars. The packaging for girl toys is usually sparkly or finely detailed using bright colors like pink, purple, and yellow. Packaging for boy toys, on the other hand, tends to be darker in color, utilizing blue, brown, silver, and black, as do the toys themselves (Zambo and Brozo 2009). Studies prove that the female retina contains more cells that respond to texture and bright colors like pink, yellow, orange, and red. The male retina contains a greater number of cells that react to darker colors like brown, dark blue, black, and silver (Zambo and Brozo 2009). Toy companies use this information to market and sell toys to one gender or the other.

Three-year-old children can predict what they think their parents would identify as "girl toys" and "boy toys" (Freeman 2007). In one study, when asked questions about "girl toys" and "boy toys," despite what their parents had reported about their preferences in buying toys for their children, more than 90 percent of the responses of three-year-olds reflected gender stereotypes of toys (Freeman 2007). Percentages were even higher for five-year-olds.

How the classroom is set up may contribute to how the children engage in play. Good classroom environments have three basic elements: time, climate, and space (Isenberg and Jalongo 2006). "Time" specifically refers to the blocks of time that the teacher allocates to individual children, routines, transitions, and the various types of play available in preschool (whole group, small individual group, and individual). Giving children long periods of time in which to engage in child-initiated play is important in any high-quality preschool classroom. In her book about the ways that girls and boys play in kindergarten, Paley (1984) found that when the time for child-initiated play was increased, boys spent more time engaging in quiet table activities. Also, providing children large blocks of time to engage in art projects and dramatic-play scenarios increases the chances for high-level questioning and extending a project over several days.

"Climate" refers to the way the classroom is organized, the rules, routines, curriculum, and the way the teacher interacts with the children. Each child should be greeted individually, and the adults in the classroom should be warm and nurturing and should display appropriate forms of affection with the children. It is important to foster an environment that allows for risk taking, in which children can work and play without the anxiety of being ridiculed or rejected. All emotions and expressions of creativity are validated in this type of classroom, and empty praise or disdain is not used. Children should be encouraged to cooperate with one another and help whenever possible. Classroom rules should be based on issues of safety and respect for one another and the classroom.

"Space" is the way the classroom is physically set up, with attention to individual areas, the needs of the children, and the room as a whole. Providing multiple areas for children to work and play alleviates many discipline problems in the classroom. Traffic flow in the classroom should move around the children's workspaces, not through them. There should be cozy spaces for time alone, a large space for gross-motor activities, and spaces where children can work in self-selected small groups. When children are comfortably seated in small groups, they often observe and discuss each other's work (White 1998). Therefore, providing this type of workspace in your classroom is conducive to high-level discussion, with children reflecting and commenting on one another's work.

Using Language That Promotes Gender Equity

There are some basic things we can remember to say to children in early childhood classrooms to support cooperation and equity (Schlank and Metzger 1997). These include the following:

- Address children as individuals, not as "girls" or "boys."
- Make comments that include both genders, rather than one or the other. For example, "The children like to play outside," instead of "The boys like to run and the girls like to swing."
- Point out incidences where boys and girls play or work together, like "Suzie and Dashawn really worked hard to clean up the block area today."

- Don't emphasize how "pretty" a girl's clothing, hair, or shoes are, or how "handsome" a boy looks. Instead, focus on specific qualities individual children show, like "Thank you, Derrick, for helping Sam zip up his coat. That was being a good friend to him."
- When you address the whole group, instead of saying "boys and girls" say "children" or "friends" or have the class come up with a class name to call themselves, like the "penguins."
- Use gender-neutral words to describe occupations, like salesperson and server.

Questions to Ask Yourself About the Classroom Environment

Think about your own classroom or observe in someone else's classroom to answer these questions:

- Are girls given as much wait time as boys to answer a question?
- Are there places in the classroom where boys (and girls) can engage in appropriate physical activities without breaking the rules?
- Are high-level answers to questions probed for in girls as well as boys (for example, "Why do you think that happened? How else could we solve that problem?")
- Are children commended on their courage and bravery not just for their physical achievements but for their emotional accomplishments as well?
- Are boys encouraged to show emotions like fear and sadness, or does a "boys don't cry" mentality prevail?
- When a girl needs help, do you automatically ask a boy to assist her?
- What opportunities are provided for children to cooperate with one another and accomplish tasks as a team (boys and girls together)?
- When issues of exclusion come up in the classroom ("You can't play because you're a girl/boy!"), do you address them immediately?

Classroom Resources

The following is a list of materials that can be added to the classroom to create a more gender-equitable environment. Carefully including these materials ensures that the classroom environment does not perpetuate gender stereotypes.

- Try to make sure the major pieces of classroom furniture are neutral in color (natural wood or white is best). You can always repaint some furniture that is already there!
- Include photographs on the walls of men and women engaging in occupations that go against old stereotypes (for example, female car mechanics and firefighters, male nurses and librarians).
- Devote one section of a wall to photos of family members of the children in the class. If some families don't have access to a camera, send home a disposable one with instructions that allow the family to take several photos, or photograph family members with your own camera, if possible.
- Create a shelf or bulletin board for families with information on child development and play.

The following sections of this chapter will address the materials and resources of typical interest areas found in preschools where children tend to segregate themselves by gender—specifically the art, dramatic play, library, block, and outdoor play areas. It has been our experience that boys and girls frequently play together at the sand and water tables, science area, and in other areas of the room.

ART AREA

Sebastian and Samuel are working in the art area during center time alongside Claudia and Ayanna. Sebastian reaches into a basket and pulls out a handful of paper to take to the table.

SAMUEL: You can't use that! That's pink for the girls. The boys don't got pink.

AYANNA: Give it here. I wanna use that pink. You get that brown, that's for you.

Children have distinct ideas about "boy" and "girl" colors. These choices are based on input from media and advertising, as well as the stimuli their eyes are pre-wired for. We have observed a large bucket of multicolored pegs being sorted by color, only to find the purple ones pushed by the wayside because "these pegs can be for the boys, but not the purple ones."

There have been records of children's drawings as early as the 1200s (Bhroin 2007). It is generally accepted that children's marks on paper begin as nonsymbolic explorations of materials, but Bhroin (2007) found connections between the art, play, and real life of young children. Although each child brings his or her own meaning to art materials (paint, crayons, markers, and so on), boys may be interested more in the symbolic depiction of some themes (vehicles and large creatures) and girls in others (people and natural objects like trees or flowers). Based on the differences between girls' and boys' brain and eye development discussed earlier, girls are more likely to depict nonlocomotor objects and people, using more intricate patterns and details. They often use a wide spectrum of bright colors. Boys tend to illustrate objects in motion or an object associated with movement and speed. They may use a single dark color to complete their illustrations, as this is what their eyes register the best (Zambo and Brozo 2009). One teacher made her art area inviting to boys by creating a "Michaelangelo Project" (Moskowitz 2008). Four children at a time were allowed in the area. They laid on their backs on scooters and maneuvered themselves with their legs to draw on paper that was taped on the underside of the table using markers and crayons.

Providing lots of very active art experiences may encourage boys to explore the art area. Working on large murals, printing with everyday objects on large paper, and making large collages with themes and materials attractive to boys will help them to know they are invited to explore the art area.

Questions to Ask Yourself About the Art Area

Think about your own classroom or observe in someone else's classroom to answer these questions:

- If a child makes a comment such as "Boys don't use pink," are there pictures in the environment to contradict such stereotypes (for example, photos of men in pink, purple, or pastel shirts)?
- Can children stand up to paint?
- Are there commercial art materials as well as natural materials available?

- Are there collage materials offered that represent different colors and textures? (feathers, glitter stickers, pom-poms, fabric, sandpaper, seed pods, pinecones, and so on)
- Are there drawing and painting utensils available in varied thicknesses (widths) and textures?
- When talking to children about their art, do you pay more attention to the girls' neat and detailed drawings and dismiss the boys' messy, abstract "junk" structures?

Resources to Add to the Art Area

The following is a list of materials that can be added to the art area to facilitate more movement in the area, which may appeal to the boys in the classroom.

- Squeeze bottles filled with tempera paint, squeezed onto paper or small trays, and plastic cars and trucks for children to roll through paint. Other "rolling" paint supplies include marbles, nubby balls, seed pods from a sycamore tree, pits from stone fruit, and rocks.
- Straws (straight ones work best) to blow on diluted paint or watercolors (NAEYC 2008).
- Baskets of wood scraps and safe, recyclable household materials for gluing into structures.
- Cut-up toy packages, video game booklets, and magazines about superheroes and trucks for cutting and gluing.
- Tools like staplers, hole punchers, and rolls of tape.
- Brass fasteners for creating movable parts on vehicles, people, or animals.

Children's Books to Add to the Art Area
Clay Boy (Ginsburg 1997)
Harold and the Purple Crayon (Johnson 1955)
Little Blue, and Little Yellow (Lionni 1959)
The Legend of Indian Paintbrush (dePaola 1988)
Henri Matisse: Drawing with Scissors (O'Connor 2002)
Camille and the Sunflowers: A Story about Vincent van Gogh (Anholt 1994)
Alexander Calder (Venezia 1999)
Paper Parade (Weeks 2004)
Counting to Tar Beach (Ringgold 1999)

DRAMATIC PLAY AREA

Jamal and Cristina are working in the dramatic play area during free play time. Jamal is adding clothes and laundry soap to the washing machine.

CRISTINA: Why you washing the clothes? You the daddy, Jamal. The mommy does that.

JAMAL: My daddy washes the clothes at the big laundry place by my house.

CRISTINA: What about your mommy? My mommy and Tia do the clothes.

JAMAL: My mommy don't live at my house. Me and my daddy and my sister do.

CRISTINA: Oh. [turns and continues feeding the baby doll seated in the high chair]

A lot of growing takes place in the dramatic play areas of preschool classrooms. Children who play there are creating social constructs that will shape the way they perceive the world and gender interactions. While it is important to allow children to freely act out the fanciful scenarios of their imaginations, they also need active guidance to help scaffold their understanding of the things they experience in their everyday lives (Copple and Bredekamp 2009). Being there for the "teachable moments" is a primary consideration in an experiential classroom. When joining in the children's pretend scenarios, teachers need to be sensitive to different family dynamics and cultural practices in terms of gender.

Boys and girls often differ in the types of play scenarios they enact and the materials they use. As mentioned earlier, girls use language more, act out roles of family members, and select themes based on everyday occurrences. Boys use less language, act out adventure themes, and are more physically active in their play (Johnson, Christie, and Wardle 2005).

In one study of how children play in the dramatic play area (N. Howe et al. 1993), the results showed that when teachers changed the theme from traditional housekeeping to novel themes (hospital, bakery, pirate ship, airplane, animal hospital, train station, fruit and vegetable store, and farm) boys were much more likely to play in the area.

Allowing children to move and share materials between the block area and dramatic play area provides opportunities for higher-level play.

Boys and girls are able to carry materials normally used in the house area to enhance their block play and provide further opportunities for them to explore gender roles.

Questions to Ask Yourself About the Dramatic Play Area

Think about your own classroom or observe in someone else's classroom to answer these questions:

- Are there both male and female dolls of various races and ethnicities?
- Are there dress-up clothes that complement various job occupations and family roles (for example, police, firefighters, doctors, and veterinarians) to be used by boys and girls?
- Are the colors in the area neutral (for example, no pink stoves)?
- Are there props that boys would enjoy (for example, suit jackets, ties, trophies, sports paraphernalia, tools)?
- When joining in the children's play scenarios, do you encourage them to take on roles that cross gender boundaries and challenge stereotypes?

Resources to Add to the Dramatic Play Area

The following is a list of materials that can be added to the dramatic play area to help create a nongender-specific environment. This may encourage boys to participate in pretend play.

- Invite a male role model (father, grandfather, retiree, family friend) to interact with the children in the dramatic play area.
- Acquire clothing, appliances, and household props for free or at minimal cost at www.freecycle.org and by shopping at garage sales.
- Display photos and posters on the surrounding walls depicting males and females in a variety of roles (for example, police officer, dentist, baker, construction worker, florist, parent).
- Gather a bucket of river stones or other smooth rocks for "cooking."
- Provide print materials that depict men with long hair or ponytails and women with short haircuts.
- Make available real cooking utensils and dishes, household appliances (iron, ironing board with neutral fabric, brooms, and mops), and telephones.

Prop Boxes to Add to the Dramatic Play Area

Prop boxes are cartons or large shoe boxes that have materials related to a specific theme that children like to act out. As children tire of the items in the dramatic play area, you can change their play by introducing new props. You can usually find materials suggested for the prop boxes through donations from families, garage sales, or dollar stores. Make sure to add children's picture books related to the theme.

- **Post office**: various types of paper, writing materials, junk mail, old greeting cards, address books, envelopes, blank self-stick labels, stickers to use as stamps, ink stamps and stamp pads, cash register with receipts and play money, mail scale, boxes, tape and packing materials, word cards with children's names and other words they may want to write in a letter, class mailbox, and mail carrier clothing (hats, blue shirts, and mail bag)
- **Supermarket or grocery store**: cardboard and plastic food boxes and containers, shelf labels to match items being sold, grocery store circulars, coupons, cash register with receipts, credit cards and play money, writing materials for grocery lists, preprinted grocery lists where shoppers check off items they buy, laundry basket strapped to a chair to use as a shopping cart, and paper and plastic grocery bags
- **Pizza shop**: menus, order pads, food packages (spices, pizza ingredients), rebus recipe cards and cookbooks, cash register with play money, credit cards and receipts, pizza boxes, aprons and chef hats, flat pizza pans, spatulas, cardstock and collage materials to make "pizzas"
- **Camera and phone repair shop**: calendar, appointment book, telephone, receipt books, writing materials for noting repairs, rebus word cards with children's names and names of items and services, preprinted rebus lists of items that children check off, old disposable cameras, old cell phones, various kinds of tape, tools such as small screwdrivers, pliers, wrenches, and tweezers, magnifying glasses, work clothing

Children's Books to Add to the Dramatic Play Area

Burger Boy (Durant 2006)
Families (Morris 2000)
Ira Sleeps Over (Waber 1972)
Loving (Morris 1994)

More More More Said the Baby (Williams 1996)
Pete's a Pizza (Steig 1998)
The Princess Knight (Funke 2004)
William's Doll (Zolotow 1972)
I Want to be a Cowgirl (Willis 2002)

LIBRARY AREA

LITISHA [holding a puppet of Sleeping Beauty]: I wanna be the beautiful princess and you have to save me from the big bad wolf.

HECTOR [holding a puppet of the Prince]: Okay. Don't worry. I'm gonna get 'em for you!

TEACHER [holding a puppet of a Troll]: Oh, no! Here comes the big, bad Troll. Princess Litisha, now it's your turn to save the day. How will you rescue the prince?

LITISHA: I'm gonna pull him up on my horse and go really fast.

In the example above, the teacher used a teachable moment to empower Litisha to be an active problem solver instead of taking a passive, submissive role. Gender role stereotypes are often echoed in the literature we read to children where boys are the heroes and girls are the victims (*Little Red Riding Hood, Sleeping Beauty,* and others). Then they are amplified as we have children act out these characters with puppets, costumes in dramatic play, flannel boards, or retellings on CD or cassette tapes. Rather than eliminating the classic fairytales that depict these scenarios, we need to balance them with other types of literature. We need to pose questions to students such as "How do you think the story would be different if Red Riding Hood was a boy?" or "How could the story end if Sleeping Beauty was Sleeping Handsome, and he was rescued by the princess?" Children can act out these versions of the stories.

Research as recent as the 1990s has shown that children's books still tend to depict girls in stereotypical roles, needing males to solve problems. However, this trend is slowly changing (Evans 1998). Teachers should evaluate children's books for gender bias (as well as other types of bias) by referring to the guidelines for selecting bias-free textbooks and storybooks (Council on Interracial Books for Children 1980):

- check the illustrations, story lines, and heroes for stereotypes
- consider the author's and illustrator's backgrounds and perspectives
- think about the effects of the story on children's self-image
- consider the descriptive adjectives used in the story
- think about the lifestyles and relationships among story characters
- check the copyright date

Children can also make their own individual and class books that share their unique family stories to challenge gender stereotypes. Making a class book with a title such as "Girls and Boys Can . . ." (Wellhousen 1996) is a good example of this activity. Each student finishes the statement and illustrates a page. Another idea for bookmaking is to help children create and read maps to find "treasure" hidden somewhere in the library area, possibly within a book. Clues can include using positional words and identifying letters or sight words. These maps can be made into a class book.

To engage boys in the library area, we need to find "entry point" books that excite their interests, contain characters with whom they can identify, and display images of positive male values (such as cooperation, courage, honesty, respectfulness, and perseverance) (Zambo and Brozo 2009). When asked, boys have reported that they like visual appeal and humor, and storybooks as well as informative books about machines, animals, and sports (Zambo and Brozo 2009). While girls developmentally pay more attention to detail in illustrations, boys are drawn by simple illustrations. Books by Mo Willems and Todd Parr have bold, graphic illustrations that attract the eyes of active young readers.

Questions to Ask Yourself About the Library Area

Think about your own classroom or observe in someone else's classroom to answer these questions:

1. Are many books available that pique the interests of both boys and girls?
2. Is there informal reading going on between children and teachers to discuss any issues that may come up in stories or illustrations?
3. Are there plenty of materials for acting out stories (puppets, a small prop kit for a favorite book)?

4. Are class-made books created by both boys and girls present in the area?

Children's Books to Add to the Library Area
David Goes to School (Shannon 2001)
The Empty Pot (Demi 1996)
Don't Let the Pigeon Drive the Bus! (Willems 2003)
Just a Dream (Van Allsburg 2002)
Pearl Barley and Charlie Parsley (Blabey 2008)
SuperHero ABC (McLeod 2006)
Yo! Yes? (Raschka 1993)
Where the Wild Things Are (Sendak 1963)
Horace and Morris but Mostly Dolores (J. Howe 1999)
Skippyjon Jones (Schachner 2003)

Resources to Add to the Library Area

The following is a list of materials that can be added to the library area to encourage more active boys to spend time in an otherwise quiet area. These materials provide opportunities for literacy experiences using hands-on materials.

- Felt pieces for favorite stories children can use to sequence.
- A basket of large foam letters and small trucks. Help children identify letters by driving the trucks over the shape of the letters.
- Books with bold, graphic drawings and finely detailed mixed media illustrations.

BLOCK AREA

Eric and Hassan are trying to build a bridge by stacking the longest blocks they can find on top of a base made of a pile of several smaller blocks. As they assemble the bridge, Carina approaches.

CARINA [holding a small doll]: Hey, I'll carry my baby over your bridge.

ERIC: Get away. We don't need no baby dolls knocking down our bridge.

CARINA: [sulks, but leaves the area]

The importance of block play in early childhood has been well documented (see chapter 10). Block play supports social-emotional, physical, language, and cognitive development. Yet, if you go into a typical preschool classroom, you will probably see many more boys than girls in this area. Boys may discourage girls who want to visit the block area (Tokarz 2008). When girls do play with blocks, their play is more focused on representing their world and their role in the world. They build homes, stores, offices, and houses of worship and engage in behaviors typically associated with the female gender (supporting, affirming, and giving assistance) (Tokarz 2008). Often, girls are observed building castles as long, low structures that represent the fictitious castles in fairytales. Boys are less interested in social roles and tend to create new and innovative types of structures, often in isolation (Tokarz 2008). Boys and girls control the space in the area differently. Boys use physical aggression, are louder, and use more space. Girls avoid confrontation, and often the boys take over the area and disrupt the girls' play (MacNaughton 1997).

MacNaughton (1997) implemented four specific strategies in the block area to help increase girls' involvement in block building. These included putting materials such as dolls, doll clothes, and decorative fabrics into the area; opening the block area only to girls on certain days or times; combining the block area with the dramatic play area; and staying in the block area to intervene each time boys interfered with the girls' play. These strategies showed only limited success. The boys often came into the block area before the girls and moved the new materials or disrupted play on the days that the girls were supposed to be the only ones visiting that center. Additionally, although girls and boys did visit the combined block/dramatic play area, for the most part, they continued playing with the same types of gender roles as before (boys were rougher, louder, and more active, while girls enacted domestic roles). MacNaughton (1997) thus concluded that perhaps the block area is a place where power relationships between boys and girls are most evident and, as such, the boys usually win. The challenge for teachers is to create a more equitable space for girls to use as well.

The block area should have lots of unit blocks of many different sizes and shapes (for a detailed description, see *The Block Book* [Hirsch 1996]) and enough space for at least three children to play together. There should be a rug to muffle the noise of the blocks and lots of accessories, including figures of many types of people (babies, men, women, and children) of various races and ethnicities, animals, vehicles, and dollhouse furniture. Paper, writing tools, and craft sticks to label buildings and create street signs and maps are also important. Having two or more types of blocks helps to expand play (unit blocks, hollow blocks, and others).

Questions to Ask Yourself About the Block Area

Think about your own classroom or observe in someone else's classroom to answer these questions:

- Is the block area near the dramatic play area so that all children can move back and forth? Have you modeled bringing materials from the two areas together?
- When joining in children's block play, do you make it a point to encourage boys and girls to play together?
- Do you encourage the girls to put away the heavier blocks as often as the boys?
- When conflicts arise between the boys and girls playing there, is creative problem solving going on to ensure that no one is excluded "because they're a girl/boy"?
- Is the block area large enough to accommodate several small structures or one large elaborate one?

Resources to Add to the Block Area

The following is a list of materials that can be added to the block area that may encourage more girls to utilize the area. It also will allow the children to explore the possibilities of unusual accessories for their block structures.

- A basket of various adornments for block structures such as strings of beads and small fabric pieces (Strasser and Koeppel 2010).
- Dolls (boys and girls of various races and ethnicities).
- Lengths of brightly colored fabric in a variety of textures and sizes.
- A "found materials" shoebox, including cardboard tubes, large pieces of Styrofoam, a pulley with rope, and a steering wheel.
- An adult female (mother, grandmother, retiree) to play in the block area, as well as the female teacher and/or assistant teacher.

- Photos of women working as mechanics, constructions workers, electricians, plumbers, and architects.

Children's Books to Add to the Block Area
This Is Our House (Rosen 2005)
Arches to Zigzags (Crosbie 2000)
Mike Mulligan and His Steam Shovel (Burton 1943)
Girls Can Be Anything (Klein 1973)
David (Shannon 1991)
Annie and Company (McPhail 1991)
Tools (Morris 1998)
Roxaboxen (McLerran 1991)
Minerva Louise and the Red Truck (Stoeke 2002)
Raise the Roof! (Suen 2003)

OUTDOOR PLAY AREA

The teacher rings the "cleanup" bell, signifying that the children will be going outside in a few minutes. As usual, the boys hurry up to put their toys away so that they can be the first ones to get to the slide, the climber, and the tricycles. When they are all in the playground the teacher sees that while the boys are very active, some of the girls are playing in the playhouse and the rest are in the sandbox.

Research has shown that boys are more active and dominant than girls in outdoor play. They are given more access to playground space and large size toys (Evans 1998). While the difference is small, boys develop gross-motor skills slightly faster than girls. On preschool playgrounds, many times you will see boys engaging in highly active play while girls play more quietly in small groups. They may find shelter under a picnic table or behind a play structure. Sometimes, one child has crossed the gender boundary and is playing with the group of the opposite sex. It may concern some teachers that the girls don't seem to be getting enough gross-motor activity. However, every child's needs are different, and as long as children engage in a reasonable amount of gross-motor activity, their needs are most likely being met.

Some equipment really supports interactive and cooperative play (Schlank and Metzger 1997). Rocking boats require that children collectively figure out how to go fast or slow or get in and out. Parachutes, bean bags, balls, tunnels, and riding vehicles encourage children to play together, take turns, and actively engage.

Questions to Ask Yourself About Outdoor Play

Think about your own classroom or observe in someone else's classroom to answer these questions:

- Are families advised to send their daughters to school in clothing appropriate for active play?
- Are girls invited to take part in the physically challenging activities along with the boys?
- When children are engaging in highly active superhero play, are creative problem solving and conflict resolution being promoted?
- Are boys praised for their strength and speed more than the girls?
- In what ways is your outdoor area appealing to boys/girls? Is there an equal balance of both?

Resources to Add to Outdoor Areas

The following is a list of materials that can be added to outdoor areas that may entice less active children to participate in more gross-motor activities.

- Large pieces of fabric for running with, draping over play structures to create tunneling effects, and cocooning.
- Long streamers for children to hold while running. Children enjoy watching the streamers flutter while they move.
- An area where children can create obstacle courses using hula hoops, cones, balance beams, and tunnels.
- An area and materials for block building. Use wooden hollow blocks or large plastic ones. Cardboard postal boxes filled with sand or paper work as a no-cost alternative.

Children's Books to Add to the Outdoor Area

From Head to Toe (Carle 1999)
Dance (Jones 1998)
Everybody Needs a Rock (Baylor 1974)
We Like to Move: Exercise Is Fun (April 2006)

A Yoga Parade of Animals: A First Picture Book of Yoga for Children
(Mainland 1999)
Salta, Ranita, Salta! (Kalan 1994)

CONCLUSIONS

While research supports the notions that boys and girls often segregate themselves by gender in different play settings, play scenarios, and
interest areas in preschool, there are many things that teachers can do
to encourage them to begin to form social relationships, cooperate, and
join one another in play.

By making the classroom environment a place where children and
adults come together in nonstereotypical roles, and by carefully listening,
observing, and understanding why children are expressing themselves
the way they do, teachers can give their young students the tools for
problem solving, decision making, compassion, courage, and expressing
themselves as individuals—not just as "girls" or "boys."

REFERENCES

Benenson, J. F., and R. Del Bianco. 1997. Sex differences in children's play:
    Boys' and girls' responses to vulnerability. *Canadian Journal of Research in
    Early Childhood Education* 6, (2): 107–25.

Bhroin, M. N. 2007. A slice of life: The interrelationships among art, play and
    "real" life of the young child. *International Journal of Education and the Arts*
    8, (16): 1–25.

Copple, C., and S. Bredekamp. 2009. *Developmentally appropriate practice in
    early childhood programs.* 3rd ed. Washington, DC: National Association
    for the Education of Young Children.

Council on Interracial Books for Children. 1980. *Guidelines for selecting bias-
    free textbooks and storybooks.* New York: Council on Interracial Books
    for Children.

Crick, N. R., J. M. Ostrov, J. E. Burr, C. Cullerton-Sen, E. Jansen-Yeh, and P.
    Ralston. 2006. A longitudinal study of relational and physical aggression
    in preschool. *Journal of Applied Developmental Psychology* 27, (3): 254–68.

Evans, K. S. 1998. Combating gender disparity in education: Guidelines for
    early childhood educators. *Early Childhood Education Journal* 26, (2):
    83–87.

Fabes, R. A., C. L. Martin, and L. D. Hanish. 2004. The next 50 years: Considering gender as a context for understanding young children's peer relationships. *Merrill-Palmer Quarterly* 50, (3): 260–73.

Freeman, N. K. 2007. Preschoolers' perceptions of gender appropriate toys and their parents' beliefs about genderized behaviors: Miscommunication, mixed messages, or hidden truths? *Early Childhood Education Journal* 34, (5): 357–66.

Fromberg, D. P. 2002. *Play and meaning in early childhood education.* Boston: Allyn and Bacon.

Frost, J. L., S. C. Wortham, and R. S. Reifel. 2001. *Play and child development.* Upper Saddle River, NJ: Merrill Prentice Hall.

Gonzalez-Mena, J. 2005. *Foundations of early childhood education: Teaching children in a diverse society.* Boston: McGraw Hill.

Hagglund, S. 1993. The gender dimension in children's learning of prosocial competence in early educational settings. *European Early Childhood Education Research Journal* 1, (2): 67–80.

Hamanaka, S. 1999. *I look like a girl.* New York: Morrow Junior Books.

Hirsch, E. S., ed. 1996. *The block book.* 3rd ed. Washington, DC: National Association for the Education of Young Children.

Hoffman, M. 1991. *Amazing Grace.* New York: Dial Books for Young Readers.

Howe, J. 1999. *Horace and Morris but mostly Dolores.* New York: Aladdin Paperbacks.

Howe, N., L. Moller, B. Chambers, and H. Petrakos. 1993. The ecology of dramatic play centers and children's social and cognitive play. *Early Childhood Research Quarterly* 8, (2): 235–51.

Hyun, E., and D. H. Choi. 2004. Examination of young children's gender-doing and gender-bending in their play dynamics: A cross-cultural exploration. *International Journal of Early Childhood* 36, (1): 49–64.

Isenberg, J. P., and M. R. Jalongo. 2006. *Creative thinking and arts-based learning: Preschool through fourth grade.* Upper Saddle River, NJ: Pearson Merrill Prentice Hall.

Johnson, J. E., J. F. Christie, and F. Wardle. 2005. *Play, development, and early education.* Boston: Pearson Education.

Laevers, F., and L. Verboven. 2000. Gender related role patterns in preschool settings: Can "experiential education" make a difference? *European Early Childhood Education Research Journal* 8, (1): 25–42.

Lindsey, E. W., and J. Mize. 2001. Contextual differences in parent-child play: Implications for children's gender role development. *Sex Roles* 44 (3/4): 155–76.

Little, H. 2006. Children's risk-taking behaviour: Implications for early child-hood policy and practice. *International Journal of Early Years Education* 14 (2): 141–54.

MacNaughton, G. 1993. Gender, power, and racism: A case study of domestic play in early childhood. *Multicultural Teaching to Combat Racism in School and Community* 11 (3): 12–15.

———. 1997. Who's got the power? Rethinking gender equity strategies in early childhood. *International Journal of Early Years Education* 5 (1): 57–66.

———. 1999. Even pink tents have glass ceilings: Crossing the gender boundaries in pretend play. In *Child's play: Revisiting play in early childhood settings,* ed. E. Dau, 81–96. York, PA: Brookes Publishing.

McMurray, P. 1993. Gender experiences in an early childhood classroom through an ethnographic lens. Paper presented at the annual Meeting of the American Educational Research Association, New Orleans, LA.

Moskowitz, L. 2008. Helping boys and girls play together. *Teaching Young Children* (August): 24.

National Association for the Education of Young Children. 2008. Ten ways to paint without brushes. *Teaching Young Children* (August): 6–7.

Paley, V. G. 1984. *Boys and girls: Superheroes in the doll corner.* Chicago: University of Chicago Press.

Sandberg, A., and I. Pramling-Samuelsson. 2005. An interview study of gender difference in preschool teachers' attitudes toward children's play. *Early Childhood Education Journal* 32, (5): 297–305.

Scarlett, W. G., S. Naudeau, D. Salonius-Pasternak, and I. Ponte. 2005. *Children's play.* Thousand Oaks, CA: Sage Publications.

Schlank, C. H., and B. Metzger. 1997. *Together and equal: Fostering cooperative play and promoting gender equity in early childhood programs.* Boston: Allyn and Bacon.

Strasser, J., and L. M. Koeppel. 2010. Supporting play in the block area for girls and dramatic play for boys. *Teaching Young Children* 3 (1).

Tokarz, B. 2008. Block play: It's not just for boys anymore—strategies for encouraging girls' block play. *Exchange* (May/June): 68–71.

Van Hoorn, J., P. M. Nourot, B. Scales, and K. R. Alward. 2003. *Play at the center of the curriculum.* 3rd ed. Upper Saddle River, NJ: Merrill Prentice Hall.

Wellhousen, K. 1996. Do's and don'ts for eliminating hidden bias. *Childhood Education* 73 (1): 36–39.

White, M. 1998. The pink's run out!: The place of artmaking in young children's construction of the gendered self. In *Gender in early childhood,* ed. N. Yelland, 223–48. New York: Routledge.

Zambo, D., and W. G. Brozo. 2009. *Bright beginnings for boys: Engaging young boys in active literacy.* Newark, DE: International Reading Association.

TWELVE

Lessons Learned Early: Girls Wait

— Sonja de Groot Kim —

BEAU: MY FOOT TALKS

Beau uses the climbing unit differently from the other toddlers. They climb up the ladder in back of the unit, while Beau runs over to the sidebars right next to the slide. He climbs up quickly, holding on with both hands. When he gets to the top, he immediately lifts his leg over the railing and places one foot on the little platform at the top of the slide. It looks as if he is claiming the space for himself. There are no arguments, no one objects. Whoever is on the platform backs off to let Beau go first. He claims the slide casually and effectively.

In the above anecdote, two-year-old Beau displayed his skills as an expert communicator without using any words. He, or rather, his foot, told the other toddlers what his "rules" were for using the climber in the gym. His rules were simple, yet powerful: "I go first." The other toddlers all understood Beau's nonverbal language. They complied each time and backed off, letting him climb up from the side of the climber and go down the slide without waiting his turn. Since it was done unobtrusively with no objections by the other toddlers, the teachers did not seem to notice and there was no intervention.

This anecdote was one of numerous observations I carried out over an extended period of time in a suburban child development center. I spent four months observing in a toddler classroom for one-and-a-half to two-and-a-half-year-old children. Then, one year later, I spent five months in the classroom for two-and-a-half to three-and-a-half-year-old children. For the sake of brevity, I will call the latter group the young threes.

In this study, my initial interest was focused on the development of communication of two- to three-year-old children. I wanted to learn more about ways in which they made themselves understood and how they came to understand the intentions of their peers and their teachers (de Groot Kim 1999).

I wanted to observe the children's interactions and learn about the ways they expressed themselves verbally as well as nonverbally. How did children make sense of their world at this young age, with both emerging language skills and their nonverbal communication such as gestures, body language, and facial expressions? How did these very young children come to understand what other children wanted or didn't want to do, either in play or with materials, indoors or outside? How could they make the other children understand and respond to what they themselves wanted to get across? How could they let their teachers know what they wanted or needed or objected to? How could they "read" the others?

I was a nonparticipant observer, which means that I did not interact with the children unless they approached me, and then only briefly. Thus, I could focus on observing the daily routine in the classroom in as much detail as possible. Each time I entered the classroom, I positioned myself in an area near the children where I could observe activities and interactions without interruption for about two hours at a time.

This was unlike the classroom teachers—who were constantly occupied with taking care of and educating their young charges. I remembered when I taught toddlers and preschool-age children. Then, my coteacher and I observed and interacted with children simultaneously, an exciting and exhausting endeavor. We observed regularly, of course, but most of the time the observations were carried out during activity time. We carried small spiral notebooks in which we quickly jotted down observations. Afterwards, we reconstructed and discussed those observations and used them for future planning.

Now, as the proverbial fly on the wall, I had plenty of time to observe and document, to look for patterns of behavior and interactions, to develop emerging themes, and to draw interpretations and implications for practice. My task was to learn to *read* the communication patterns of the children and their teachers. I collected reams of observations about the toddler group. In my ongoing analysis and final interpretation, I noted the many ways in which these toddlers communicated with each other and with their teachers, but at that time, I did not connect them to any gender-related behavior. It was not until I observed for several weeks in the young threes classroom that I began to see behavior patterns in some of the three-year-old boys that jolted me back to memories of different yet similar ways of communicating by some toddler boys a year earlier.

I started reading the toddler field logs again. This "revisiting" the data proved to be critically important in allowing me to make gender-related connections between the behavior patterns of some of the toddlers and some of the young threes. I found that, both in the toddler room and in the young threes room, some boisterous boys (I called them the "loud boys") took part in very energetic play near the classroom door that led to the hallway. Each time, this type of play happened during transition time when the children changed from one activity to another, either going outdoors to the playground, to the gym (during inclement weather), or in small groups to the hallway for a play activity with one of the teachers. In each instance, the active boys left the classroom first. Leaving first gave these boys a number of advantages, which I will discuss later in this chapter.

Though the title of this chapter is "Lessons learned early: Girls wait," I did not arrive at this interpretation until I was well into my study. This might have been because I had become so accustomed to children's ways of interacting with each other that I missed clues as to what was going on below the surface. It was only when I returned to my earlier toddler observations and reanalyzed them that patterns of behavior that seemed gender-related emerged. In this chapter, I explore the myriad ways young children communicate their intentions with others, beginning in infancy. It is only when we recognize in ourselves, and in the children we care for, the desire and the capacity to make meaningful connections that we can truly help the children in our care learn and grow.

YOUNG CHILDREN'S BODY TALK—INFANTS AS SKILLED COMMUNICATORS

We know that infants from birth are social beings and are very responsive to people interacting with them. They coo, babble, and smile, and their caregivers interpret their sounds, movements, and gestures. All these interactive, nonverbal signs help to create close emotional ties between the adult and the child. Bennett (1993, 42) notes that "it can be argued that a rich store of interpersonal knowledge develops in the first year." Evidence of infants as social beings continues to emerge. According to McHale et al. (2008, 459), "These data may indicate that infants begin in the earliest months of life to grasp relationships and to exercise group sociability."

By eighteen months, the beginning of toddlerhood, the ability to create and maintain nonverbal connections with others is very strong. However, toddlers are now a bit more experienced with verbal language and many have some first words. It seems that we as adults are so excited when infants and toddlers begin to utter their first words that mean something, like "mama," "dada," "bye-bye," that we tend to concentrate on and encourage this verbal communication, and slowly begin to pay less attention to the ways children communicate nonverbally—their body talk—which is still present in abundance.

I did not observe in the older infant room for children from twelve to eighteen months. However, I did observe children this age (the "waddlers," as they were aptly called by the teachers in this center) on the playground where they sometimes joined the toddlers for outdoor play activities. One day, as I was observing, I noticed one of the waddlers walking by. It was Bobby, the same boy I had observed in the gym a few weeks earlier, when he had drawn my attention to the ceiling lights. He looked to be about fourteen months old and was an expert at communicating his intentions. When such a young child notices something of interest and, through pointing and gazing, shares this experience with others, it is considered a milestone in communication. It is also called "joint attention." Slaughter and McConnell (2003, 68) state, "There is no doubt that the behaviors of joint attention that are achieved by infants by the end of the first year of life allow them to engage in relatively complex social-communicative interactions."

In joint attention, the child draws another person's attention to something or some place, to share enjoyment of an object or of something she sees. She attracts the other person's attention by looking intently at that person and then pointing her finger at something or somebody she wants the other person to see as well. Parents and caregivers do the same when they say to the child, "Look at that," while pointing their finger at something a distance away, a passing car for example. The child then follows the direction of the finger and looks at the object. This joint attention behavior emerges between the ages of nine and fifteen months. It is considered such an important milestone that the absence of this kind of behavior is a reason for concern. According to Durocher (2005, 1), "Impairments in the development of joint attention skills are a hallmark of children with autism spectrum disorders." In the following vignette, we see how skilled Bobby was in using point and gaze to attract and hold my attention.

I'M TALKING TO THAT LADY

Sonja's Observation

One of the younger children, about fourteen months old, walks through the play yard. He looks at me and then up at the sky. He points his finger up and looks at me again. He says, "Eh, eh." He takes a few more steps, then he checks with me again, the same way. He smiles and keeps his finger stretched in the air. Once more he says, "Eh, eh."

Now I remember! This same boy, a few weeks ago, walked past me in the gym as I stood watching. He walked under the ceiling lights, looked at me, pointed up at the lights, and said, "Eh, eh." Now, he keeps looking at me while he walks, pointing his finger straight up in the air. He is talking to me!

A teacher walks over, and without talking, takes his hand, which is still pointing skyward, and walks with him to the gate. Why is he leaving like that?

Sonja: Speaking for Bobby

I know how to talk to people. You just keep looking at them and looking at them and then they see you. I know how to do that. I want to show that lady the sky. Look at that sky! I point my finger at the sky and tell her what I see. I smile and say, "Eh, eh." That means, "Look at that sky up there." She sees it too. She smiles. Now we're both looking at the sky. I like to tell people about all the things I see.

I showed her the lights in the gym the other day. I put my arm up and pointed at the lights and I said, "Eh, eh." I love to tell people about things I like! I like talking to that lady.

Hey, someone is taking my hand. I'm busy, I wasn't finished talking to that lady. Where are we going? Why are we leaving?

In the above vignette of Bobby in the gym and on the playground, we see him as a highly skilled communicator by the ripe old age of fourteen months! These examples may not seem directly related to gender in early childhood. However, in a very real sense, it is the essence of it. It demonstrates that we need to observe closely and patiently to understand what these very young children are trying to communicate, which is an attempt at creating and maintaining meaningful, interpersonal relationships with others (Berk 2008; Bruner 1990). They also learn that they can *talk* to us, using their body language, and that we acknowledge and respond to it. What a wonderful, empowering feeling for a young child!

In the vignette about Bobby, I gave verbal expression to this one-year-old's nonverbal communication. Giving voice to children's nonverbal ways of communicating is a challenge. We are not mind readers, and therefore it is a heavy responsibility for the person(s) studying these very young children to do so cautiously and with integrity. Speaking for the child rests on close study of children over a period of time and on careful interpretation of their behavior.

When I reread the vignette, I recalled that, at the time of the observation, I was annoyed at the teacher for interrupting my exchange with Bobby. She took his hand and, without saying a word, walked him out of the playground. She did not appear to realize that Bobby was in the middle of a conversation with me. She may not have understood what Bobby's gestures and facial expressions—in this case the pointing and gazing—meant in the context of development. Yet, in the busy life of an infant teacher, essential needs such as diapering and feeding the children are certainly a priority.

IN THE TODDLER ROOM: CHILDREN SENDING SIGNALS

The toddlers time and again found ways to let their teachers know what they needed. Oftentimes the teachers noticed and responded to their nonverbal requests for help. The toddlers' signals were frequently very subtle, such as moving a little closer to a teacher, displaying small movements, or making soft sounds, but the teachers recognized them and quickly responded. The following vignette shows how Kurt and Beau, two of the toddlers, quickly received the assistance they needed from their teachers Emma and Karen.

KURT: MY HAT IS STUCK

Kurt is the last child to finish the cupcake that Lea's mother brought in for Lea's birthday party. There are birthday hats as well, which Emma and Karen have put on each child. After eating and singing— the children eat, the teachers sing—the children leave the table for other activities. When Kurt is finished, he walks over to where I am sitting, points a finger at his head, and smiles. He is showing me his birthday hat. Next, he raises both hands slowly over his head, touches his hat, and very, very slowly first stretches it up and then forward a few inches. As he pulls, the expression on his face changes slowly. His eyes and eyebrows tighten into a frown and his mouth forms a tight little circle. He seems to anticipate something will happen, and he is correct. The rubber band gets stuck behind one ear. He freezes, holding the hat in the air with both hands. "Oh, oh," he says softly. Then again quietly, "Oh, oh." Karen looks in his direction and immediately walks over saying, "Oh, the rubber band got stuck?" She carefully removes the hat and brings it over to the counter. Kurt then wanders off.

BEAU: LIFT ME UP

In the gym, Beau is trying to climb on a soft foam structure about two feet high. His hands are planted firmly on the top and he unsuccessfully tries to swing his leg onto the foam structure too. The teacher stands a few feet away from him and doesn't seem to notice his efforts. Almost imperceptibly, Beau moves closer to her and again attempts to swing his leg onto the structure. This time the teacher notices, picks him up, and hoists him onto the structure.

This body talk was something I noticed throughout my observations in the toddler room as well as in the young threes room, and it led to my interpretation of "girls wait." During transition times, before leaving the classroom, three of the more active boys in the toddler room engaged in rough-and-tumble play (Garvey, 1990; Pellegrini and Smith 2005). The quieter boys and the girls never participated in this type of play even though they paid close attention to it. Most early childhood teachers are quite familiar with the appearance of rough-and-tumble play in their classrooms. It looks like fighting, but it is not real fighting—even though the children push and pull at each other, sometimes even rolling on the floor. Most of the time, there is little chance that play fighting turns into real fighting (Smith and Pellegrini 2008).

The active boys in the toddler room seemed to understand very well that it was not real fighting but pretend fighting, and their facial expressions showed this. They were laughing or had a nonthreatening expression on their faces as they tussled about. In my writing, I called it "puppy wrestling," since that seemed to be a more accurate description of the playfulness in the boys' actions. For them, it was a way to get to know each other.

I noted that the only time of the day this puppy wrestling occurred was just before outdoors time when the teachers were busy getting the children diapered and dressed for outdoor play or for the gym. The three puppy wrestlers—Eddy, Beau, and Ben—seemed to have a mutual understanding that the purpose of the activity was playful, pretend aggression. Miller, Trautner, and Ruble (2006, 295) note that "observational learning is important in conveying gender-typed information. Through these social experiences, children develop expectations and beliefs in themselves that are related to sex-typed behaviors."

During this transition time, one of the teachers changed diapers and dressed individual children, while the other teacher buttoned and zippered children's jackets and put on their hats. Usually, some of the children who were ready to go outdoors wandered over to the two fish tanks that stood, like guardians, on either side of the door. Each tank was filled with several goldfish and sat on a small table. The children who watched the fish seemed productively occupied while they waited to go outdoors. Here as well, I observed how some two-year-olds communicated with each other using sounds, facial expressions, gestures, and movements.

GETTING TO KNOW YOU

Mae and Kurt are standing together by one of the fish tanks. They seem to have their own little game going. Mae touches the fish tank and says, "Oh," while she laughs loudly. Kurt looks at Mae intently and imitates her exact actions and sounds. Mae watches him closely. Then, laughing loudly again, she touches the fish tank in another spot. Kurt immediately does the same. Now Mae places both hands on the table that holds the fish tank and begins to make some hopping, frog-like motions with her legs. Kurt looks at this as well and makes the same movements with his legs. They both laugh loudly, with Mae throwing her head back.

Then Emma asks Mae to go potty and the play ends.

While some children waited, Ben, Beau, and Eddy were the exceptions. As soon as they were dressed, they quickly ran to the door, where they began to push, shove, shake, and grab each other by the arms and shoulders. For a moment it looked as if there would be a real fight, but when I looked at the boys' facial expressions and their gestures and movements, there were no angry expressions nor was there anger in their pushing and pulling movements. On the contrary, they were laughing, and their movements seemed relaxed.

The teachers seemed to understand this and did not appear to be concerned. As a matter of fact, they ignored it, at least at first. The first time I observed this commotion, I tensed up and sat at the edge of my little chair, ready to jump up and intervene in case it was necessary. However, when I observed the reactions of Karen and Emma and recognized the playfulness in the boys' behavior, I sat back and relaxed as well. Ben, Beau, and Eddy (who were doing their puppy wrestling near the door) were the children the teacher regularly selected to go outdoors first.

While I documented that it was usually the same boys who left the classroom first, there was no evidence, during the time I was present, that the same boys had other gender-related advantages during their daily life in this classroom. Thus, I did not draw any conclusions about gender-related advantages for these three toddlers. However, in the course of this study, my focus began to include the teachers' interactions with the children, because their interactions seemed to set the tone for what transpired in the classroom. Was there evidence that Karen and Emma themselves sent messages to the children that could be construed as *gendered* messages, however subtle? The following anecdote presents an example of teachers bantering with each other.

FLOWERED PANTS FOR KURT?

What Happens

"Oh, you have flowers on your pants," Emma says to Kurt. "Are you wearing your sister's pants?" Kurt lies on the table, looking up at Emma. He does not respond. She finishes changing him, watches him walk away, and says to Karen, with a questioning look and in a doubtful voice, "They don't look worn though; they look new." Karen responds, "Well, maybe she bought them at a garage sale. Sometimes you get new things there."

My Comments

From Emma's and Karen's back-and-forth bantering within earshot of the children, it seemed that, according to their reasoning, flowered pants were not for boys. They could only be hand-me-downs or were bought at a garage sale. One would not buy new pants for boys that had a flower pattern.

My Questions

These conversations seem innocent, but I'm curious what messages they convey over time to young children about their gender identity. I ask myself, What does Kurt absorb and understand?

I interpreted Emma's casual comments about Kurt's flowered pants as gender-related. When Kurt had his diaper changed, he lay motionless on the dressing table looking straight up at Emma while she carried on a conversation with Karen across the room about his flowered pants. Since the room was small and the teachers talked across the room, most children could hear. So could I. At first, I listened with amusement to their seemingly innocent bantering. Then, suddenly, I wondered, "What are they *really* saying?" It seemed that Emma and Karen were transmitting subtle gender messages to Kurt as well as to other toddlers in this small room about what were and were not appropriate clothes for boys.

Memories washed over me as I recalled an earlier time in my life when I went shopping with our baby daughter, dressed in her blue snowsuit. I recalled people's comments, "What a nice little boy," and "Look at his eyes." They assumed that children dressed in blue were boys. We know that children under age two are already exposed to differences in their environment, such as clothes and toys, depending on whether they are boys or girls (Pomerleau et al. 1990). Harris (1998, 19) says that in the United States, parents treat their children the same, whether they are boys or girls, except for jobs around the house and the toys they buy for their children. Therefore, we can assume that young children grow up being surrounded by subtle and not-so-subtle gender-related messages.

IN THE YOUNG THREES CLASSROOM: HIGH-FIVING WORKS

The child development center where I carried out my observations had several large enclosed play yards as well as a large gymnasium where the teachers took the children during inclement weather. Sally and Bonny, the teachers of the young threes, seemed to be the only teachers in this center who took children to play in the hallway right outside the classroom. The hallways were wide, and one teacher took two or three children at a time into the hallway, playing active games such as hockey or sliding objects down an incline she had set up for them with blocks and planks from the gym.

Here I began to see an important phenomenon. When one of the teachers announced that it was time to clean up because they were going outdoors or to the gym, four of the active boys—Dean, Eddy, Freddy, and Kurt—quickly congregated near the door and started to act in physical, though controlled, ways. It was different from the rough-and-tumble play, the puppy wrestling as I called it, in the toddler room. I did not observe rough-and-tumble play (which is pretend aggression, not real aggression) in the young threes classroom at all. This was surprising to me, because this type of play tends to increase, not decrease, during children's early years (Bjorklund and Brown 1998; Pellegrini 2006).

Instead, I saw the active boys stand close to each other, talking very loudly and animatedly about going outside and what they were going to do when they got there. They did not push or shove or roll around on the floor as the toddlers had done, but they jumped up and down and touched each other in controlled ways—they held their arms up high and slapped each other's palms, giving each other "high-fives." Having spent several weeks in this classroom absorbing the culture and observing the communication patterns, I concluded that, most likely, the boys generally were not allowed to engage in this physical rough-and-tumble play. One of the teachers, Bonny, placed a strong emphasis on "being nice and playing nice" and rough-and-tumble did not exactly look "nice," even if it was good-natured.

I noticed that the teachers in the young threes classroom took the physically active boys out of the classroom first. After I'd observed this several weeks in a row, I suddenly had an "aha" moment. I had seen this happen before in the toddler room. Here, as in the toddler classroom, no girls were involved in rough-and-tumble play. It is the type of play that active boys typically engage in, whereas girls rarely do (Fromberg, 2005; Pellegrini, 2006). I also observed that the girls in this room were hanging back, waiting along the wall and away from all the commotion. In the toddler room, the girls were also staying away from the activity. They waited near the fish tanks. Thus, gender seemed to play an important role in social development (Banerjee and Lintern 2000; Maccoby 2000).

As I mentioned earlier, not all the boys were involved in the rough-and-tumble toddler play or the high-fives play of the young threes. The younger and the more reticent boys stayed back from the fray as well. There were many more boys than girls in the young threes classroom, so the girls were easy to spot during these transitions from one activity to another, and they were never in the first group leaving the classroom—with one exception. On this one occasion, one of the girls, Bridget, stood near the "high-fiving" boys and, when Sally opened the door, she dashed out with these boys. Bonny, the other teacher, called her back to help clean up, but she did not seem to hear it. Bridget made it out of the classroom with the boys, the only time that happened during my five months of observations in the young threes classroom.

Bridget Makes It Out First

I watch to see if any girls leave with the first group of boys. It seems, from what I have observed over time, that the girls wind up in the last group, waiting with a teacher for Tim and Ted (the boys who have been receiving speech therapy) to arrive at 11 a.m. Mandy and Elly are standing by the wall, patiently waiting, but Bridget seems determined to be with the first group. As she is heading out the door, I hear Bonny say, "Bridget, come back here." But Bridget doesn't hear (or pretends not to hear?) and disappears out the door in the surge of boys.

WHO'S IN CHARGE?

From what I observed, it seemed that the teachers were in charge of selecting children to leave the classroom to play in the gym or on the playground. At least, that is how it appeared in the toddler room and how I interpreted it. For the first few weeks in the young threes room, it seemed the teachers were in charge of selecting children as well. In addition to going to the gym or the playground, Sally, one of the teachers, regularly selected a few children to join her for a play activity in the hallway.

However, when I realized that the active boys in both the toddler and the young threes classrooms, using different methods, achieved the same result—going out first—I focused more closely on these transition times and documented the children's behaviors and the teachers' responses. In addition, I reexamined and reinterpreted my data from the toddler room. At first, it seemed that the teachers were selecting children to leave the classroom. After all, they were the adults, and they were the ones saying, "I'll take these children out first." The children just followed the adults' instructions. But did they really? Did loud boys unknowingly elicit certain responses from teachers? I wondered whether it could be the other way around: Did their behavior become purposeful once they learned it worked?

The classroom is the children's social world in which they learn to function competently as they gain skills in living with other children and their teachers on a daily basis. The children, however young they are, are not passive participants in this classroom culture. This would mean that they have no control over what goes on in their environment. When children are together with a group of their peers, they actively participate in constructing their own social world and in modifying, or getting around, adult rules to meet their own needs (Corsaro 2005). Denham (2006, 87) notes that "young children are learning to use emotional communication to express clear nonverbal messages about a social situation or relationship—for example, stamping feet or giving a hug." It seemed that the boys showed competence in applying what worked for them—loud behavior—so they could leave the classroom first.

In the case of the toddler boys, puppy wrestling was entirely typical behavior. At first, it may have occurred unintentionally near the door. However, when it resulted in the teacher taking them out first each time, the boys may have grasped that their behavior might have had something to do with it. Thus, unintentional behavior could have been transformed into intentional behavior.

In the case of the young threes, there was no puppy wrestling, possibly because the teachers' social rules in this classroom emphasized "being nice." Therefore, physical activity play seemed to have morphed into a more acceptable form of noisy behavior near the door. The end result was the same as in the toddler room. These boys went to the gym or outdoors or participated in hallway activities first. I documented how they spent a longer time outdoors, had earlier access to the most desirable toys, and, in hallway play, received more frequent and longer turns as well as more instruction and verbal feedback from their teachers.

WE WANNA RIDE!

Bridget, Elly, and Mandy's sad complaint, "We wanna ride!" which I describe next, was a significant moment. It symbolized a pattern whereby children often seemed to be selected for outdoors and special activities based on their gender, and it established how this gendered selection brought about fewer opportunities for girls. Most likely, the teachers were not aware of what was happening at these times. Whatever the motivation, the girls absorbed the message that "girls wait." Their turn might come later or, as shown below, it might not. The girls complied most of the time.

"WE WANNA RIDE!"

Bea, the temporary teacher, comes outside with several boys. They ride their tricycles with gusto up and down an incline in the yard for about twenty minutes. Then, Bridget, Eddy, Elly, and Mandy come outside and find tricycles to ride too. They start riding up and down the incline as well. Now there are eight children in that area. It's very crowded. Elly and Eddy each topple over once. They are not hurt and continue riding. Bea says there are too many children on tricycles and sends Bridget, Elly, and Mandy to another fenced-in area on the playground where they stand watching, their noses pressed against the fence. They yell, "We wanna ride, we wanna ride!" Bea tells them there are too many children on tricycles and they have to wait their turn. Kurt has left, but Dean, Freddy, and Eddy continue to ride. When it's time to go indoors for lunch, the girls haven't had a turn.

The teacher did not seem to consider the impact of her decision. When the girls loudly told her their request, "We wanna ride!" she told them to wait for their turn. The boys, three of whom had arrived twenty minutes before the girls came outside, continued riding until lunchtime. The three girls—Bridget, Elly, and Mandy—never did get their turn. This was the clearest example during my observations of the effect that the gendered selection of children for out-of-classroom play had on young girls. It seemed to be firmly established by the time I finished my study.

Social rules for expected behavior are, of course, a necessity in any environment where groups of people, in this case young children, spend a good portion of their day together playing, eating, and napping. Many social rules are explicit—they are clearly stated. Other social rules, such as the one informally established in these classrooms having to do with who left the classroom first, are more ambiguous since they are not explicit rules. They are a kind of hidden, underground rule. Neither children nor teachers may have been aware of it on a conscious level. But it was a rule nonetheless, and it was implemented regularly, with implications for some of the boys and for the girls. For the loud boys, it seemed to be "We go first," and for the girls, it seemed to be "Girls wait."

As I described in this chapter, it took me a painfully long time to begin to understand that very young children were, at a very early, impressionable age, exposed to gender-related messages in classrooms run by competent, caring, and conscientious teachers who seemed to be unaware of sending these messages. My goal is to share what I learned, with you, the reader, in anticipation that you will become more aware of your own and others' differentiated responses to the boys and girls in your care.

REFERENCES

Banerjee, R., and V. Lintern. 2000. Boys will be boys: The effect of social evaluation concerns on gender-typing. *Social Development* 9: 397–408.

Bennett, M., ed. 1993. *The development of social cognition: The child as psychologist.* New York: The Guilford Press.

Berk, L. E. 2008. *Child Development.* 8th ed. New York: Allyn and Bacon.

Bjorklund, D. F., and R. D. Brown. 1998. Physical play and cognitive development: Integrating activity, cognition, and education. *Child Development* 69: 604–6.

Bruner, J. 1990. *Acts of meaning.* Cambridge, MA: Harvard University Press.

Corsaro, W. A. 2005. *The sociology of childhood.* 2nd ed. Thousand Oaks, CA: Pine Forge Press.

de Groot Kim, S. 1999. Making sense of my world: The development of communication in two- and three-year-old children in a childcare center. PhD diss., New York University.

Denham, S. 2006. The emotional basis of learning and development in early childhood education. In *Handbook of research on the education of young children.* 2nd ed., ed. B. Spodek and O. N. Saracho, 85–103. Mahwah, NJ: Erlbaum.

Durocher, J. S. 2005. The critical role of joint attention in the treatment of children with autism spectrum disorders. Paper presented at the Autism Society of America's 36th National Conference on Autism Spectrum, Boston, MA.

Fromberg, D. P. 2005. The power of play: Gender issues in early childhood education. In *Gender and schooling in the early years,* ed. J. Koch and B. J. Irby, 1–27. Charlotte, NC: Information Age Publishing.

Garvey, C. 1990. *Play.* Cambridge: Harvard University Press.

Harris, J. R. 1998. *The nurture assumption: Why children turn out the way they do.* New York: Free Press.

Maccoby, E. E. 2000. *The two sexes: Growing apart and coming together.* Cambridge, MA: Harvard University Press.

McHale, J., E. Fivaz-Depeursinge, S. Dickstein, and M. Daley. 2008. New evidence for the social embeddedness of infants' early triangular capacities. *Family Process* 47 (4): 445–63.

Miller, C. F., H. M. Trautner, and D. Ruble. 2006. The role of stereotypes in children's preferences and behavior. In *Child psychology: A handbook of contemporary issues.* 2nd ed., ed. L. Balter and C. Tamis-Le Monda, 295. New York: Psychology Press/Taylor and Francis.

Pellegrini, A. D. 2006. Rough-and-tumble play from childhood through adolescence. In *Play from birth to twelve and beyond: Contexts, perspectives and meanings.* 2nd ed., ed. D. P. Fromberg and D. Bergen, 111–18. New York: Routledge.

Pellegrini, A. D., and P. K. Smith. 2005. *The nature of play: Great apes and humans.* New York: Guilford Press.

Pomerleau, A., D. Bolduc, G. Malcuit, and L. Cossette. 1990. Pink or blue: Environmental gender stereotypes in the first two years of life. *Sex Roles* 22 (5–6): 359–367.

Slaughter, V., and D. McConnell. 2003. Emergence of joint attention: Relationships between gaze following, social referencing, imitation, and naming in infancy. *Journal of Genetic Psychology* 164, (1): 54–71.

Smith, P. K., and A. Pellegrini. 2008. Learning through play. In *Encyclopedia on early childhood development* [online], ed. R. E. Tremblay, R. DeV. Peters, M. Boivin, 1–6. Montreal, Quebec: Centre of Excellence for Early Childhood Development. http://www.child-encyclopedia.com/documents/ Smith-PellegriniANGxp.pdf.

THIRTEEN

Men in Education:

REFRAMING THE GENDER ISSUE

— Shaun Johnson —

Much of what is written about male teachers follows a similar storyline: against a menacing tide of false accusations, scrutiny from colleagues, and skepticism from family and friends, the heroic male teacher forges ahead because of his unyielding dedication to the shaping of young minds. Stories of approbation amidst barriers to participation are a common theme in the male teacher research literature (see, for example, Cushman 2005; Mills, Hasse, and Charlton 2008; Smedley, 2007). It is likely these stories are meant to illustrate the significant obstacles precluding men from teaching, particularly at the early childhood and elementary levels. Foster and Newman (2005, 341) even coined the term "identity bruising," which "describes the 'knock backs' that male trainees and teachers receive during their initial experiences of the 'female' culture of the primary school."

I do not suggest that these stories are illegitimate or that they be ignored. In a later section of this chapter, I recommend ways to eliminate the negative experiences reported by many men in the classroom. I do, however, propose an alternative narrative to missing men in schools. Continued focus on the fear, false accusations, and suspicion surrounding male participation in education is problematic for two reasons. First, it is important not to valorize the caring that men do at the expense of the women teachers who already work hard with limited resources to teach children. Gaskell and Mullen (2006, 453) observed that female teachers are the ones associated "with low status and income, while the teaching men do garner more power and esteem."

The second problem deals with simply moving on with the discussion. The research literature has adequately addressed the issue of the unique obstacles that men face when entering the classroom (Cushman 2005; Coulter 1993; DeCorse and Vogtle 1997; Francis and Skelton 2001; Frank and Martino 2006; Goodman and Kelly 1988; King 1998; Mills, Hasse, and Charlton 2008; Montecinos and Nielson 2004; Roulston and Mills 2000; Sargent 2001; Skelton 2003; Smedley and Pepperell 2000; Sumison 1999). Perhaps there is some room for further investigation, yet it is well documented why men do not consider teaching as a career: gender stereotypes, fear of accusations, low status, and low remuneration relative to alternative careers. There is also evidence that the debate over the perilous conditions, the so-called "woman peril," caused by an overabundance of "feminizing" influences in public schools in the United States, already took place around the turn of the twentieth century (Hansot 1993). Given that the downward trend of men in classrooms persists after more than a century, it is obvious that focusing the discussion on peril, crisis, fear, and suspicion is not constructive, so perhaps it is time to change tactics.

CHAPTER LAYOUT

This chapter begins with a brief overview of the important distinctions between the male teacher problem and the larger conversation surrounding men in education. Also, for readers unfamiliar with the literature, there is a brief discussion of the typical reasons why men do not teach.

Subsequent to the overview of the problem is a proposed reframing of the discourse on men in education, which is necessary to breathe new life into the dialogue and solutions for the entrenched divisions of labor in teaching. The reframing focuses on why the prevailing conversation is problematic and what an alternative narrative has to offer.

Finally, it is essential in the collective enthusiasm to encourage more men to teach that educators do not reaffirm the same sexist, misogynistic, and conservative views of gender that end up reinforcing the disparities in teaching professions—that is, "gender categoricalism"—or separate roles for men and women, and caring for and nurturing children as "women's work." Much more than just programs to welcome men into schools and support their participation is needed. This chapter emphasizes how educators must be better prepared to discuss gender in the classroom so they no longer promote the kinds of traditional gender roles that prohibit education from becoming a more inclusive institution.

Problem and Conversation

Regarding male teachers, I refer on many occasions throughout this text to the distinct terms "problem" versus "conversation." Many in the education research community at home and abroad agree that the lack of male teachers is indeed a problem (see, for example, Carrington and Tomlin 2000; Driessen 2007; Lahelma 2000; Martino 2008; Mills 2004; Thornton and Bricheno 2006). There are two layers to this problem. On the one hand, it is certainly a problem of demographics: the statistical reality is that the fewness of male teachers is a global concern. Data from the United Nations Educational, Scientific and Cultural Organization (UNESCO) in 2005, for instance, showed a nearly universal disparity in instructional personnel from the pre-primary to upper-secondary levels in all so-called "developed countries." Specific to the United States, the National Education Association (NEA) reported during the 2005–6 school year that 24.4 percent of all teachers were male. The Bureau of Labor Statistics (BLS) reported in 2007 a negative trajectory for male teachers in postsecondary, secondary, elementary and middle school, and preschool respectively: 53.8, 43.1, 19.1, and 2.7 percent.

The first layer, or the demographic nature of the male teacher problem, is fairly obvious. The second and subtler layer to the male teacher problem is one of contradiction: the gender disparity in teaching is inconsistent with public education's mission of promoting democratic values, namely equity, equal opportunity, and egalitarianism. How can we take seriously the counsel of educators that children can grow up to be whomever they want to be if the educators' own profession is marred by an ongoing adherence to traditional and conservative gender values? In other words, the overwhelming lack of diversity in the teaching profession, which also pertains to gender, race, class, and sexual orientation, is out of sync with core democratic principles.

The male teacher conversation refers to the surrounding discourse of the problem, the reasons for its existence, and the solutions to getting more men into schools and child care centers. The themes within the prevailing conversation in the United States—boys' underachievement and male role modeling—are problematic in ways that confirm rather than challenge the sexist stereotypes telling men that teaching or caring professions are not for them.

In this chapter, I offer an alternative conversation emphasizing multiple gendered subjectivities and inclusivity of difference, which is more consistent with core democratic values. As with most things in life, those who call for more male teachers cannot have it both ways: prioritizing a single version of masculinity, defending traditional gender roles, and exploiting preexisting stereotypes for the purposes of recruitment will not bring more men into teaching. Moreover, preserving the status quo concerning gender and sexuality will likely continue the cycle of fear, suspicion, and scrutiny that follows male teachers and keeps other men from even considering teaching in the first place.

MEN OVER TIME

It is outside the scope of this chapter to reproduce an extensive history of men teaching. Nevertheless, to provide some historical context to the problem, two important observations must be included: the large-scale changes that drove men out of teaching in the latter half of the nineteenth century, and the possibility that the conventional wisdom of men "owning" the teaching profession before women took it over is partly false.

Teaching had always been considered a "procession more than a profession" (Clifford 1989, 319). Men in particular saw teaching as noble part-time work or a stepping-stone to bigger and better things. Grumet (1988, 37) observed that "the men who taught in these schools were often itinerants, working to finance their own college educations or preparation for the ministry or other professions." A confluence of rapid industrialization, urbanization, immigration, and an overall increase in the demand for compulsory education changed teaching's transient nature. The school population swelled as a result of rising interest, and the need for teachers soared throughout the late nineteenth and early twentieth centuries (Rury 1989). As society became more industrialized, other institutions followed suit, adopting the vocabularies and structure of "social efficiency" and the factory floor. This in turn transformed the hiring and credentialing of teachers from a "relatively loose" and "private affair" to something more rigorous and standardized (Sedlak 1989).

Becoming a teacher was a lengthier and more difficult process, requiring examinations and obligatory professional development. Educational professions followed the trends of other learned occupations regarding the abandonment of idiosyncratic hiring and licensure procedures in lieu of standardized credentials or certifications. These changes, along with the lengthening of the compulsory school year, made the short-term, part-time, stepping-stone possibilities of teaching impossible. A proliferation of higher-paid industrial jobs simply made teaching no longer worth the trouble, at least for many men.

How education reformers dealt with the staffing problem in teaching at this time dovetails with the problematic conventional wisdom that men dominated the teaching profession before women. Apple (1988, 58) urged us to "ask whether what has unfortunately been called the feminization of teaching actually concerns the same job." That is, the teaching profession did not exist before the large-scale changes that occurred leading to its predominantly female employ in the latter half of the nineteenth century. Previous to urbanization and industrialization, for example, teaching was a largely undemanding, short-term, nepotistic, and localized occupation. The professionalization of teaching could thusly be read as a "greater formalization of the educational system" overall; the hiring of cheaper labor, particularly women, lead to a "greater pressure for rationalization" so that this workforce could be satisfactorily controlled (64).

Simultaneous to the "professionalization" of teaching came its feminine ascendance. The teaching profession that we know today did not exist prior to this point. More rigorous credentialing, longer school terms, and an increased demand for compulsory schooling by the general public created a tremendous need for teachers (Carter 1989). Given that the opportunity cost of teaching was too high for many men where better-paid industrial labor was an option, the only way this demand could be assuaged was to hire droves of newly educated women to staff classrooms—at roughly a third of the cost. In effect, touting the feminine virtues of teaching and caring for children, which solidified its traditional status as "women's work," could be considered a convenient marketing ploy by early public education reformers to fill the school staffing void with a glut of fresh-faced female recruits whose career options were limited.

This historical analysis first implies that nothing is inherently feminine about the teaching profession. In fact, some pro-feminist scholars argued that the supervision of a mass of female subordinates by largely male administrators reflects a long-standing patriarchal or "masculinized" tradition within education at an institutional level (Grumet 1988; Keddie and Mills 2009; Walkerdine 1990). Teaching as "women's work" is simply a quaint relic of a time roughly around the turn of the twentieth century where the demand for teachers dovetailed with a league of newly educated women with limited career options.

Additionally, and a bit more controversially, Sugg (1978, 109) argued that "the feminization of teachers was an effectual solution to American ambivalence about education." In other words, allowing the overwhelming gender disparities in teaching to continue mirrors perfectly the low status and prestige of education. Even if the feminization of teaching emerged over one hundred years ago amidst sexism and stereotype, its perpetuation and acceptance reflects an institutionalized and professionally acceptable malaise toward who teaches children. It is now for us to decide: Is there something inherent about teaching that makes it more attractive to women or are we as its professionals defining teaching so narrowly that only a slim sliver of the male population joins it?

REASONS FOR SCARCITY

A considerable proportion of the male teacher literature focuses on the specific experiences of men in teaching: what were their thoughts at the time of entrance into preparation programs (Brookhart and Loadman 1996; Goodman 1987; Hansen and Mulholland 2005; Johnston, McKeown, and McEwen 1999; Montecinos and Nielson 2004; Smedley 2006) or an accounting of their negative encounters on the job (Cushman 2005; DeCorse and Vogtle 1997; Foster and Newman 2005; Mills, Haase, and Charlton 2008; Sargent 2001). These literatures boil down to two logical propositions: on the one hand, detailing the unique decision-making processes of current male teachers in the hopes of flipping those same switches in other men; and on the other, saving from attrition what few male teachers are left by ameliorating negative experiences. For those readers unfamiliar with this literature, the common reasons given for a lack of men in teaching as corroborated by a number of sources are low status or prestige, low salary and benefits, physical contact with children, and gender stereotypes (Cushman 2005; Drudy et al. 2005; Nelson 2002; Thornton and Bricheno 2006; Sargent 2001).

Status and Prestige

Ingersoll (2003, 2) cites "teacher bashing" as our second national pastime in the United States, finding "a pervasive sense of disparagement for teachers and the teaching occupation. [The author] would often hear that teachers did not work very hard, were not very smart, were overpaid and had easy jobs because of their long summer vacations." Such rage about teachers may indeed come from the lay attitude that anyone can teach. According to Lortie (1975), this precludes the teaching profession from developing a highly specialized "technical subculture" inaccessible to the average person. "A specialized knowledge base" is only one among other characteristics that Talbert and McLaughlin (1994, 126) argued as limiting teaching to semiprofessional status: "Shared standards of practice, a strong service ethic, or commitment to meeting clients' needs, strong personal identity with, and commitment to, the occupation, and collegial versus bureaucratic control over entry, performance evaluations, and retention in the profession."

Currently, even men in the profession who themselves flouted a degree of gender stereotyping to enter the classroom try to exploit those same stereotypes to find higher-status positions. Men who want to stay in education compensate by taking better-paid and higher-status administrative positions. It is also not unusual for male teachers to be coerced out of the classroom and into administration (Thornton and Bricheno 2000). Williams (1992, 297) defined this phenomenon of coercive promotion specific to men as the "glass escalator effect." In this case, working in a predominantly female profession causes internal conflicts of masculinity that are resolved by channeling men into more masculine specialties, "which ironically [means] being 'tracked' into better paying and more prestigious specialties." The implication here is that a process of discrimination based on sex exists within the teaching profession itself. Allan (1994, 126) corroborated the presence of several distinct advantages to being a male in the teaching profession, such as "initial advantages offered by affirmative action, welcoming male principals, and widespread public perception of the need for more male role models in the socialization of young children."

Salary and Benefits

Lack of financial incentives to teach relative to other professional occupations is one important reason why the nonpecuniary rewards of teaching are typically emphasized, such as interpersonal relationships with children and a close bond to the community (Carter 1989). Many teachers cite their desire to work with children as one of the most important reasons they chose the profession (Drudy et al. 2005). But the salary or wage issue is problematized because it may affect men and women teachers differently. Lortie (1975) contended that the opportunity costs of teaching are higher for men, since they value the financial rewards of their work and seek occupations that pay more. Women experience fewer career options overall and might not seek professions that directly lead to vast material wealth.

Because of competing opportunities for men, teaching is ultimately less financially attractive. In an economic analysis of various occupational salaries in Britain, Dolton and Chung (2004) calculated a more substantial loss of lifetime earnings for men if they became schoolteachers. Verdugo and Schneider (1994) even discovered wage discrimination within the teaching profession, a disparity benefiting men up to at least 5 percent of contract salary. As history demonstrated, however, there are continually stereotypical ways to subsidize male participation in teaching, such as the differential access to promotional opportunities (Jacobs 1993; Williams 1992). DeCorse and Vogtle (1997) contended that many men in teaching highly value alternatives to compensation found in the frequent holiday vacations, summers off, and even ease of transition to teaching as a second career. Ultimately, some men already in teaching do acknowledge that teaching is a well-paying job (Johnston, McKeown, and McEwen 1999). This is certainly true for many men that I interviewed in my dissertation research on men in education. So, it may be all a matter of perspective. If the salary keeps men out, the ones who get in end up feeling quite comfortable.

Physical Contact with Children

Regarding what discussion there is in the male teacher literature about perceived improprieties, Sumison (1999, 459) made an interesting observation in her single case study about a male early childhood worker: "The relatively low pay and status, and lack of other socially acceptable rewards for men who choose to work in childcare fuel these inherent suspicions." It is thusly implied that no man in his right mind would put up with any of what has been discussed already if he was not a pedophile and wanted ready access to children. Men certainly utilize caution when it comes to even the most innocuous forms of care and interaction with students. A male teacher in an interview study by Smedley and Pepperell (2000) referred to this position as a "no man's land." This image implies a stalemate or limbo between what many male teachers feel in their heart as the right thing to do for their students and the arm's length at which many others in society feel these men need to be kept.

Further evidence from the empirical literature suggests that suspicions of child abuse or other potential improprieties lead to greater scrutiny of men from peers and the larger community (Sargent 2001). Extra surveillance motivates men to engage in a number of compensatory habits, such as an overreliance on verbal forms of praise or an active avoidance of discomforting situations altogether. Other teachers may respond "by punishing student displays of affection. They also increased surveillance of student activities. In the end, teachers may have deflected attention from questions about their own desires by focusing on those of students" (Blount 2005, 2). Regardless of these efforts, many men find it difficult to escape the deeply ingrained fear of male teachers as potential child abusers, even if this flies in the face of statistics about actual abuse risk (Cushman 2005).

Complicating the matter further is the erroneous connection between child abuse and sexuality, or that the possibility of being gay makes one a pedophile and vice versa, which is a fear expressed by many male teachers (Skelton 2003). Fear of caring for younger children is part and parcel of a pervasive homophobia in society and the avoidance of behaviors inconsistent with a stereotyped version of masculinity. Anxieties over being seen as gay or a "soft male" continue to confront current male teachers and likely discourage others from teaching (Sargent 2001). One silver lining in all of this is the contention that apprehension about caring for children and the concomitant suspicions are highest for preservice and new teachers, abating somewhat as those teachers get more experience (Hansen and Mulholland 2005). The question remains: Is that because the male teachers get over their fears or that the school community at large needs time to get over their own? King (1998, 82) cautioned that as long as "care is a domain or relationship that is ascribed to women, then men's enactment of care behavior will be marginalized and viewed with suspicion."

Gender Stereotypes

Patriarchy as a system of power and oppression has over time defined and enforced an acceptable set of masculine practices (Connell 1987). This also means avoiding the feminine, which includes teaching because it is considered women's work. Combine that with the lowered prestige of the profession due to associations with second-class femininity along with the pressures for men to seek esteem through their work, and we ultimately have the masculine third rail that is classroom teaching. Additionally, stereotypes discourage a preponderance of men from teaching because of pressures to be the breadwinner—which in turn confers status—and out of fear of approbation for perceived sexual deviance incorporating both homosexuality and child sexual abuse.

The concept of hegemonic masculinity extensively theorized by Australian sociologist Connell (1987, 74) alludes to a system of power relations that establishes clear divisions of labor and shapes sexual desire to subordinate women and dominate men. A spate of relatively recent literature on male teachers (most of which was done overseas) increasingly utilizes the concepts hegemonic masculinity and multiple masculine subjectivities in analyses of the gender disparities in teaching (Carrington and Skelton 2003; Francis and Skelton 2001; Lingard 2003; Martino 2008; Martino and Kheler 2006; Mills 2000; Mills, Hasse, and Charlton 2008; Mills 2004; Roulston and Mills 2000; Skelton 1998, 2003; Sumison 1999, 2000). The fact that teaching violates masculine norms is a central organizing construct of this literature.

Education and its professionals play a significant role in shaping cultural attitudes. Moreover, schools in particular are powerful agents of socialization and work closely in a systemic relationship with other institutions to create a harmonious front of acceptable gender roles (Connell 1987). As such, according to Keddie (2008, 581), "teaching-as-usual discourses can be transformed to allow an environment that is conducive to teachers and students theorizing themselves in ways that problematize and transform the inequitable relations that contribute to gender injustice." Male teachers are to an extent transformative figures in the classroom. It may behoove them to accept some responsibility for interrupting the scripts of traditional masculinity (Frank and Martino 2006; Martino and Berrill 2003); it may also be important for entire schools to critically examine how their programs espouse only certain types of masculinity (Martino, Lingard, and Mills 2004).

This leadership role—that both male teachers and schools can take—of encouraging more progressive gender values treads dangerously close to the role-modeling debate that I discuss shortly. One fundamental problem with espousing male teachers as masculine role models is the absence of a precise definition for reformers, educators, and policymakers of what is to be modeled and how to go about modeling it (Francis and Skelton 2001). The bottom line is that educators and the general public should not become so enthusiastic about attracting men to education without acknowledging what values these teachers, or all teachers for that matter, have about gender and masculinity, in particular. Without focusing on the values, cultural norms, and stereotypes that contribute to the male teacher problem initially, the disparity will likely continue as it has for yet another century.

REFRAMING THE CONVERSATION

As stated previously, the male teacher problem is one of both demographics and contradiction. The persistent gender disparity in teaching conflicts with the messages and values we expect our schools to promote. If education and its professionals play a significant role in shaping cultural attitudes, then it should concern us that the current attitudes implied by teacher demographics are fraught with sexism, stereotype, and a division of labor based on traditional gender roles. Despite good intentions, the mainstream calls to reform teacher demographics (or the conversation surrounding male teachers in particular) rely on sexism and stereotype to instill some urgency and attract males to the profession.

The "Boys Crisis"

A relatively recent shift in education policy circles in the United States and around the world focuses attention on the specific needs of boys in schools (Francis and Skelton 2005). Such a shift is likely part of the larger "backlash" against feminist progress, a movement brought to the forefront of feminism by journalist Susan Faludi (1991, 1999). This discourse on boys is preoccupied with student achievement and standardized testing. Its primary communicative vehicle is what Weaver-Hightower (2003, 476) called "popular rhetorical literature" that appeals to backlash politics, populist panic propagated by the mainstream media, parental concerns over their child's education, and spices up old ideas with the "thrill of the new." Mills (2003, 59) aptly terms texts focused on an unconfirmed crisis of male underachievement as "backlash blockbusters" because they are emblematic of the antifeminist movement Faludi warned us about and attempt to popularize the discussion to "re-establish boys and men as the privileged subjects within educational discourse."

The call for male teachers is inevitably wrapped up into crisis discourse because men in education are going to apparently resuscitate young males from the clutches of a misguided feminism within our nation's public schools. On the one hand, many crisis proponents use standardized test data, school dropout rates, college entrance demographics, and suspension or expulsion statistics to justify a crisis. Some evidence in the numbers indicates that males currently do less well in school, be it grades, class rank, retention, graduation, or college entrance (Kimmel 2006). One significant problem with a reliance on the raw statistical data is the overwhelming ambiguity. According to the National Center for Education Statistics (NCES), in 2007, 52.5 percent of all males versus 63 percent of all females between the ages of twenty-five to twenty-nine completed some college. For young men, this has been a decrease in only three percentage points from its 55.1 percent high in 2000. One question: What constitutes use of the term crisis? In addition, less than half (45.9 percent) of black males and a dismal 28.2 percent of Hispanic males completed some college in the same age range. Second question: What boys are they talking about?

Another justification for more male teachers given by boys-crisis proponents deals with male role modeling: an increase in the numbers of men in classrooms somehow leads to greater school satisfaction for boys, in turn benefiting their overall achievement. This is further folded into concerns raised about fatherlessness and the ascendance of nontraditional family structures (Martino and Kehler 2006). Crisis authors suggest that only men can model a "gentlemanly attitude" for young boys, which ultimately leads to success in school and life (Sax 2008, 166). More specifically, crisis author Sommers (2000, 162) underscored the perfect classroom environment for boys as only a male teacher could bring: "The class is didactic and teacher-fronted. It involves sharp questions and answers, and constantly checking understanding. Discipline is clear-cut—if homework isn't presented, it is completed in a detention. There is no discussion."

There are several problems with the male role modeling argument. First, Bricheno and Thornton (2007, 394) discovered that very few students actually view their teachers as role models; boys overwhelmingly cited athletes as people they most admire, although—the authors contend—"the term 'role model' can be interpreted in several different ways, with differential emphasis placed on different parts of the definition ('respect,' 'follow,' 'look up to' or 'want to be like')." Another problem is the untenable link between the gender of the teacher and overall student achievement or satisfaction measures (Carrington, Tymms, and Merrell 2005; Ehrenberg, Goldhaber, and Brewer 1995; Francis et al. 2008; Gold and Reis 1982). A boon to student achievement, especially for boys, is a fundamental part of the role modeling view: boys will like school more and thus be more successful if they see a man in the classroom.

There is finally the untested assumption that men actually know what it means to be a role model in the classroom. Ultimately, who gets to decide how manhood is modeled in the classroom and what salient features are necessary for it to be successful? Sargent (2001, 118) in his discussions with male teachers found their descriptions of role modeling for boys devoid of specific details and stunningly "colorless and vague and [lacking] any sense of being proactive." There is also abundant evidence, moreover, from the research literature that male teachers may actually reinforce rather than challenge sexist stereotypes (Allan 1994; Cook 1997; DeCorse and Vogtle 1997; Goodman 1987; Jamison 2000; Montecinos and Nielsen 2004; Roulston and Mills 2000; Skelton 2003).

What does all of this mean? To put it bluntly, solving the male teacher problem is unlikely if it continues to be debated based on the terms set by crisis proponents. Their justifications for more male teachers are predicated on one real definition of masculinity that must be modeled for young boys in the classroom. However, not many can agree on either how this works or what exactly should be modeled. Crisis proponents also claim that the feminist project is complete and boys should now be the focus. But it is unclear what boys are being discussed and whether a crisis actually exists. Given the prevalence of this kind of rhetoric in the United States and the continuation of the male teacher problem, it is clear that an alternative way to discuss male teachers is warranted.

ALTERNATIVE CONVERSATION

An alternative narrative is needed for discussing the male teacher problem that places more of the onus on the cultural values precluding males' participation rather than exploiting stereotypes to make teaching more attractive to men. In emphasizing the cultural values that discourage diversity in education's workforce, all of society and especially educators are responsible for turning the tide. This new perspective also cautions that values are more important than demographics. That is, change needs to come from a shift in the conversation rather than simply having more men in schools. If newly hired male teachers are either ineffective or reinforce traditional stereotypes, then it is better not to have them at all. With that, there are two fundamental concepts to this alternative conversation on male teachers. I will first give a brief overview of the key concept and then discuss how it works regarding men in education.

The first layer to the alternative narrative deals with multiple subjectivities, a concept that relies heavily on "hegemonic masculinity," as developed by Connell (1987, 1995). Through a complex web of social, political, economic, and institutional forces, this hegemonic or dominant form of masculinity marginalizes other men and subordinates women, leaving the door open to an exciting proposition: that multiple forms of masculine subjectivities exist apart from the cultural ideal constantly espoused in the media and defended by social norms. To pluralize masculinity to "masculinities" is a simple grammatical change, yet a huge conceptual leap for many people traditionally accustomed to the essentialist categories of man and woman.

A great deal of research has already begun the collective embrace of the male teacher problem, boys' education, and progressive or profeminist work on masculinity (Connell 1996; Francis and Skelton 2005; Johannesson 2004; Keddie 2006, 2008; Kimmel 1996, 2006; Lingard and Douglas 1999; Mac An Ghaill 1996; Martino 2008; Martino and Berril 2003; Martino, Lingard, and Mills 2004; Mead 2006; Mills 2004; Renold 2004; Titus 2004). This literature and the alternative perspective presented here contend that men are encouraged by society to avoid the feminine. Given that teaching is considered "women's work," men must avoid this kind of work lest they be scrutinized. Teaching also suffers low status and low pay relative to other career options open to men. Persistent pressures to provide for their families as the primary wage earner add to the problem. Embracing the concept of multiple masculine subjectivities means there are numerous ways to forge one's path as a male in society, which include working with children and young people. Defending a single definition of masculinity closes opportunities; accepting multiple masculine practices encourages new ones without the fear of reprobation that discourages many men from teaching.

The second fundamental concept is the inclusivity of difference, which highlights the need to remove any social hierarchy that legitimizes one practice of gender over another. Specifically regarding masculinity, for example, excessive consumption of meat products, a custom of traditional manhood, would not be valued any more highly than an affinity for arugula, the effete salad green highlighted in the 2008 presidential election to "feminize" Barack Obama. A culture of inclusivity and legitimacy of differences based on class, race, gender, and sexual orientation takes democracy as a political structure and translates it to a cultural framework that governs our everyday lives and how we treat one another (Maloutas 2006). Thus, democratic values in governance must be additionally transmutable to cultural values, or how we live our social lives within a democracy. To create a gender-inclusive society, the power of the people to govern themselves instantaneously translates to the power of all gendered subjectivities to access equal opportunities without recrimination.

The acknowledgment that men can teach and care for children must be supported by a larger society that legitimizes the inevitable differences that each individual citizen brings to the table. No one should feel they are incapable of seeking out desirable opportunities because that practice would violate cultural norms against their participation. More specifically, men who teach or engage in other so-called feminine practices are choosing a different path regarding their gender because it challenges prevailing norms. The negative experiences, scrutiny, or outright avoidance of teaching altogether by men is evidence of society's continued inability to legitimize alternatives to mainstream masculinity.

Rerooting Solutions

We must usher in a new era concerning the male teacher problem and how it is discussed. The demographic trends within the profession show that whatever is being done is not working. The alternative narrative encourages male teachers based on an ethos of possibility as opposed to an ethic of balance. In other words, the boys' crisis commentary encourages male teachers based on parity, but does so in a manner that reinforces stereotypes, namely that the male role must be adequately represented in an institution dominated by women. This says nothing of the kinds of teachers involved or what these men are necessarily doing in their roles as male educators—just that they are in the company of children and that is enough. Shifting the debate away from simply attracting male teachers and focusing more on their presence is symptomatic of a greater shift in prevailing gender values and that both men and women teachers can propagate that shift for future generations.

By rerooting solutions I mean that future efforts to make teaching a more diverse profession should be based on languages and vocabularies consistent with multiple subjectivities and an inclusivity of difference. First, it is problematic to, for instance, complain that men do not teach while simultaneously recommending that the profession be described in more "active" terms or tout the ability of men to coach sports teams. All this says is that men are inherently active and love watching sports. There are plenty of men who dislike sports, so how can they be included? Second, it is essential to encourage other kinds of diversities in teaching complementary to gender. Encouraging multiple ways of being and legitimizing those differences covers everything from gender and social class to sexual orientation. Basing solutions to the male teacher problem on a new conversation may look different in various locations within P-16 education, yet these must work in concert if there is going to be progress.

Teacher Preparation

Gender is not adequately dealt with at the teacher preparation level, where most of the discussions focus on feminist equity and school law in terms of sexual harassment. Regarding the latter, male preservice teachers typically hear about how they are not to be alone in the classroom with a female student. This is about as far as many teacher trainees get in discussing gender.

Teacher preparation programs need to include new areas of scholarship in gender studies such as recent sociologies of masculinity and queer theories. Treating boys and girls equally in classrooms is certainly an important problem and should continue to be discussed in colleges of education. But many new teachers are lured into the same trap of the gender binary that defines separate roles for men and women. These are precisely the kinds of ideas that discourage men from teaching. Teachers need to question their own assumptions about gender and recognize their power to end the cycles of homophobia and misogyny in their classrooms. This is unlikely to happen if the conversation is limited to equality.

New courses need to be designed and interdisciplinary relation-ships should be forged so education professors or lecturers are no longer closed off from new gender scholarship and research. Ongoing profes-sional development for teachers currently in the classroom can be initi-ated, but these need not focus simply on boy- or girl-friendly teaching strategies. It is more often the case that gender-specific teaching strate-gies sound a lot like good teaching and can work for all students. The fundamental idea here is to focus less on the male teachers—the fear and scrutiny—and alternatively refocus on the cultural conditions that leave them out of the classroom in the first place.

CONCLUSION

It certainly is mysterious that so many men refuse teaching as a pro-fession while a great number of women choose it. If not for power-ful social, cultural, and economic factors precluding male participation and shuffling women to the classrooms, things might be very different. Consider the following quote from Rubin's (1975, 87) essay on women: "A woman is a woman. She only becomes a domestic, a wife, a chattel, a playboy bunny, a prostitute, or a human Dictaphone in certain relations. Torn from these relationships, she is no more the helpmate of man than gold in itself is money." "Teacher" could easily substitute "woman" and with the addition of a litany of denigrating stereotypes about educa-tors. The whole notion that a teacher is a woman and only becomes a highly scrutinized state employee, a glorified babysitter, a schoolmarm, a twenty-something MRS major waiting for a husband, or a business school write-off is only true because of socially constructed ideas. Imag-ine for a moment that certain authorities, say the president of the United States, declared that from this day forward teaching finally earned its rightful status as an intellectual profession, with all the commensurate rights and privileges. Suddenly, from one minute to the next, the United States would find itself with millions of new female intellectuals, which would be a frightening proposition for some people.

Understanding the singular experiences of male educators should continue to be an important empirical exercise within the research on gender and education, particularly regarding the ongoing populist com-mentary surrounding the so-called "boys crisis." The focus, however, should be neither entirely on the experiences of men in classrooms nor necessarily on improving their lot. This is not to say that I am insensitive to the negative experiences of men in the classroom or issues of homophobia, pedophilia, and the insidious connections between the two that in many cases lead to a greater scrutiny of the teaching that men perform. To the contrary, I consider myself to be part of a profeminist ideological camp that is intent on attenuating the negative scrutiny based on gender and sexuality.

The sexist conditions that valorize hegemonic forms of masculine practice are the same conditions precluding men from teaching because of its classification as women's work. Thus, the focus needs to be on identifying the cultural conditions limiting male participation in teaching, how they prohibit teaching as masculine practice, and how to adjust those conditions so that teaching becomes a more diverse profession. A greater proportion of men in teaching, in conjunction with a commensurate welcoming of intersectional identities (for example, race, class, and sexual orientation) might be an important first step in an overall shift in gender relations. This would lead to a valuation of multiple ways of expressing one's gendered identity and the available opportunity to practice within the marketplace forms of identity that are contrary to dominant expectations. Thus, a larger number of men may feel comfortable working with children once the fear of approbation and negative scrutiny have been lifted.

The field of early childhood education plays a crucial role in changing the current predicament. Young children take their first wobbly steps into this gendered world through the doors of our elementary classrooms and child care centers. The public and parents trust that educators are going to bestow on their children the adventure of new content and understanding, of math and language, as well as the basic values that forge a common humanity. Parents do not, however, expect that their children's teachers expose them to division and discrimination.

At the present time the mainstream discussion occurring in our schools emphasizes separate roles for boys and girls, separate toys, hobbies, and even separate colors. Given that the jury is still largely out on the scientific or biological basis for these gendered divisions, the situation plays out just the same year after year. Why does this continue? Moreover, when will we learn that something as seemingly flippant as "boys will be boys" will, compounded over several years with interest, encourage the same kinds of division and discrimination that teaches children, namely young boys, that teaching, caring, and nurturance are simply not for them?

To promote the kind of change necessary to make teaching a more inclusive profession, we as a society—especially educators—must rethink how we can model a more inclusive and nondiscriminatory perception of gender for children. Early childhood educators in particular direct in both explicit and implicit ways how children perform and perceive their gendered identities at a very crucial time in their lives—one that they do not get to repeat. Before education reformers look to the next program or initiative to solve the male teacher problem, it is perhaps best to start immediately as educators by looking at what kinds of values we model for children for several hours every day.

REFERENCES

Allan, J. 1994. Anomaly as exemplar: The meanings of role modeling for men elementary teachers. Dubuque, IA: Tri-College Department of Education (Eric Document Reproduction Service No. ED 378 190).

Apple, M. 1988. *Teachers and texts: A political economy of class and gender relations in education.* New York: Routledge.

Blount, J. 2005. *Fit to teach: Same-sex desire, gender, and school work in the twentieth century.* New York: State University of New York Press.

Bricheno, P., and M. Thornton. 2007. Role model, hero or champion? Children's views concerning role models. *Educational Research* 49 (4): 383–96.

Brookhart, S., and W. Loadman. 1996. Characteristics of male elementary teachers in the U.S.A. at teacher education program entry and exit. *Teaching and Teacher Education* 12 (2): 197–210.

Bureau of Labor Statistics. 2007. Employed persons by detailed occupation, sex, race, and Hispanic or Latino ethnicity, 2007. http://www.bls.gov/cps/cpsaat11.pdf.

Carrington, B., and C. Skelton. 2003. Re-thinking "role models": Equal opportunities in teacher recruitment in England and Wales. *Journal of Education Policy* 18 (3): 253–65.

Carrington, B., and R. Tomlin. 2000. Towards a more inclusive profession: Teacher recruitment and ethnicity. *European Journal of Teacher Education* 23 (2): 139–57.

Carrington, B., P. Tymms, and C. Merrell. 2005. Role models, school improvement and the "gender gap"—Do men bring out the best in boys and women the best in girls? Paper presented at the European Association for Research on Learning and Instruction 2005 Conference, University of Nicosia.

Carter, S. B. 1989. Incentives and rewards to teaching. In *American teachers: Histories of a profession at work,* D. Warren, ed., 49–62. New York: MacMillan.

Clifford, G. J. 1989. Man/woman/teacher: Gender, family, and career in American educational history. In *American teachers: Histories of a profession at work,* D. Warren, ed., 293–343. New York: MacMillan.

Connell, R. W. 1987. *Gender and power: Society, the person, and sexual politics.* Stanford: Stanford University Press.

———. 1995. *Masculinities.* Berkeley: University of California Press.

———. 1996. Teaching the boys: New Research on masculinity, and gender strategies for schools. *Teachers College Record* 98 (2): 206–35.

Cook, A. F. 1997. Perceptions and beliefs regarding men in elementary and early childhood education. *Eastern Education Journal* 26:29–33.

Coulter, R. P., and M. McNay. 1993. Exploring men's experiences as elementary school teachers. *Canadian Journal of Education* 18 (4): 398–413.

Cushman, P. 2005. Let's hear it from the males: Issues facing male primary school teachers. *Teaching and Teacher Education* 21 (3): 227–40.

DeCorse, C. J., and S. Vogtle. 1997. In a complex voice: The contradictions of male elementary teachers' career choice and professional identity. *Journal of Teacher Education* 48:37–46.

Dolton, P., and T. P. Chung. 2004. The rate of return on teaching: How does it compare to other graduate jobs? *National Institute Economic Review* 190 (1): 89–103.

Driessen, G. 2007. The feminization of primary education: Effects of teachers' sex on pupil achievement, attitudes and behavior. *Review of Education* 53: 183–203.

Drudy, S., M. Martin, M. Woods, and J. O'Flynn. 2005. *Men in the classroom: Gender imbalances in teaching.* London: Routledge.

Ehrenberg, R. G., D. Goldhaber, and D. J. Brewer. 1995. Do teachers' race, gender, and ethnicity matter? Evidence from the national educational longitudinal study of 1988. *Industrial and Labor Relations Review* 48 (3): 547–61.

Faludi, S. 1991. *Backlash: The undeclared war against American women.* New York: Doubleday.

———. 1999. *Stiffed: The betrayal of the American man.* New York: Perennial.

Foster, T., and E. Newman. 2005. Just a knock back? Identity bruising on the route to becoming a male primary school teacher. *Teachers and Teaching: Theory and Practice* 11 (4): 341–58.

Francis, B., and C. Skelton. 2001. Men teachers and the construction of heterosexual masculinity in the classroom. *Sex Education* 1 (1): 9–21.

———. 2005. *Reassessing gender and achievement: Questioning contemporary key debates.* New York: Routledge.

Francis, B., C. Skelton, B. Carrington, M. Hutchings, and B. Read. 2008. A perfect match? Pupils' and teachers' views of the impact of matching educators and learners by gender. *Research Papers in Education* 23 (1): 21–36.

Frank, B., and W. Martino. 2006. The tyranny of surveillance: Male teachers and the policing of masculinities in a single sex school. *Gender and Education* 18 (1): 17–33.

Gaskell, J., and A. L. Mullen. 2006. Women in teaching: Participation, power and possibility. In *The Sage handbook of gender and education,* eds. C. Skelton, B. Francis, and L. Smulyan, 453–68. Thousand Oaks: Sage Publications.

Gold, D., and M. Reis. 1982. Male teacher effects on young children: A theoretical and empirical consideration. *Sex Roles* 8 (5): 493–513.

Goodman, J. 1987. Masculinity, feminism, and the male elementary school teacher: A case study of preservice teachers' perspectives. *Journal of Curriculum Theorizing* 7 (2): 30–55.

Goodman, J., and T. Kelly. 1988. Out of the mainstream: Issues confronting the male profeminist elementary school teacher. *Interchange* 19 (2): 1–14.

Grumet, M. 1988. *Bitter milk: Women and teaching.* Amherst: The University of Massachusetts Press.

Gutmann, A. 1987. *Democratic education.* Princeton: Princeton University Press.

Hansen, P., and J. A. Mulholland. 2005. Caring and elementary teaching: The concerns of male beginning teachers. *Journal of Teacher Education* 56:119–31.

Hansot, E. 1993. Historical and contemporary views of gender and education. In *Gender and Education: Ninety-second Yearbook of the National Society for the Study of Education,* eds. S. K. Bilken and D. Pollard, 12–24. Chicago: University of Chicago Press.

Ingersoll, R. 2003. *Who controls teachers' work: Power and accountability in America's schools.* Cambridge: Harvard University Press.

Jacobs, J. A. 1993. Men in female-dominated fields: trends and turnover. In *Doing "women's work": Men in nontraditional occupations,* ed. C. L. Williams. Newbury Park: Sage Publications.

Jamison, J. 2000. Negotiating otherness: A male early childhood educator's gender positioning. *International Journal of Early Years Education,* 8 (2): 129–39.

Johannesson, I. A. 2004. To teach boys and girls: A pro-feminist perspective on the boys' debate in Iceland. *Educational Review* 56 (1): 33–42.

Johnston, J., E. McKeown, and A. McEwen. 1999. Choosing primary teaching as a career: The perspectives of males and females in training. *Journal of Education for Teaching* 25 (1): 56–64.

Keddie, A. 2006. Pedagogies and critical reflection: Key understandings for transformative gender justice. *Gender and Education* 18 (1): 99–114.

———. 2008. Teacher stories of collusion and transformation: A feminist pedagogical framework and meta-language for cultural gender justice. *Journal of Education Policy* 23 (4): 343–57.

Keddie, A., and M. Mills. 2009. Disrupting masculinized spaces: Teachers working for gender justice. *Research Papers in Education* 24 (1): 29–43.

Kimmel, M. S. 1996. *Manhood in America: A cultural history.* 2nd ed. Oxford: Oxford University Press.

———. 2006. A war against boys? *Dissent* (fall): 1–6.

King, J. R. 1998. *Uncommon caring: Learning from men who teach young children.* New York: Teachers College Press.

Lahelma, E. 2000. Lack of male teachers: A problem for students or teachers? *Pedagogy, Culture and Society* 8 (2): 173–86.

Lingard, B. 2003. Where to in gender policy in education after recuperative masculinity politics? *International Journal of Inclusive Education* 7 (1): 33–56.

Lingard, B., and P. Douglas. 1999. *Men engaging feminisms.* Buckingham: Open University Press.

Lortie, D. C. 1975. *Schoolteacher.* Chicago: University of Chicago Press.

———. 2002. *Schoolteacher: A sociological study.* 2nd ed. Chicago: University of Chicago Press.

Mac An Ghaill, M. 1996. "What about the boys?": Schooling, class, and crisis masculinity. *The Editorial Board of the Sociological Review*, 381–97.

Maloutas, M. P. (2006). *The gender of democracy.* New York: Routledge.

Mancus, D. S. 1992. Influence of male teachers on elementary school children's stereotyping of teacher competence. *Sex Roles* 26 (3/4): 109–28.

Martino, W. J. 2008. Male teachers as role models: Addressing issues of masculinity, pedagogy and the re-masculinization of schooling. *Curriculum Inquiry* 38 (2): 189–223.

Martino, W., and D. Berril. 2003. Boys, schooling and masculinities: Interrogating the "right" way to educate boys. *Educational Review* 55 (2): 99–117.

Martino, W., and M. Kehler. 2006. Male teachers and the "boy problem": An issue of recuperative masculinity politics. *McGill Journal of Education* 41 (2): 113–31.

Martino, W., B. Lingard, and M. Mills. 2004. Issues in boys' education: A question of teacher threshold knowledges? *Gender and Education* 16 (4): 435–54.

Mead, S. 2006. *The evidence suggests otherwise: The truth about boys and girls.* Washington, DC: Education Sector.

Mills, M. 2000. Issues in implementing boys' programme in schools: Male teachers and empowerment. *Gender and Education* 12 (2): 221–38.

Mills, M. 2003. Shaping the boys' agenda: The backlash blockbusters. *International Journal of Inclusive Education* 7 (1): 57–73.

———. 2004. Male teachers, homophobia, misogyny, and teacher education. *Teaching Education* 15 (1): 27–39.

Mills, M., M. Haase, and E. Charlton. 2008. Being the "right" kind of male teacher: The disciplining of John. *Pedagogy, Culture and Society* 16 (1): 71–84.

Montecinos, C., and L. Nielson. 2004. Male elementary pre-service teachers' gendering of teaching. *Multicultural Perspectives* 6 (2): 3–9.

National Center for Education Statistics. 2007. Schools and staffing survey, 2003–2004. http://nces.ed.gov/surveys/sass/index.asp (retrieved January 1, 2009).

National Education Association. 2007. Rankings and estimates of the states 2006 and estimates of school statistics 2007. http://www.nea.org/edstats.

Nelson, B. G. 2002. The importance of men teachers and reasons why there are so few. Minneapolis: MenTeach.org.

Renold, E. 2004. "Other" boys: Negotiating non-hegemonic masculinities in the primary school. *Gender and Education* 16 (2): 247–66.

Roulston, K., and M. Mills. 2000. Male teachers in feminized teaching areas: Marching to the beat of the men's movement drums? *Oxford Review of Education* 26 (2): 221–37.

Rubin, G. 1975. The traffic in women: Notes on the "political economy" of sex. In R. R. Reiter, ed., *Toward an anthropology of women*, 157–210. New York: Monthly Review Press.

Rury, J. L. 1989. Who became teachers?: The social characteristics of teachers in American history. In D. Warren, ed., *American teachers: Histories of a profession at work,* 9–48. New York: MacMillan.

Sargent, P. 2001. *Real men or real teachers: Contradictions in the lives of men elementary school teachers.* Harriman, TN: Men's Studies Press.

Sax, L. 2008. *Boys adrift: The five factors driving the growing epidemic of unmotivated boys and underachieving young men.* New York: Basic Books.

Sedlak, M. W. 1989. "Let us go and buy a school master": Historical perspectives on the hiring of teachers in the Unites States, 1750–1980. In D. Warren, ed., *American teachers: Histories of a profession at work*, 257–90. New York: MacMillan.

Skelton, C. 1998. Feminism and research into masculinities and schooling. *Gender and Education* 10 (2): 217–27.

————. 2003. Male primary teachers and perceptions of masculinity. *Educational Review* 55 (2): 195–209.

Smedley, S. 2006. Listening to men student primary school teachers: Some thoughts on pedagogy. *Changing English* 13 (1): 125–35.

————. 2007. Learning to be a primary school teacher: Reading one man's story. *Gender and Education* 19 (3): 369–85.

Smedley, S., and S. Pepperell. 2000. No man's land: Caring and male student primary teachers. *Teachers and Teaching: Theory and Practice* 6 (3): 259–77.

Sommers, C. H. 2000. *The war against boys: How misguided feminism is harming our young men.* New York: Simon & Schuster.

Sugg, R. S. Jr. 1978. *Motherteacher: The feminization of American education.* Charlottesville: University Press of Virginia.

Sumison, J. 1999. Critical reflections on the experiences of a male early childhood worker. *Gender and Education* 11 (4): 455–68.

————. 2000. Motivations for the career choice of preservice teachers in New South Wales, Australia and Ontario, Canada. American Educational Research Association. New Orleans, LA.

Talbert, J. E., and M. W. McLaughlin. 1994. Teacher professionalism in local school contexts. *American Journal of Education* 102:123–53.

Thornton, M., and P. Bricheno. 2000. Primary school teachers' careers in England and Wales: The relationship between gender, role, position and promotion aspirations. *Pedagogy, Culture and Society* 8 (2): 187–206.

————. 2006. *Missing men in education.* Sterling: Trentham Books.

Titus, J. J. 2004. Boy trouble: Rhetorical framing of boys' underachievement. *Discourse: Studies in the Cultural Politics of Education* 25 (2): 145–69.

UNESCO. 2008. United Nations Educational, Scientific and Cultural Organization world education indicators percentage of female teachers in the school years 2004–2005. http://www.uis.unesco.org.

Verdugo, S., and J. Schneider. 1994. Gender inequality in female-dominated occupations: The earnings of male and female teachers. *Economics of Education Review* 13 (3): 251–64.

Walkerdine, V. 1990. *Schoolgirl fictions.* London: Verso.

Weaver-Hightower, M. 2003. The "boy turn" in research on gender and education. *Review of Educational Research* 73 (4): 471–98.

Williams, C. L. 1992. The glass escalator: Hidden advantages for men in the "female" professions. *Social Problems* 39 (3): 253–67.

CONTRIBUTORS

Gail Masuchika Boldt is an associate professor of education at Penn State University. She is on the affiliated faculty for women's studies. Her most recent book, coedited with Paula Salvio, is *Love's Return: Psychoanalytic Essays on Teaching and Learning*. She is currently researching a book on the history of contemporary elementary school literacy practices.

Sylvia Bulgar is a professor of mathematics education at Rider University in Lawrenceville, New Jersey. She has also spent over two decades teaching elementary self-contained classes and middle and high school mathematics. She has published numerous papers and book chapters on how children learn mathematics, how teachers can use this knowledge in their teaching, and the impact of testing and gifted education and is currently editing a book about fractions. She has presented her work in the United States and in other countries. The underlying goal of her work is to help provide democratic access of quality mathematics instruction to all students. Bulgar is married with two grown daughters and six grandchildren.

Kent Chrisman is a professor of early childhood education at Shippensburg University of Pennsylvania and served as the campus lab school director at Stephen F. Austin State University in Texas from 1976 to

1988. Chrisman has served as the Pennsylvania cochair of the Early Childhood Career Preparation and Development Advisory Committee for the last three years and serves on the state's Early Learning Council. He has been involved in working with school districts and early childhood programs with alignment and transitioning for the past three years and has also served as a consultant to various Head Start programs. He is also the current president of the Pennsylvania Association of Early Childhood Teacher Educators.

Donna Couchenour, PhD, is a professor of teacher education in the early childhood education program at Shippensburg University of Pennsylvania, a certified family life educator, and has served as a Head Start teacher and laboratory school director at West Virginia University and Oklahoma State University. Couchenour has served as an early childhood consultant with Head Start, child care, and public school prekindergarten through third grade programs. After serving on the NCATE panel for the National Association for the Education of Young Children (NAEYC) for eight years as a lead reviewer for higher education program reviews, Couchenour was recently nominated by NAEYC and appointed to serve as an NCATE Board of Examiners member. She has held a variety of positions in state and local AEYC affiliates, including president, secretary, and vice president for advocacy. Couchenour has published three books with her coauthor (and spouse) Kent Chrisman: *Families, Schools and Communities: Together for Young Children* (2010, Wadsworth), *Healthy Sexuality Development: A Guide for Early Childhood Educators and Families* (NAEYC, 2002), and *In the Field: Readings and Guided Field Experiences in Early Childhood Education* (Delmar Thomson Learning, 2007).

Sonja de Groot Kim, PhD, is an experienced early childhood educator. She has been an early childhood teacher, a director of a laboratory nursery school at Vassar College and at Teachers College, and a teacher educator. She teaches undergraduate and graduate courses in early childhood education and early childhood administration in the Department of Early Childhood and Family Studies at Kean University. Her interests include studying the intersection of age, gender, and culture in young children's development—especially their communicative development—and their peer relationships. She has been involved in studying and adapting the Reggio Emilia approach in early childhood programs as well as in teacher education programs.

Debra Dyer, EdD, is an assistant professor in both the early childhood education and graduate literacy programs in Keuka College, Keuka Park, New York. She received her master's of science in education and doctorate from Binghamton University. Dyer's interests lie in culturally compatible early childhood curriculum and instruction, inquiry-based collaborative learning communities in early childhood, and building university-community partnerships.

Eila Estola, PhD, has been a senior researcher in the Department of Teacher Education and Educational Sciences, University of Oulu, Finland, since 1995. Estola was originally an early childhood teacher and has also worked as a lecturer in the program of early childhood teacher education at the University of Oulu. In addition, she was a principal of the early childhood teacher education college in Oulu. Her main research interests focus on teachers' identities, relational and moral gender issues, and narrative research.

Stephen Garretson is a faculty member in early childhood education at the University of Texas at Arlington. Garretson's interest in fatherhood stems from experiences with his own father, male role models in his life, and his current experiences as a father of three young boys. As a PhD student in child development at Texas Woman's University, Garretson focuses much of his research and studies on fatherhood and the impact fathers have on young children.

Dorothy W. Hewes, PhD, has held various positions in early childhood education programs during the past sixty-five years. She has been professor emeritus at San Diego State University since 1992. Her areas of specialization are the administration of preschool centers and the history of early childhood education. Her most recent books are *An Administrator's Guidebook to Early Care and Education Programs*, with Jane Leatherman (Allyn and Bacon, 2005), and *W. N. Hailman: Defender of Froebel* (Froebel Foundation, 2001). She has received numerous achievement awards, including those from the International Froebel Society (2009), OMEP, and the National Association for the Education of Young Children (2007).

Blythe F. Hinitz is professor of elementary and early childhood education at the College of New Jersey and the author of *Teaching Social Studies to the Young Child*. Hinitz has also authored the chapters "Historical

Research in Early Childhood Education" in *Handbook of Research on the Education of Young Children* and "History of Early Childhood Education in Multicultural Perspective" in *Approaches to Early Childhood Education.* She is a coauthor of *History of Early Childhood Education* and *The Anti-Bullying and Teasing Book for Preschool Classrooms.* Hinitz is a member of the Boys Project of the Educational Equity Center at AED, and she currently coordinates an international study on antibullying and anti-harassment. As a board member of H-Education, the World Organization for Early Childhood Education [OMEP]-USNC, and Professional Impact New Jersey, she has given numerous presentations around the world. She is a chapter officer of the Honor Society of Phi Kappa Phi and the 2007 recipient of the NAECTE Outstanding Teacher Educator Award.

Jeanne Marie Iorio is an assistant professor in early childhood education at the University of Hawaii–West Oahu. Before completing her doctorate at Teachers College, Columbia University, she worked as a classroom teacher, administrator, and teacher educator in a variety of settings, always seeking school environments that honor and listen to children. Through her research, Iorio attempts to rethink early childhood practice and theory, often disrupting traditional power hierarchies. Her research interests include child-adult/teacher conversations as aesthetic experiences, democratic classrooms, arts and education, and inspiring teachers as agents of change through advocacy and action research. Currently, she is involved in several research projects, including a longitudinal study of kindergarten in the state of Hawaii and an arts-based analysis of year-long preschool stories reflecting the complexity of children's experiences and thought processes within emergent curriculum.

Tamar Jacobson, PhD, is associate professor, department chair, and director of the early childhood program in the Teacher Education Department at Rider University, New Jersey. Currently, Jacobson serves on the Advocacy Committee of the National Association of Early Childhood Teacher Educators (NAECTE). She was selected to participate on the Consulting Editors Panel for the NAEYC, and is a Fellow in the Child Trauma Academy. Her first book, *Confronting Our Discomfort: Clearing the Way For Anti-Bias,* was published by Heinemann in 2003. Her second book, *Don't Get So Upset! Help Young Children Manage Their Feelings By Understanding Your Own,* was published by Redleaf Press in September 2008.

Shaun Johnson is an assistant professor of elementary education at Towson University in Baltimore, Maryland. He previously taught fifth grade in Washington, DC, and Montgomery County, Maryland, and received his PhD in curriculum and instruction at Indiana University in June 2009. His dissertation investigated the lack of men in education.

Lisa Mufson Koeppel is a preschool teacher in Passaic, New Jersey, and has a master's degree in early childhood education from William Paterson University. She has published numerous articles on early childhood topics. She lives in Bergen County, New Jersey, with her husband and two sons, Levi and Jacob.

Cynthia A. Roberts is a behavioral science doctoral student in the Psychology Department at the University of Rhode Island. In her previous work she helped center-based and family child care providers become nationally accredited, and facilitated a statewide early care and education project to develop core competencies for ECE professionals in Rhode Island. She is the mother of a three-year-old son and surrounds him with books that portray an array of roles and possibilities for him.

Janis Strasser is a professor of early childhood education at William Paterson University. She has been in the field for more than thirty years as a preschool, kindergarten, and music teacher, and also as a Head Start education coordinator. She has been a consulting editor for *Young Children*, is a member of the advisory board of *Teaching Young Children*, and frequently presents workshops at state and national conferences. She has written more than thirty journal articles, several book chapters, and coauthored *The Essential Literacy Workshop Book* (Gryphon House, 2007).

Josh Thompson is his kids' kindergarten teacher. All four of his children were in the Montessori three- to six-year-old classroom where he taught for fourteen years. He moved into higher education ten years ago to teach early childhood teachers, currently at Texas A&M University–Commerce, where teachers come to learn.

Clarissa M. Uttley, PhD, is an assistant professor in the Education Department at Plymouth State University in Plymouth, New Hampshire, where she teaches courses in the early childhood studies program. Her main focus is the social emotional development of young children and how early childhood educators support and optimize healthy child development. Prior to attending graduate school Uttley worked as a preschool teacher in Massachusetts. Concepts of gender in childhood have been a focus of her research and stem back to her own childhood, with the challenges of growing up as a tomboy catching frogs and toads at the neighborhood pond.

Hema Visweswaraiah moved to Denver, Colorado, in August 2009 and now works in a preschool classroom at the Ricks Center for Gifted Children at the University of Denver. Prior to that, she taught preschool for four years at the Rita Gold Early Childhood Center at Teachers College, Columbia University, in New York City. She received her bachelor of arts from the University of Rochester in Rochester, New York, and completed her master of arts at Teachers College, with teaching certifications in early childhood general education and early childhood special education. Visweswaraiah's role in the classroom as a teacher-researcher has been fueled by her interest in better understanding young children's perceptions of their world through play, conversation, and careful observation in an effort to provide them with the best environment for learning and growing.

Debby Zambo teaches courses in educational psychology at Arizona State University in the College of Teacher Education and Leadership. She has also taught master's reading courses in best practices, essential elements, and differentiated instruction. Before joining the university Zambo taught in public schools for more than eight years and at a private school for adolescents with learning needs for one year. Most of her public school experience has been working with children in kindergarten through third grade who face learning and emotional challenges. Zambo cowrote *Bright Beginnings for Boys: Engaging Boys with Active Literacy* with William G. Brozo (International Reading Association, 2009). Her e-mail address is debby.zambo@asu.edu.

INDEX